Mark Twain

Twayne's United States Authors Series

David J. Nordloh, Editor

Indiana University, Bloomington

TUSAS 535

MARK TWAIN
(1835–1910)
Courtesy of the Bancroft Library, University of California, Berkeley

Mark Twain

By John C. Gerber

The University of Iowa

CARNEGIE LIBRARY
LIVINGSTONE COLLEGE
SALISBURY, N. C. 28144

Twayne Publishers
A Division of G.K. Hall & Co. • *Boston*

121050

Mark Twain
John C. Gerber

Copyright 1988 by G.K. Hall & Co.
All rights reserved.
Published by Twayne Publishers
A Division of G.K. Hall & Co.
70 Lincoln Street
Boston, Massachusetts 02111

Copyediting supervised by Barbara Sutton
Book production by Janet Zietowski
Book design by Barbara Anderson

Typeset in 11 pt. Garamond
by Compset, Inc., of Beverly, Massachusetts

Printed on permanent/durable acid-free paper
and bound in the United States of America

Library of Congress Cataloging in Publication Data

Gerber, John C.
  Mark Twain / by John C. Gerber.
    p. cm.—(Twayne's United States authors series ; TUSAS 535)
  Bibliography: p.
  Includes index.
  ISBN 0-8057-7518-8 (alk. paper)
  1. Twain, Mark, 1835–1910—Criticism and interpretation.
I. Title. II. Series.
  PS1338.G47 1988
  818'.409—dc19

87-28816
CIP

For Peggy, Barbara, and Ann

Contents

About the Author

John C. Gerber is M. F. Carpenter professor emeritus of English at the University of Iowa and professor emeritus of English at the State University of New York at Albany. He has taught at the universities of Pittsburgh, Chicago, California (Berkeley), Iowa (where he was head of the Department of English and of the School of Letters), and at the State University of New York at Albany (where he was also head of the Department of English). In addition, he has taught or lectured (principally on Mark Twain) at many other universities in the United States as well as universities in Egypt, France, Korea, the People's Republic of China, and the Philippines. His scholarly articles and reviews have appeared in such journals as *American Literature, American Literary Realism, Books at Iowa, Civil War History, College English, New England Quarterly, PMLA, Proof,* and *Studies in American Humor.* He has also written essays for such collections as *The Centenary of Huckleberry Finn, Essays in American and English Literature, The Mythologizing of Mark Twain,* and *Style of Prose Fiction: English Institute Essays 1958.* In 1971 he edited *Studies in "Huckleberry Finn,"* and from 1962 to 1968 wrote the chapter on Mark Twain for *American Literary Scholarship: An Annual.* From 1962 to 1982 he was chairman of the editorial board for the Iowa-California Edition of the Works of Mark Twain, and was historical editor for the volume containing the Tom Sawyer novels.

Preface

This volume is intended as an introduction for the general reader to the major works of Mark Twain. Taking up the works in chronological order, it provides for each an historical context, a summary of the contents, and a commentary on the craftsmanship and ideas. In presenting this sequence I try to show the development of Twain's extraordinary literary skill and to suggest the importance of each work to his passage from a young man keenly aware of the jokes of life to an old man who is convinced that life itself is a joke. Even from the beginning Mark Twain shows himself as a moralist as well as a humorist. Indeed, he believed his main function was to teach. Additionally, he reveals himself as a romantic as well as a realist, an idealist as well as a materialist, a Western democrat as well as one who sought the approval of the genteel aristocrats of the East. Increasingly, he becomes the pessimist and the determinist, and emerges overall as both a Tom Sawyer glorying in show and acclaim and a Huckleberry Finn wracked by inner anxieties. Such complexities and contradictions deserve a more detailed consideration than the limitations of this study make possible. I hope, however, that I have been detailed enough to be fair to the author—and to the reader.

It is a pleasure to acknowledge the debts that I have accumulated in the process of writing this book. Not only are there the specific borrowings cited in the footnotes but also the pervasive ideas and attitudes gained from such longtime Mark Twain scholars as Walter Blair, Henry Nash Smith, and William M. Gibson. In addition, I want to express my thanks for encouragement in completing the book to Vice President Richard D. Remington and Dean Fredrick Woodard of the University of Iowa; to Dale M. Bentz, University Librarian, and Margaret E. Richardson, Book Stacks Librarian for making the days in the University of Iowa library so pleasant; and to Maureen Schaefer, secretary of the Department of English at S.U.N.Y. Albany for the help she provided in the early stages of the manuscript. David Nordloh, the Twayne editor for this volume, not only invited me to be its author but also has provided most useful guidance along the way. For the photograph of Mark Twain I am indebted to Robert H. Hirst and Robert P. Browning of the Mark Twain Papers, The Bancroft Library,

University of California, Berkeley. Holly Carver helped to cut down the manuscript to size, and John and Barbara Barrett scanned it for errors. My special thanks go to Carolyn B. Brown for her patience and skill as both editor and typist. Without her help I would have had to ask for yet another extension on the deadline. Finally, I gratefully acknowledge the support of my wife, who over the years has cheerfully accommodated the family schedule to the vagaries of research and composition.

John C. Gerber

University of Iowa

Chronology

1835   Samuel Langhorne Clemens born, 30 November, in Florida, Missouri, to John Marshall Clemens and Jane Lampton Clemens.

1839   Family moves to Hannibal, Missouri, on the west bank of the Mississippi River.

1847   John Clemens dies, 24 March.

1848   Sam goes to work for Joseph P. Ament, Hannibal printer.

1851   "A Gallant Fireman," Clemen's first known sketch, published in his brother Orion's *Western Union*.

1852   "The Dandy Frightening the Squatter."

1853–1857   Printer in St. Louis; New York; Philadelphia; Keokuk, Iowa; and Cincinnati. Publishes three Thomas Jefferson Snodgrass letters in *Keokuk Post* in 1856.

1857–1861   Persuades Horace Bixby, senior pilot on the *Paul Jones*, to take him on as an apprentice pilot. Becomes a licensed pilot 9 April 1859. Leaves river when Union gunboats close it to commercial traffic.

1861–1862   June, "trains" for about two weeks with the Marion Rangers, Confederate volunteer group. Late July–early August, travels by stagecoach with brother Orion to Carson City, Nevada. Fails at staking timber claim and in prospecting for silver.

1862–1864   August 1862–May 1864, reporter and free-lance writer on the staff of *Territorial Enterprise* (Virginia City). 3 February 1863, signs himself for the first time "Mark Twain" on a burlesque account of the doings of the Nevada legislature.

1864–1865   Local reporter for the *San Francisco Morning Call*. Contributes to such literary periodicals as the *Golden Era* and the *Californian*. "Jim Smiley and His Jumping Frog."

1866   Spends four months in Sandwich Islands (Hawaii) as cor-
        respondent for the *Sacramento Union*. Back in San Fran-
        cisco, delivers first of many lectures on the Islands.
        December, sails for New York under contract to the *San
        Francisco Alta Californian* as roving correspondent.

1867   *The Celebrated Jumping Frog of Calaveras County, and Other
        Sketches*. 8 June sails to Europe and Holy Land as news-
        paper correspondent on *Quaker City*. November, serves
        briefly in Washington, D.C., as secretary to Senator
        William M. Stewart of Nevada.

1868   Works on manuscript of *The Innocents Abroad* and lectures
        on *The American Vandal Abroad*.

1869   *The Innocents Abroad*. February, engaged to Olivia Lang-
        don of Elmira, New York. Purchases partnership in *Buf-
        falo Express* with help of loan from Jervis Langdon,
        Olivia's father. Lectures under the management of James
        Redpath.

1870   Marries Olivia on 2 February. Writes for *Buffalo Express*
        and *New York Galaxy*. First child and only son, Langdon
        Clemens, prematurely born 7 November.

1871   Family rents Hooker house in Nook Farm area of Hart-
        ford, Connecticut.

1872   *Roughing It*. Susan Olivia Clemens (Susy) born 19
        March. June, Langdon dies.

1873   *The Gilded Age*, in collaboration with Charles Dudley
        Warner. Clemens family to Europe for first of several
        visits there.

1874   June, daughter Clara born. Late September, family
        moves into new house in Nook Farm area of Hartford.

1875   *Old Time on the Mississippi* serialized in *Atlantic Monthly;
        Sketches, New and Old*.

1876   *The Adventures of Tom Sawyer*.

1877   *A True Story and the Recent Carnival of Crime*. 7 May, *Ah
        Sin*, a play, written in collaboration with Bret Harte,
        opens in Washington. Whittier birthday dinner speech,
        17 December.

1878–1879   Travels with family in Europe. Takes walking trip with the Reverend Joseph Twichell in Germany and Switzerland.

1880   *A Tramp Abroad.* Daughter Jean born 26 July. Begins investing in the Paige typesetting machine.

1882   *The Prince and The Pauper. The Stolen White Elephant.* April–May boat trip on the Mississippi.

1883   *Life on the Mississippi.*

1884   Campaigns for Grover Cleveland. November 1884 to February 1885, reading tour with George Washington Cable.

1885   *Adventures of Huckleberry Finn.*

1889   *A Connecticut Yankee in King Arthur's Court.*

1891   Family to Europe, where they live for most of the 1890s.

1892   *The American Claimant.*

1893   *The £1,000,000 Bank-Note.*

1894   *Tom Sawyer Abroad. The Tragedy of Pudd'nhead Wilson and the Comedy of Those Extraordinary Twins.* April, Twain's publishing house declares itself bankrupt. Meets H. H. Rogers, vice president of Standard Oil, who over the next four years helps him regain his solvency.

1895–1896   Lecture trip around the world to raise funds to repay creditors.

1896   *Personal Recollections of Joan of Arc; Tom Sawyer Abroad, Tom Sawyer, Detective, and Other Stories.* Susy Clemens dies of meningitis, 18 August.

1897   *How to Tell a Story and Other Essays; Following the Equator.*

1900   *The Man That Corrupted Hadleyburg and Other Stories and Essays.* Returns to America to a national welcome.

1901   Litt.D. degree from Yale.

1902   LL.D. degree from University of Missouri.

1903   Takes a villa in Florence for Mrs. Clemens's health.

1904   Mrs. Clemens dies, 5 June.

1906   *What Is Man?* published privately and anonymously.

1907   Litt.D. degree from Oxford.

1908   Moves to Stormfield, Redding, Connecticut.

1909   Clara marries Ossip Gabrilowitsch, pianist and conduc-
       tor. Jean Clemens dies, 23 December.

1910   Mark Twain dies, 21 April, and is buried at Elmira,
       New York.

Chapter One
The Good Time Years

"What is human life?" Mark Twain asked in one of his maxims, and promptly supplied the answer himself. "The first third a good time; the rest remembering about it."[1] Intentionally or not, he was describing his own life, even though it never turned out to be quite so neatly divided. From 1835 to 1866 he led a colorful and relatively footloose existence as a boy, printer, pilot, miner, newspaperman, West Coast bohemian, and traveling correspondent. From 1866 to his death in 1910 he kept recalling the experiences of the earlier years and fashioning them into oral yarns, lectures, newspaper and magazine sketches, travel books, and novels. Invariably, the best of his writing developed at least in part out of the "good time years." For this reason, if for no other, the facts of his early life merit considerable attention.

Boyhood, 1835–47

Actually the "good time" years were not all that good. Even the frolics of boyhood so vividly re-created in *The Adventures of Tom Sawyer* were tempered in the author's real life by a frail childhood, near poverty, four deaths in the immediate family, and a multitude of anxieties, some of them so deeply troubling that he never fully got over them. The truth is that almost from the first Sam Clemens's life was a mixture of contradictions.

The contradictions began with his parents. John Marshall Clemens was solemn, austere, disciplined, and almost fanatical in his rectitude. Jane Lampton Clemens, on the other hand, was impulsive, affectionate, and a good storyteller. The father was a freethinker, the mother a Calvinist. Originally from Virginia, they had married in Kentucky and had moved to Tennessee where for a short time John Clemens as postmaster, storekeeper, and lawyer had done rather well. For several hundred dollars he had even bought 70,000 acres of land in the Knob country, the "Tennessee land" that was alternately to be the hope and despair of the Clemenses for decades to come. As their family grew,

1

however, the Clemens fortunes dwindled so markedly that when an enthusiastic invitation came from John Quarles, Jane Clemens's brother-in-law, to join them in Florida, Missouri, the Clemenses responded with alacrity. They arrived there about 1 June 1835, the family then consisting of Orion (with the accent on the first syllable) almost ten, Pamela seven, Margaret five, and Benjamin three. There was also a slave girl named Jenny.

In Florida, which consisted of little more than a clearing between two forks of the Salt River, the Clemenses moved into a small two-room frame building. It was in this house that Samuel Langhorne Clemens was born on 30 November 1835.[2] The parents named him for his paternal grandfather and an old family friend back in Virginia. The baby barely made it through the first two winters. Even his mother thought him a poor looking object to raise. The Clemenses stayed in Florida only four years. Henry was born there and Margaret, the little beauty of the family, died there in 1839. Again the father failed in business, and again the family moved, this time to Hannibal, Missouri, a town of about a thousand situated on the west bank of the Mississippi at a break in the escarpment carved out by Bear Creek. It was the town that as St. Petersburg Mark Twain would make world famous.

For the impressionable boy, Hannibal had both its bright and its dark side. There were endless opportunities for swimming, fishing, skating, climbing, and exploring caves and islands. Especially there were the chances to watch the gaudy river packets that stopped at the Hannibal wharf daily to exchange passengers and freight and take on wood. Every boy, Mark Twain later recalled, had one ambition and that was to work on a steamboat, preferably as a pilot. But in Hannibal there were also murders, knifings, the fears of the Morrell gang and "butcher-knife boys" who preyed on river towns, and incidents of slaves being whipped and chained together for shipment to the deep South. There were also the horrors of the regular visitations of cholera, smallpox, and yellow fever. The contrast between light and dark in the St. Petersburg of *Tom Sawyer* captures well the spirit of that real Hannibal.

Every summer vacation until he was twelve, Sam went back to his Uncle John Quarles's farm in Florida, and his reminiscences of his experiences there are among the happiest in his autobiography. He recalls with special joy the prodigious meals, the escapades with his many cousins, and especially the fascinating hours spent listening to the songs and stories of the slaves. Aunt Hannah and Uncle Dan'l were his favorites, the latter eventually serving as the model for Jim in *Huckle-berry Finn*. Puss Quarles, his favorite cousin, remembered Sam particularly for his love of cats and for his slow talk. Evidently he was already affecting the drawl that was to become his trademark.

Except as a speller Sam failed to distinguish himself as a scholar. At the age of four and a half he began attending a small school in Hannibal conducted by two rather severe maiden ladies, Elizabeth Horr and Mary Ann Newcomb. He was remembered by them as being slow of speech but "certainly not slow about thinking up ways of getting out of studying."[3] Later, he enrolled in William O. Cross's "good common school" for boys and girls, and still later in J. D. Dawson's school for young ladies and a few boys of "good morals." During his early years Sam preferred paperback thrillers, but his mother insisted that he become intimately acquainted with the Bible; his father subscribed to *Peter Parley's Magazine* for the children and shared a copy of *Don Quixote* with Sam; and Orion and Pamela did their best to make him fond of the works of such other authors as Bunyan, Dickens, and Ossian, not to mention *Godey's Lady's Book* and the Sunday School magazines. Too, there was always the example of young Henry, who was the bookworm of the family.

For the inquisitive boy who doted on the offbeat, however, the "cultural" events of the town often seemed more exciting than books. Some that Mark Twain particularly recalled in his later writing were the circus and showboat performances, minstrel shows, political parades and speeches, Fourth of July celebrations, and lectures on such awesome subjects as witchcraft and phrenology. Sam joined the Cadets of Temperance in order to wear the organization's red merino sash in parades, and at one demonstration of mesmerism he faked hypnosis so dramatically that the lecturer invited him back on succeeding nights. He never missed out, moreover, on the old-time religion. Jane Clemens saw to that. Shortly after the family arrived in Hannibal she started the children in the Methodist Sunday School. Several years later, she moved them to the Presbyterian Sunday School and insisted, as they grew older, that they stay for church too. The Calvinistic training Sam experienced in the Presbyterian church, abetted undoubtedly by instruction from his mother and school teachers, drilled deeply and lastingly into the boy's mind. "Mine was a trained Presbyterian conscience," he later wrote, "and knew but the one duty—to hunt and harry its slave upon all pretexts and on all occasions, particularly when there was no sense nor reason in it."[4] The Calvinistic doctrines of depravity and predestination created an intellectual context from which he never escaped. Yet Sam Clemens was never a believer in an orthodox sense, and this fact, too, may be traced to his early training. The faith of his mother must surely have been countered by the skepticism of his father and of Uncle John Quarles, a man whom he adored. His religious ambivalences started early.

While the boy grew and prospered, the father was discovering Hannibal to be a good deal less than the El Dorado he had hoped for. Again he opened a law office and tried store keeping, but after an early spurt his business affairs went badly. His store lost money, and the tenants in the rental property in which he had invested did not pay. The ultimate crusher came when a business partner, a notorious deadbeat for whom he had given security, declared bankruptcy. True to his gentry code, John Clemens sold every possession he possibly could in order to meet the demands of his creditors—an act that must have served as a model for Mark Twain when fifty years later he, too, faced bankruptcy. John Clemens might have pulled clear—he was almost certain to be selected clerk of the county court—but in March 1847 he contracted pneumonia and died. Jane Clemens was left with four children[5] and little else. Well before he was twelve, young Sam Clemens had to begin accepting family responsibilities. His boyhood was over, the boyhood he would later romanticize and use again and again, not only as material for his fiction but also as a psychical refuge from the assaults of the adult world.

Printer, 1847–56: Humorous Sketches

After his father died, Sam Clemens apparently stayed in school about a year, though working part-time as a printer's devil in the office of the *Hannibal Gazette.* In June 1848 he went to work full time for Joseph P. Ament, publisher of the *Missouri Courier,* and in 1851 for Orion on the *Western Union,* later the *Journal.* Orion testified that in setting type and printing Sam was both swift and clean. Although setting type must have sharpened Sam's respect for economy of phrasing and precision in punctuation, it was setting type on newspapers, not typesetting per se, that encouraged him to read more widely and that propelled him into authorship. Like other small-town newspapers of the 1850s, Hannibal papers featured news that was mainly local, excerpts from political speeches, highly personal editorials, correspondence, advertisements for everything from the *Edinburgh Review* to cures for the piles, and short literary and humorous pieces inserted to fill the blank spaces. It was this "filler" that was most important for Sam's development. Sam set type on such respected material as quotations from the Bible, episodes from classical mythology, and selections from the works of famous English and American writers. He became familiar, also, with such humorists as Seba Smith, Benjamin P. Shillaber, and William Tappan Thompson, and such humorous publications as *The Carpet Bag, Brother Jonathan,* and *The Spirit of the Times.*

Reading led inevitably to authorship. Sam Clemens's first published sketch, so far as is known, was "A Gallant Fireman," which appeared in Orion's *Western Union* on 16 January 1851. This was a single paragraph telling how Jim Wolf, a fellow apprentice, rushed out of the shop when a fire broke out next door carrying a broom, an old mallet, a wash-pan, and a dirty towel. After an hour he returned and "thinking he had immortalized himself, threw his giant frame in a tragic attitude, and exclaimed, with an eloquent expression: 'If that thar fire hadn't bin put out, thar'd a' bin the greatest *confirmation* of the age!'"[6] Such an anecdote with its oral tone, juxtaposition of rustic and literary language, puns, and silly catalog clearly reflects the Western humor of the time.

Sam's next two sketches indicate that by the age of sixteen he was already looking beyond Hannibal for an audience. "The Dandy Frightening the Squatter" appeared in Boston in Shillaber's *Carpet-Bag* for 1 May 1852, and "Hannibal, Missouri" turned up a week later in the Philadelphia *American Courier.* There was little about the "Dandy" that was original. The anecdote of a city fop being bested by a backwoodsman had for years been a favorite of Western humorists. Halting in action and trite in language, the sketch would not be known today if it had not been signed "S. L. C." In "Hannibal, Missouri" Sam attempted to provide Eastern readers with a short account of the history, geography, and business enterprise of Hannibal.

Doubtless Sam composed many of the news items that appeared in Orion's *Journal* in the early 1850s, but the contributions that identify him as something more than an ordinary apprentice are some twenty short pieces in which he exploited an already irrepressible delight in satire and burlesque. Five of these appeared in the *Journal* in September 1852 while Orion was in Tennessee unsuccessfully trying to make a deal for the family land. When he returned he found that Sam had printed three rather outrageous satires on local affairs over the name of W. Epaminondas Adrastus Blab, and two attacks on J. T. Hinton, the

editor of the rival *Tri-Weekly Messenger.* Worse, in a woodcut, he had
ridiculed Hinton for having tried to drown himself in Bear Creek after
being jilted. It was probably no coincidence that nothing more of any
importance by Sam appeared in the *Journal* until May 1853 when his
brother once more went out of town. This time Sam printed a poem
entitled "Love Concealed: To Miss Katie of H——l," a title he
thought "a perfect thunder-bolt of humor."[7] In succeeding issues he
published letters from three fictional correspondents, containing testy
arguments as to whether "H——l" meant Hannibal or Hell. Again
Orion was miffed. But this time he had to admit that Sam brought
life—and subscribers—to the paper. He elevated him to the post of
assistant editor and gave him a column of his own to fill. Sam proceeded to jam everything into it from river information to accounts of
local mayhem.

Restless and venturesome, however, Sam tired of Hannibal and,
more particularly, of working for his solemn and impractical brother.
Even having his own column could not hold him beyond its third
appearance. So by promising his mother not to raise a glass or throw a
card he won her reluctant approval for him to seek work in St. Louis
where his sister—now Mrs. William A. Moffett—had moved. There
he worked briefly as a compositor on the *Evening News.* But St. Louis
had never been his intended destination, as his mother learned to her
astonishment when she received a letter dated 24 August 1853 from
New York. The letter, telling principally of the rigors of travel, was a
show-offy bit, but Orion printed it in the *Journal* and thereby unwit-
tingly launched his brother on a career of travel writing that extended
well into the 1890s.

By March 1854 Sam was back in the Midwest, visiting his mother
and probably helping Orion and Henry with their Muscatine paper.
Before winter set in, however, he had returned to the staff of the *Evening News* in St. Louis. Two letters from that city to Orion's paper show
a growing delight in the theater and a modest concern about local
crime, poverty, and business affairs. His perspectives were enlarging.

Before leaving the family for good, Sam made one more attempt to
become an integral part of it. In the summer of 1855 he joined Orion
and Henry in Keokuk, Iowa, where Orion had bought out the Franklin
Book and Job-Printing Office. For a while Keokuk delighted Sam. It
was a boom town, and since much of his work was at night he had
plenty of time to read and to socialize. Except for a letter to an Annie
Taylor in Mount Pleasant, Iowa, what he wrote in Keokuk was negli-

gible. With great good humor he described for Annie the "jubilee" of bugs that clustered around him as he set type at night under a flaring gas lamp. The description still remains one of his most ingenious uses of personification, for the bugs in their pomposity and pretensions are clearly stand-ins for human beings.[8]

By the spring of 1856 Sam had once more had all that he could take of his older brother. Besides, he again wanted to travel. In such a restless mood he was especially susceptible to a current account of fortunes to be made importing coca from the upper Amazon. Miraculously, the means for at least the first leg of the trip suddenly materialized when he found a fifty dollar bill on a Keokuk street. Although he advertised for the owner, to his infinite relief no claimant turned up. In October he visited his mother, who had moved to St. Louis to be with Pamela, and then set out for the Amazon by the still unexplained route of Chicago and Cincinnati. Before he left Keokuk, however, he arranged to write a series of humorous letters for the *Keokuk Post* at five dollars a letter, his first financial deal with a publisher. As it happened, he wrote only three such letters—one from St. Louis and two from Cincinnati—because the deal collapsed when he tried to push the editor of the *Post* into doubling the fee. There was little that was original about these "Thomas Jefferson Snodgrass Letters" except, maybe, their uninhibited gusto. Clemens lifted the surname of his narrator from Dickens's *Pickwick Papers,* and for the character of the narrator he turned to the stereotype brash, uneducated, country yokel to be found in much of the humor of the so-called literary comedians of the time. He borrowed their stylistic tricks too: mangled spelling, erratic grammar and punctuation, overused capitalization, puns, misquotations, and the literal application of trite figurative expressions. Even the episodes in the Snodgrass letters were hackneyed. Snodgrass was no comic persona to treasure, and happily Mark Twain never attempted to use it again. In fact, years later he never even claimed the Snodgrass letters as his. He did later claim (in his *Autobiography*) that while in Cincinnati he met a Mr. Macfarlane from whom he first acquired his pessimistic doctrine. But there is good reason to believe that Mr. Macfarlane was a fiction.[9]

One should not make too many claims for Sam Clemens at the age of twenty-one. His sights were not set high, nor were they finely focused. He was impressionable, nervous, and more than a trifle lazy. If he had any central ambition it was to see more of the world. Yet this is not the whole story. During this period he shucked off much of his provincialism and began to develop a sense for regional and social differences. He learned the ins and outs of printing and publishing. He developed a fondness for the theater and nothing less than a passion for books. Admittedly, the some two dozens sketches and travel letters he wrote from 1847 to 1856 are distinguished neither in quantity nor quality. Yet they all show him exploiting that blend of realism, satire, and fantasy that was the mark of Western humor. However tentatively, by 1856 his immediate course was set.

Pilot, 1857–61: Two Letters to the Newspaper

When the ice broke on the Ohio River at Cincinnati in the spring of 1857, Clemens boarded the packet *Paul Jones* for the trip to New Orleans, still with the romantic dream of exploring the Amazon. Somewhere on the Mississippi below Cairo, however, an older dream of being a riverboat pilot took over. With persistence he managed to persuade Horace Bixby, the pilot of the *Paul Jones*, to take him on as an apprentice. The agreement called for him to pay Bixby a hundred dollars down (which he had to borrow from Pamela's husband) and four hundred dollars from his first earnings as a licensed pilot. Although he exaggerated the travails of a cub pilot in the early chapters of *Life on the Mississippi*, the notebooks that Bixby ordered him to keep show that learning the idiosyncrasies of the Mississippi was a demanding and often frightening experience. He worked as a cub until 9 April 1859, when he was licensed as a pilot on the stretch from St. Louis to New Orleans.

As a full-fledged pilot Clemens achieved the prestige and authority that the Tom Sawyer in him loved. He was a pilot on twenty-one different boats and the evidence indicates that he was a competent one. "Piloting on the Mississippi River," he wrote, "was not work to me; it was play—delightful play, vigorous play, adventurous play—and I loved it."[10] But it was by no means all play. No one so high strung as Sam Clemens could regularly respond to the ever-present dangers of the river with the sublime confidence Mark Twain attributed to Horace Bixby in *Life on the Mississippi*. The jottings in his notebook for 1860 suggest a caution bordering on timidity. Throughout his life he had recurrent nightmares about ramming a boat into the shore.

The most traumatic experience he had during his pilot days was to sit by helplessly and watch his brother Henry die of a scalding he suffered when the steamboat *Pennsylvania* blew up just south of Memphis. He had helped to get Henry a job as assistant "mud-clerk" on the *Pennsylvania*. Then, on a trip downriver he had knocked down the chief pilot, a man named Brown, when Brown for no good reason struck Henry in the face. As a result Brown refused to allow Clemens aboard when the *Pennsylvania* started back north from New Orleans. He had to follow, two days later, as a passenger on the *A. T. Lacey*. By the time the *Lacey* got to Memphis, Clemens had learned that the *Pennsylvania* had blown up and that Henry was one of the injured. He found him in a makeshift hospital and sat beside him off and on for four days until the end came. Later he tortured himself with the thought that a young orderly—or even he—had caused the death by giving Henry an overdose of morphine. Henry's death was but the first of a series of tragic events for which Clemens felt himself at least partly to blame, and which in the 1890s helped to set him raging against the universe itself.

He published only two pieces of imaginative prose during his days as a pilot.[11] The first was "River Intelligence," a burlesque letter printed by the *New Orleans Crescent* on 17 May 1859. The target of the attack was one Isaiah Sellers, a self-important older pilot who had been on the river since keelboat days. Over a year later Twain and J. W. Hood, his fellow pilot on the *Arago,* wrote a spoof of the memoranda pilots customarily provided for their colleagues. Appearing in union halls and in newspapers in cities along the river, these memoranda contained such information as the names of boats sighted, the depth of the river at various points, special dangers to be aware of, and so on. The Clemens and Hood burlesque appeared in the St. Louis *Missouri Republican* for 30 August 1860. Meant for other pilots, it is almost unintelligible today without a glossary. Anyone can guess, though, that Clemens and Hood were up to something when they report passing "the Skylight and the Twilight and the Daylight at Mud Bar."[12] The blend of fact and fancy in this burlesque—for there is fact—more truly anticipated what Clemens would write for Western newspapers than did the out-and-out clowning of "River Intelligence."

Whatever claims can be made for these two river pieces, they constitute a slim output for the four years Clemens spent as a pilot. Paradoxically, though, the experiences of these years provided an essential element in Mark Twain's development as an author and lecturer. They gave him not only a deep sense for the beauties and dangers of the Mississippi, but also a sharp perception of the people who traveled the river and lived along its banks. "In that brief, sharp schooling," he later wrote, "I got personally and familiarly acquainted with about all the different types of human nature that are to be found in fiction, biography, or history."[13]

Finally, being a pilot encouraged Clemens to perfect his skill as a yarnspinner. Mississippi riverboat pilots whiled away much of their time trading stories—tall tales, chiefly—about the river and rivermen. Pitted against such pros in the art of short narration, Sam Clemens honed his own powers until he could more than hold his own. It was hardly a coincidence that later, as both a lecturer and a writer, he was at his best in telling (or writing) short prose sketches.

"Soldier," 1861

The outbreak of the Civil War brought an end to Sam Clemens's days as a pilot. In April 1861 he went north as a passenger on the *Uncle Sam,* arriving in St. Louis one week after the firing on Fort Sumter. Soon thereafter he joined a dozen or more of his old friends in Hannibal who were Confederate sympathizers in organizing the "Marion Rangers." Because Hannibal was controlled by Union Home Guards, they had to slip south into Ralls County to be sworn in. They started off in a lighthearted mood but rain and the rumors of Union troops in the vicinity discouraged them, and they disbanded before they took part in any engagement. He could not have spent much more than two weeks campaigning. In 1877 he asserted that "we were the first men that went into the service in Missouri; we were the first that went out of it anywhere."[14]

Newspaperman, 1861–64: Journalistic Writings

By adding the West to Hannibal and the Mississippi River Sam Clemens created a third reservoir of American life for the books he eventually wrote. It was in the West that he decided upon writing as his profession, and it was there that he adopted his famous pseudonym. Western publications, too, shaped his early style. Attempting to win the acclaim of readers in Nevada and California, he exaggerated heavily and resorted frequently to burlesque and occasionally even to hoaxes. There is no doubt that he gained the reputation in these years of a young man on the make. Because of his wit and audacity he was admired, respected, feared, and, at times, thoroughly disliked. Interestingly, the only sketch of truly literary worth from this period, "The

Celebrated Jumping Frog of Calaveras County," was one he intended for Eastern readers.

It was Orion who made the trip west possible. In 1860 he had campaigned vigorously for Abraham Lincoln. When Lincoln won and appointed Edward Bates of St. Louis attorney general, Orion quickly got in touch with Bates in whose office he had briefly studied law in the 1840s. For once Orion was lucky. Bates appointed him secretary for the Territory of Nevada. Since he did not have the funds necessary for the trip from St. Louis to Carson City, capital of the Territory, Orion urged Sam to accompany him and presumably pay the fare for both of them. The brothers left St. Louis for St. Joseph, Missouri, on a Missouri River steamboat on 18 July 1861. From St. Joe they took a stage coach to Carson City, where they arrived 14 August. In his account of his trip in *Roughing It* Mark Twain wrote that they were "fed fat on wonders every day."[15]

For almost a year after reaching Washoe (the local name for Nevada), Clemens tried to make his fortune in timber claims and silver mining—and went broke. By the summer of 1862 he was ready to throw in the towel. In true melodramatic fashion, however, help arrived just before catastrophe. While mining near Aurora he had occasionally sent off a humorous letter, which he signed "Josh," to the *Territorial Enterprise* in Virginia City. No copies of these "Josh" letters survive, but we may assume that they were not intended for Victorian ladies, for Sam wrote Orion not to send back even excerpts to the family. Apparently, though, they delighted the editors of the *Territorial Enterprise,* for Joseph T. Goodman, the paper's co-owner, not only printed them but also wrote Clemens offering him a job as a local reporter and free-lance writer at a salary of twenty-five dollars a week. The lure of gold was hard to put down, but Clemens had no choice. He accepted Goodman's offer and arrived in the *Enterprise* office in August 1862 looking like nothing so much as a worn down and disreputable tramp.

Those were the glory days for Virginia City. Miners had discovered the Comstock Lode there just three years before. It was the richest silver vein ever to be found in North America, and the result was a rush reminiscent of the one at Sutter's Mill in 1848. For an imaginative young reporter Virginia City was paradise. Clemens was fortunate, too, in his associates on the *Enterprise.* The staff included the two owners, Joseph T. Goodman and Denis E. McCarthy; Steve Gillis, a compositor and irrepressible practical joker; Rollin M. Dagget, formerly the founder of the *Golden Era* in San Francisco; and Dan DeQuille (William

Wright), a much respected humorist who became Clemens's closest friend. These were not small-town operators. Although still relatively young, they all had newspaper experience and knew a readable story when they saw one. Into such a group Sam Clemens fitted perfectly. He was too cocksure to be generally liked, but the friendships he established with these men of the *Enterprise* were firm and lasting. Professionally they helped him too, especially Joe Goodman, who schooled him in the importance of proper names and concrete details. They knocked out most of his few remaining lapses in grammar, and by example or instruction they reinforced in him the notion that writing to be successful must stir the reader.

Since no file of the *Territorial Enterprise* survives, it is impossible to be exact about all that Clemens wrote for it. Some fifty items are extant because they were reprinted in other papers or were saved as clippings by Orion and Pamela or appear in a few copies of the *Enterprise* that somehow kept clear of the trash barrel. These tend to be the more humorous or sensational pieces. They too easily skew our impressions of Clemens's total effort for the paper. Day in and day out, though, while he was in Virginia City he spent his time writing for local readers about such events as mine developments, incorporations, fights, earthquakes, court trials, Indian activities, elections, concerts, and stock transactions. One estimate had it that he turned out between 1,500 and 2,000 local items. Such items as exist show that he enlivened even some of these run-of-mine accounts with exaggerated details, incongruous phrasing, and personal opinion. Nevertheless, it would be a mistake to conclude that he served the *Enterprise* simply as a jester.

Yet it was as a jester that he became known. He had not been with the *Enterprise* much more than a month when he published a hoax entitled "Petrified Man" that started his reputation for audacity. In it he announced the discovery near Humboldt City of a petrified man. It was sitting in a pensive attitude, he wrote, and a coroner's jury had determined that the unfortunate gentleman had died of "protracted exposure." At least eight papers in Nevada and California reprinted the story in good faith, though a careful reading would have disclosed that the petrified man was winking and thumbing his nose—and had a wooden leg. In midwinter Goodwin sent Clemens to Carson City to cover the activities of the territorial legislature. He did the job so well that the Legislative Council cited him for full and accurate reports of the proceedings. Along with these "straight" reports, he filed hilarious accounts of the people he encountered in Carson City; especially he lampooned Clement T. Rice, the reporter for the *Virginia City Union,* whom he dubbed "The Unreliable." The "feud" between Rice and Clemens continued until Clemens left Virginia City. The thrust of it was that Clemens, as a courtly gentleman, was gravely offended by Rice's oafish improprieties. [16] In late January 1863 Clemens filed a new spate of humorous letters from Carson City about the social activities there and the further embarrassments caused by the Unreliable's coarse behavior. In the letter published 3 February he signed himself for the first time, so far as we know, "Mark Twain." Not only that, but in the body of the letter he had the Unreliable greet him with, "How are you, Mark, old boy?" [17]

The practice of using pseudonyms was widespread among American newspaper humorists. For a precedent Sam Clemens needed to go no further than his roommate, William Wright, who was known almost solely by the pen name (pen name indeed!) of Dan DeQuille. From the outset Clemens used "Mark Twain" simply to indicate a humorist at work. He never attached it to his more serious dispatches to the *Enterprise.* But since the humorous pieces were what attracted readers, the pen name quickly displaced the real one—just as "Artemus Ward" took over for Charles Farrar Browne, "Petroleum Vesuvius Nasby" for David Ross Locke, and "Josh Billings" for Henry W. Shaw. Clemens's adoption of a nom de plume is understandable, but why "Mark Twain"? The most widely accepted explanation is that he lifted it from the cry of the leadsman on a Mississippi River boat. "Mark Twain!" meant two fathoms, twelve feet, or safe water. Another explanation is that he took the expression from the order one gave the bartender in a Virginia City saloon when treating a friend. It instructed the bartender to put two marks after one's name on a running tab. This explanation suggests that the pseudonym was an in-joke among Sam Clemens's drinking companions. Of course, both of these explanations may have validity. A third seems to be groundless, though it was the one that Mark Twain himself always gave. He claimed "Mark Twain" was a pseudonym used by Isaiah Sellers, the older pilot whom he had ridiculed in the *New Orleans Crescent.* He added that since Sellers had died and no longer needed a pen name, he simply appropriated it. But careful investigation has turned up no evidence that Sellers ever used the name. Whatever its source, "Mark Twain" soon became familiar in the West, whereas "Samuel L. Clemens" was known only to a few. [18]

In October Twain indulged himself in another hoax, one that created such an uproar that he had to publish an immediate retraction. Enti-

tled "A Bloody Massacre near Carson," it told of a Philip Hopkins who
brained seven of his nine children, scalped his wife, and dashed into
Carson City on horseback with his own throat cut from ear to ear. The
account attributed his derangement to the fact that Hopkins had lost
his money in the Spring Valley Water Company, whose dividends had
been "cooked," that is, falsely inflated. The horror of the supposed
incident completely obscured the quite legitimate attack on "cooking."
Reprinted widely in both Nevada and California papers, the hoax resulted in such a flood of criticism that even his retraction failed to stem
it. Editors who had been taken in—and they were in the majority—
blasted him as an "idiot," "lunatic," and "silly ass." When the criticism turned on the *Territorial Enterprise* Twain offered to resign, but
both Goodman and DeQuille advised him to forget it.

Slightly tamed, Mark Twain went to Carson City in the winter of
1863–64 to cover both the Constitutional Convention and the third
session of the territorial legislature. He needed to improve his image
as a journalist and he did. His accounts of legislative activities won
him the commendation of the legislature. At the same time his off-
duty antics resulted in his being elected "Governor" of the Third
House, a burlesque assembly composed of newspapermen, business
men, lawyers, and even some legislators.

For the three weeks between the Constitutional Convention and a
regular session of the legislature, he returned to Virginia City to help
entertain Artemus Ward. Meeting Ward was one of the most fortuitous
experiences in Mark Twain's life. Ward was at the top of his career,
both as a newspaper humorist and as a comic lecturer. His "letters"
written to the *Cleveland Plain Dealer* and reprinted throughout the
North and West were sheer linguistic lunacy, but underneath the non-
sense lay an appealing folk wisdom and an arresting satire on wartime
events. As a lecturer Ward filled houses wherever he appeared, invariably convulsing his listeners with his combination of wild illogic and
a shy, diffident delivery. He had been a sensation in San Francisco and
Carson City, and his arrival in Virginia City almost occasioned a civic
celebration. He quickly "adopted" the *Enterprise* staff, especially Mark
Twain and Dan DeQuille, and led them through an almost unending
series of tipsy revels. Ward was only a year older than Twain but their
relationship was that of master and apprentice. No one can fully gauge
the resolve that Ward in his off-beat fashion instilled in Mark Twain,
but Twain himself by comment and imitation gave credit to Ward for
some of his own most successful lecturing techniques: the emphasis on

the pause, the non sequitur and anticlimax, and especially the frozen face delivery.

Whatever happened, Mark Twain would probably have left Virginia City before the end of 1864. The Comstock veins were beginning to play out and the town's unbridled exuberance to diminish. But a new gaffe—this one really unforgivable—caused him to depart more abruptly than he had intended. On 16 May, while hardly sober, he wrote a paragraph in which he reported hearing that the money raised at a fancy dress ball in Carson City for the United States Sanitary Commission (the Red Cross of the time) had been diverted to aid a Miscegenation Society "somewhere in the East." The resulting uproar overwhelmed him. The ladies who sponsored the ball, including his sister-in-law Mollie Clemens, were scandalized. Moreover, since approval of miscegenation was a label that Copperheads had been trying to pin on Unionists, his use of the word drew Twain into a political fight he had been attempting to avoid. When he first arrived in Virginia City he had been blatantly Southern in his sympathies, but he soon found that there was more to be gained by being a Unionist, and as a result had quietly changed his allegiance. Now, he found himself identified again with the Confederacy. The Virginia City *Union,* in particular, tried to demolish him. In the letters and editorials that followed, each nastier than the last, he almost managed with the urging of Steve Gillis to maneuver himself into a duel with James L. Laird, the publisher of the *Union.* Growing talk of this duel—and rumors of other challenges—brought matters to a head. Fearful of even greater ridicule and of the possibility of a jail sentence for breaking the law against duels, Twain and Gillis quietly left Virginia City on the morning of 29 May.

San Francisco: Literary Burlesques and "The Celebrated Jumping Frog of Calaveras County"

Except for three months spent in the Tuolumne Hills, Mark Twain lived in San Francisco from May 1864 to March 1866. It was not one of the happiest periods of his life. Of necessity he took a job as local reporter with the *Morning Call,* the "washerwoman's paper." Most of what he wrote for the *Call* was routine reporting. But as daily contact with the sour underbelly of city life strengthened his impatience with cruelty and corruption, his treatment of such topics as street crime and police court procedures increasingly sharpened into satire.

As soon as he could, he left the *Call* and began to write for two literary journals, the *Californian* and the *Dramatic Chronicle.* These arrangements improved his income and provided a chance to write literary sketches and burlesques. Some twenty of the sketches he wrote for the *Californian* appeared while Bret Harte was editor. Twain later told T. B. Aldrich that Harte changed him from "an awkward utterer of coarse grotesquenesses to a writer of paragraphs and chapters that have found a certain favor in the eyes of even some of the very decentest people in the land."[19] Few have been able to detect such a splendid debt to Harte. In fact, Franklin R. Rogers argues that Twain owed more to Charles Henry Webb, another editor of the *Californian.* Rogers believes that Webb was especially helpful in getting Twain to drop what remained of his bumpkin style and to play more imaginatively with the sounds and rhythms of his words.[20]

Neither Harte nor Webb, however, cured Twain of his grotesqueries—if indeed they tried—for his sketches in the San Francisco weeklies were probably the silliest stuff he ever turned out: farces, burlesques, and, an old favorite, attacks on a rival editor. In one lampoon of advice to the lovelorn he recommended to a correspondent named Aurelia that she do the best she could under the circumstances though her lover had lost his smooth complexion, one leg, both arms, an eye, the other leg, and his scalp.[21]

By late 1865 Mark Twain was fed up with San Francisco. Once more Steve Gillis brought matters to a head. Arrested for taking part in a barroom brawl, he asked Twain to supply the bail bond. When Twain complied, Gillis skipped town. So did Twain, though it is not clear whether he feared the police or simply wanted fresh adventure. He left San Francisco with Jim Gillis, Steve's brother, for Jim's cabin on Jackass Hill in the Tuolomne Hills. They arrived there on 4 December, and Twain stayed until late February. Although he occasionally panned for gold with Gillis, Dick Stoker, and others, the stay on Jackass Hill was more important for him as a refresher course in Southwestern yarn-spinning. Gillis was a master storyteller,[22] and so were the locals with whom they swapped yarns in the tavern at Angel's Camp on rainy afternoons. One afternoon they heard a solemn duffer named Ben Coon tell a story about a frog that lost a jumping contest because his belly had been filled with shot by the owner of a competing frog.[23] Coon related the anecdote as though he were reciting statistics, offering no indication that he thought there was anything the least funny about it. Later, back on Jackass Hill, Twain and Gillis kept quoting from the yarn and laughing over it. What tickled them was not the yarn itself so much as Ben Coon's grave manner in telling it.

In late February Twain returned to San Francisco, where he found waiting for him a request from Artemus Ward, then in New York, for a sketch that Ward could include in a collection on travel in Nevada. Twain wrote back that he could not possibly meet Ward's deadline, but Ward persisted, and after still more delay Twain responded with "Jim Smiley and His Jumping Frog," cast as a letter to Ward.[24] Although it arrived too late to be included in the collection, Ward liked it so well that he gave it to Henry Clapp, who published it in his *Saturday Press* for 18 November 1865. Immediately, with allowance for the hyperbole, it "set all New York in a roar,"[25] and did the same in San Francisco when Bret Harte reprinted it in the *Californian*. Soon, as it began appearing in other papers throughout the country, "Mark Twain" became a name known nationwide.

The "Jumping Frog" is probably Mark Twain's most firmly organized sketch. For its basic structure he borrowed the frame device that other Southwestern humorists commonly used to introduce and close stories told as oral tales. Thus in the introduction to his tale Mark Twain tells how he encountered a garrulous old fellow named Simon Wheeler in the decaying mining village of Angel's Camp, and in the conclusion he relates his difficulty in breaking away from Wheeler, who was set to talk for hours. Between these two parts of the "frame," Twain without interruption lets Wheeler spin a long yarn about a Jim Smiley. This overall organization is clear enough; less obvious is the tight control the author keeps on Wheeler's monologue, which on the surface seems wholly directionless. Actually, it is carefully molded for climax. After identifying Smiley as a man who would bet on anything, Wheeler offers a series of examples, moving from the most common thing to bet on (horse racing) to something quite uncommon (the health of Parson Walker's wife). He repeats this climactic pattern in telling about the pets that Smiley kept for betting purposes, again moving from the ordinary (a nag) to the less ordinary (a bull pup) to the least ordinary (a frog he had trained to jump). To heighten the sense of progression Wheeler provides more details about the bull pup than he does about the nag, more about the frog than he does about the pup. The high spot comes when the frog, secretly filled with buckshot, can do no more than "hyst" his shoulders when commanded to jump. The sketch is three fifths over before the original frog story surfaces.

In centering his story on his narrators rather than on the jumping contest, Twain turns the old joke into a comic character study. He focuses, as he later said all humorists should do, on the manner of telling rather than on the matter of what is told.[26] In this instance, he focuses on two quite different manners. In the frame story he assumes the persona of an educated but stuffy visitor to Angel's Camp who at the request of a friend from the East is looking for the Reverend Leonidas W. Smiley. He is obviously miffed because he suspects that there is no Reverend Smiley there, and that his friend (Artemus Ward in the first version of the story) has deliberately sent him on a fool's errand so that he will be cornered by Simon Wheeler and have to listen to an interminable account of Jim Smiley. As narrator of the frame Mark Twain writes a stiff, literal, and bureaucratic style that serves dramatically as a foil for the richly figurative vernacular of the main story. As Simon Wheeler, narrator of the main story, Twain pretends to be an old loafer who in his simple and earnest way loves nothing more than regaling a new listener with his oft-repeated yarns. Basic to the fun, then, is the incongruity between the two points of view and the two styles that result. But an additional incongruity enhances the fun, and that is the contrast between the contents of Wheeler's yarn and his manner of telling it. Like Ben Coon, Wheeler is totally unconscious of anything ridiculous in the accomplishments of Jim Smiley. Wheeler thinks Smiley a person of transcendent genius, and tells about him with the gravity and earnestness ordinarily reserved for the relating of great events. Similarly, he views the frog with awe and wonderment. The persona of Simon Wheeler thus forces Mark Twain into doing what he would always do best, tell about ridiculous happenings gravely and in the vernacular. Twenty years later another earnest and humorless persona would result in *Adventures of Huckleberry Finn.*

In San Francisco, in the spring of 1866, though, Mark Twain was far from optimistic about his future. He wrote daily letters to the *Territorial Enterprise,* and started jabbing so vigorously at corruption in San Francisco that readers began viewing him as a reformer as well as a humorist. Yet he could not suppress the notion that he had committed himself to writing of a low order. In such a mood he could call even the "Jumping Frog" story a "villainous backwoods sketch." "Verily," he wrote his mother, "all is vanity and little worth—save piloting."[27]

The Hawaiian Islands, 1866: Travel Letters

He quickly rebounded when he obtained a job that took him off the mainland. Steamship service between San Francisco and Honolulu had just been established, and interest in the Sandwich Islands (later the Hawaiian Islands) as a place for travel and commercial investment was fast developing. Twain had relatively little difficulty, therefore, in persuading the owners of the *Sacramento Union* to send him to "ransack the islands," as he wrote his mother, and send back twenty or thirty letters for which he would get "as much money as I would get if I staid at home,"[28] describing what he found. Thus, in high spirits once more, he left San Francisco on 7 March on the *Ajax,* a combination steamer and sailing vessel. Although he planned to spend only a month in the Islands, he in fact spent four months there. They were probably the happiest months of his adult life.

His sightseeing in the Islands extended beyond Oahu to Maui and Hawaii, even though he soon discovered that travel on none of them was easy. Outside of Honolulu and Hilo he had to travel by horseback and put up in homes rather than hotels. As an outer garment he wore a long linen duster that was so heavily starched that it was often more of a nuisance than a help. But there were no glum letters home, and his notebooks show an insatiable curiosity and a lively amusement. Two events in the Islands affected his career profoundly. One was meeting Anson Burlingame, the brilliant American minister to China, and the other was being the first to report the burning at sea of the clipper ship *Hornet.* Twain had just returned to Honolulu from the island of Hawaii and was in bed with saddle sores when a message arrived that Burlingame and his son wished to visit him. The son had read the "Jumping Frog" and was eager to meet the author. Overwhelmed that such distinguished persons should wish to see him, Twain managed to get out of bed and visit the Burlingames instead of waiting for them to come to him. The meeting was a complete success; despite his pain Twain kept his hosts howling with laughter.

A day or so later came a chance to interview survivors of the *Hornet* disaster. On 3 March the *Hornet* had caught fire near the equator, and the crew and two passengers had to take to the boats. Those in the two quarterboats perished, but all fifteen of those in the longboat survived forty-three days at sea and a journey covering almost four thousand miles. Starved and helpless, they sighted the peak of Mauna Loa and were able to drift ashore on the island of Hawaii, where rescuers helped them ashore and transferred the third mate and the seamen to a hospital in Honolulu. The story was a reporter's dream, but Twain, having aggravated his boils in visiting the Burlingames, was bedfast. Made aware of the situation, Burlingame contrived to have Twain carried on his cot to the hospital. He even questioned the seamen himself so that Twain could simply listen and take notes. Twain then spent the night writing up this account for the *Union* and succeeded the next morning in having it thrown on the deck of the *Milton Badger* just as the ship was casting off for San Francisco. Since no other reporter had been so enterprising, Twain scored a terrific scoop, one that is still legendary on the Pacific Coast.

In one of their conversations Burlingame complimented Twain highly on his talent, going so far as to call him a genius, but adding that he should associate more with persons of refinement and intellect. It was friendly and much needed counsel, but only a man of Burlingame's stature could have offered it without precipitating a stormy response. As it was, Twain accepted the advice gratefully and treasured it literally the rest of his life. If it did nothing else, it strengthened his hunch that he must move from California to the East if he was to establish himself as something more than a newspaper humorist.

Mark Twain fulfilled his contract with the *Sacramento Union* by writing twenty-five letters, at least eight of them after he left Honolulu. Three of the letters dealt with commercial prospects, especially those in sugar, coffee, and whaling. One, of course, contained the story of the *Hornet* survivors. The others were colorful extensions of his Nevada and California writings. But there were marked differences. Nothing he had done before had evoked the descriptive power stimulated by the beauties of the Islands or the narrative power brought out by the story of the *Hornet* survivors. And little that he had done before had such promise for his humor as the role-playing that resulted from the introduction in his letters of a Mr. Brown, a fictitious traveling companion. To Mr. Brown he assigned the grosser remarks that he obviously thought funny but hesitated to claim for himself. The presence of Mr. Brown forces Twain to play a counterrole, that of a cultured gentleman. Thus a series of minidramas results that were the beginnings of the role-playing that eventually makes *Innocents Abroad* so comic and so dramatic. Furthermore, these minidramas show Twain indulging in a rudimentary type of self-censorship. In 1866 he was still not willing to eliminate the gamier remarks, partly because he knew that they would delight the readers of the *Sacramento Union*. But he was beginning to disassociate himself from them. The process of refining "Mark Twain," in short, began before Clemens went East to live.

On the voyage back to the mainland Mark Twain took advantage of the fact that Captain Mitchell of the *Hornet* was a fellow passenger along with the Ferguson brothers, who had been the passengers on the ship. He talked with them at length about their experiences and copied the diaries they generously lent him. Once back in San Francisco, he developed a much more detailed narrative of their ordeal and sent it to *Harper's Monthly* since, as he said, he wanted it to appear in the best of the Eastern journals. Its appearance in December 1866, Twain always felt, was his literary debut—as indeed it was. Even the fact that *Harper's* listed him in the index as "Mark Swain" crushed him only temporarily.

After the freedom of the islands Mark Twain found San Francisco even more depressing. Almost as a joke he mentioned the possibility of lecturing about the Islands to John McCabe, editor of the *Alta California*. McCabe's response was so enthusiastic that Twain hired Maguire's Academy of Music for the evening of 2 October and spread handbills around the town with the still famous last line: "Doors open at 7 o'clock. The trouble to begin at 8 o'clock." At the appointed time the Academy was jammed—and Mark Twain was frightened. But when he stepped on the stage to a storm of applause, the stage fright vanished. He could not have had a more appreciative audience or more favorable reviews. Invitations began to come in asking that he repeat the lecture in other places. Eventually he spoke in over a dozen towns and mining camps, ending the tour with triumphant appearances in Virginia City and, again, in San Francisco. He had finally struck gold. The lectures not only paid far better than newspaper work but also, as he was quick to realize, they created a "voice" or personality for "Mark Twain." Ever after, he used his Missouri drawl both to make his lectures uniquely entertaining and to give his writing a tempo and rhythm that no other humorist could match.

When he left San Francisco in December 1866 Mark Twain was sky high. He had money in his pocket and an assured income because he had arranged with the *Alta California* to mail them weekly letters of the kind he had sent from the Sandwich Islands. He was going to New York, then back to the Midwest to see his family, and then maybe even around the world. With such prospects he could once more think kindly of San Francisco. He wrote his family that he was leaving more friends than "any newspaper man that ever sailed out of the Golden

Gate."[29] His euphoria, however, had a deeper source. He had finally demonstrated to himself that at least in the West he could be a successful writer and lecturer, and the reception in New York of the "Jumping Frog" sketch as well as the *Hornet* account suggested that he could successfully challenge the East. To be sure, he had not changed greatly as a person. He could be the most entertaining of companions, but in return he required attention and praise. He was lazy except when excited about what he was doing, moody, nervous, and basically insecure. He smoked incessantly, drank a good deal, though normally not to the point of being maudlin, and was often brilliantly profane. He was ambitious for fame and money, was a victim of wanderlust, and was beginning to display the streak of pessimism that would eventually grow and ride him to his grave. He had few close friends but maintained warm ties with his mother and sister. When he detected hypocrisy, cruelty, or corruption, he spontaneously exploded into indignation against those responsible and sympathy for the victims. Life bothered him. Happily, though, his sense for the comic induced a large measure of the detachment that his psyche needed for protection against the onslaughts of the outside world. In sum, when he left the West at thirty-one, he was the gifted but unsettled and ornery person he would always be. The East would refine him somewhat but never basically change him.

Chapter Two

The Innocents Abroad

Between December 1866 and August 1869, Mark Twain returned east, visited his family in St. Louis, joined an excursion to Europe and the Holy Land, wrote almost a hundred travel letters for San Francisco and New York newspapers, converted many of these letters into *The Innocents Abroad,* returned briefly to the West Coast, ventured on a minor and a major lecture tour, and fell in love. Not even he could complain about the lack of novelty.

Having agreed to write a weekly travel letter for the *Alta California,* Twain left San Francisco in 15 December 1866. The trip required sailing south to Nicaragua, crossing Nicaragua by horseback and steamer, and then sailing north on the Atlantic to New York, hardly the easiest of journeys. On the stretch to Nicaragua a storm tossed the ship about so fiercely that Twain was convinced they all would have drowned had it not been for the skill of Captain Edgar ("Ned") Wakeman. Later he depicted Wakeman admiringly as Captain Blakely in *Roughing It,* as Hurricane Jones in "Some Rambling Notes of an Idle Excursion," and as the protagonist in *Extract from Captain Stormfield's Visit to Heaven.* After the sea voyage, the lakes and lush valleys of Nicaragua seemed heavenly. But there was little lightheartedness on the trip north after cholera broke out on shipboard. Five passengers died and many more became ill. But Twain did not join those who fled the ship at Key West, and so arrived in New York on 12 January 1867. He stayed there long enough to catch up on the letters he owed the *Alta* and to arrange with Charles Henry Webb, who had preceded him East, to publish his first book, *The Celebrated Jumping Frog of Calaveras County, and Other Sketches,* a collection of twenty-seven pieces most of which had appeared in the *Golden Era* and the *Californian.* It was in the preface to this little volume that Webb called Mark Twain the "Wild Humorist of the Pacific Slope" and the "Moralist of the Main," a dichotomy repeated in many books about Twain, including this one. During this period, too, he learned of a summer excursion to Europe and the Holy Land, and wrote in the *Alta* letter of 2 March that he

would join the expedition as a reporter unless the editors vetoed the
idea. The ploy worked. In printing the letter the *Alta* editors added,
"No Veto," and sent him the cost of the voyage, $1,250. The rest of
the deal was that he was to send back fifty letters at twenty dollars a
letter.

In mid-March Twain took the train to St. Louis to see his mother
and sister and while in the Midwest lectured on the Sandwich Islands
in St. Louis, Hannibal, Keokuk, and Quincy. By mid-April he was
back in New York looking for more adventures that might interest the
Alta readers. He undoubtedly succeeded with his accounts of seeing
the Black Crook, New York's first lavish girlie show, and of spending
a night in jail after he and a friend had tried to break up a street fight
and had managed only to get themselves arrested. All told, he wrote
twenty-six letters for the *Alta,* seven on the trip East, four on the
postwar Mississippi valley, and the remaining fifteen on New York
City. Much like the letters from the Sandwich Islands, these accounts
combine factual information with personal impression, social criticism,
and Washoe-type humor. The inimitable Mr. Brown appears again
with his cynical and raffish remarks, and there is a new character called
"the Bore," who will crop up under different names in future travel
accounts. Something of the bounce of the Sandwich Island letters is
missing in these, however, for the trip home was hardly a picnic, and
both New York and the Midwest seemed to him to have deteriorated.
Curiously Twain describes little of the one experience that greatly
braced his ego: an enthusiastically received lecture on the Sandwich
Islands that he gave at the Cooper Union in New York.

The idea of the excursion had originated among the parishioners of
Henry Ward Beecher's Plymouth Congregational Church in Brooklyn,
and had the strong support of Beecher himself. In charge was Captain
Charles C. Duncan, a member of the church and a sailor and shipping
merchant. For the trip Duncan obtained the thirteen-year-old *Quaker
City*, a 1,900-ton side-wheeler with auxiliary sails fore and aft. He
publicized the trip widely as a luxury cruise, the first of its kind, and
promised such niceties as a library, a physician, and the Plymouth
Collection of Hymns. At first he even promised that General Sherman
would be aboard, and possible Beecher, but both withdrew their names
from the passenger list well before the date of departure. Principally
the expedition attracted ministers, former army officers, and physi-
cians, many of them with wives, and several persons with newspaper
attachments. It was a well-to-do, leisured, and eminently "respectable"

group in which Mark Twain was clearly a maverick, but as close to a celebrity as the company could boast.

The *Quaker City* sailed from New York on 8 June 1867 and was gone almost five and a half months. As advertised, it stopped in the Azores and then continued to Gibraltar where it remained several days to take on coal. Many of the passengers chose to head immediately for Paris through Spain, but Twain and five others with "five bottles and 75 cigars" took a small steamer for Tangier, a city that delighted Twain because it was so thoroughly different from any he had ever visited before. After a day and a half there, they crossed back to Marseilles and boarded a train for Paris where they stopped for a little more than a week before returning to Marseilles to rejoin the ship and most of the passengers for the trip to Genoa. There, largely by rail but partly by stagecoach, they followed the popular tourist trail through Italy to Milan, Venice, Florence, Rome, Pompeii, and Naples. From Naples the full company sailed for Piraeus, the port of Athens, where to their dismay they were not allowed to land because the authorities feared they might be bringing cholera from Italy. But Twain and three others slipped ashore at night and, Tom Sawyer–like, eluded the police successfully enough to climb the Acropolis and be back on shipboard by dawn. From Athens they steamed to Constantinople and into the Black Sea where at Odessa they were received by the czar in his summer palace. The company asked Twain to write the greetings to be read to the czar in their behalf. He complied with so sophomoric a statement that even the ship's crew made fun of it, and Twain subsequently played it down in *The Innocents Abroad*. At Smyrna, Twain joined those making a short trip by train to Ephesus. And at Beirut he became part of a group of eight that hired a dragoman to lead them on an unmercifully long and hot donkey-ride east to Damascus and then south to such biblical towns as Bethlehem, Jericho, and Jerusalem. Bone-weary, they finally rejoined the ship at the port of Jaffa and sailed for Egypt. From there the ship proceeded westward to Gibraltar. While the ship was in port, Twain and three others spent seven delightful days in Seville, Cordova, Cadiz, and the countryside of Andalusia, but in neither the *Alta* letters nor in the book did he elaborate on this side trip. One suspects that in both instances he was simply too fatigued to add another major segment. Finally, the ship started the long voyage back across the Atlantic, and after touching in Bermuda docked in New York on 19 November.

Of the seventy-four passengers on board there were only eight for whom Mark Twain professed much liking. Three of these were his drinking and cardplaying companions: Dan Slote, an earthy New York banker who was Twain's closest friend on the trip, Julius ("Moult") Moulton, and Jack Van Nostrand. In addition, there were Dr. Abraham Reeves Jackson, the surgeon of the ship and a companion on the Acropolis and other escapades; Mr. and Mrs. Solon Severance and Mrs. Mary Mason Fairbanks from Cleveland; and Charles Jervis Langdon (the "cub") from Elmira, New York. The last two remained permanently important in Mark Twain's life. "Mother" Fairbanks, as Twain always called her though she was only seven years older than he, was on the trip as a correspondent for her husband's *Cleveland Herald*. Apparently Twain and she did not become close friends until the ship reached Egypt, but at that point he began regularly to seek her advice on his writing. Her immediate influence on him is debatable. She criticized a score of his letters, one so severely that he threw it away. He said she "weeded" his work of slang, yet there seems to be little discernible change in his style between the *Alta* letters he wrote before and those he wrote after he became one of her "cubs." Whatever her effect on his writing, however, there is no question that she became a force for gentility in his life. Their correspondence, which continued until a few years before she died, shows that he frequently sought her approval, though he never became so proper and refined as she would have had him be. Fortunately for him, Mrs. Fairbanks was just as aware of and responsive to his talents as she was to what she considered to be his crudities.

Young Charles Langdon played an even more important role in Twain's life. Though he early sought Twain's company on the cruise, Twain gave him short shrift until one day in the Bay of Smyrna Langdon showed him an ivory miniature of his sister Olivia. Then and there the storybook romance began. Twain fell in love with Olivia on the spot—or so he said after he married her. Certainly on the rest of the voyage he discovered that the "cub" was far more interesting then he had first suspected. Most of the passengers, though, he found too solemn and pious for his taste. Especially he disliked Captain Cutter not only for his unbearable piety but for his cupidity as well. Then there were the Oracle who pontificated endlessly without benefit of facts, and the Poet Lariat, a "born ass" who memorialized every important event in execrable verse.

Unlike most of the passengers on the *Quaker City,* Mark Twain was not only a tourist but a working journalist. He kept regular notes and wrote well over 100,000 words while abroad. Fifty of his letters appeared in the *Alta California* (plus one he wrote after the cruise was over), six in the *New York Tribune,* and three, that appeared anonymously, in the *New York Herald.* Actually, he had to write sixty-four letters for the *Alta,* because while in Alexandria he learned to his horror that fourteen of his earlier letters never reached San Francisco. Thus, after leaving Alexandria, instead of turning out eight letters as he had planned, he had to produce twenty-two. When the *Quaker City* finally docked in New York, Twain was weary of the whole business. The first night home he stayed up to contrive a letter for the *Herald* in which he blistered the cruise as a "Grand Holy Land Funeral Procession" and charged that life with the "pilgrims" consisted of little more than "solemnity, decorum, dinner, dominoes, prayers, slander."[1] However much he criticised the prim and pious among the passengers, though, neither in the *Herald* letter nor elsewhere did he ever mention fraternizing with the crew. Mark Twain was quite willing to seem a maverick in polite society, but unlike Whitman he never claimed to be one of the roughs.

As for the letters themselves, the combination of fact and fancy that had worked so successfully in previous travel correspondence served equally well in describing the *Quaker City* adventures. Again, information derived from both reading and personal experience established a stable counterpoint for the rowdy humor that Western readers expected. The cynical Mr. Brown was back, this time accompanied by a simpleton named Blucher who could not understand why his watch kept losing time as the ship traveled eastward. Again, too, Twain as the Moralist of the Main attacked corruption and sham wherever he found it. A big advantage the *Quaker City* letters had over the ones from the Sandwich Islands was that they included Old World history and biblical lore, material of great intrinsic interest to American readers. Moreover, they were on the whole more perceptive. As one would expect, though, of a traveler who is sometimes exhilarated, sometimes tired, the letters were uneven in quality. Those written to substitute for the ones that had gone astray were obviously padded with material from such works as J. L. Porter's *Murray's Guide* (used without credit, incidentally) and William Prime's *Tent Life in the Holy Land,* which Twain quoted primarily in order to ridicule Prime's saccharine style. Prime, he asserted cried so much over the holy sites that he irrigated Palestine from one end to the other.

After a day with the Slote family in New York, Twain headed for

Washington and a job as a secretary for Senator William Stewart of Nevada. The two men quickly quarreled and parted, but not before the experience provided material for later satirical treatment in *The Gilded Age* and elsewhere. In the meantime Twain became an "occasional" writer for both the *New York Tribune* and the *Herald*. During the Christmas holidays he went back to New York to attend a reunion of the *Quaker City* nighthawks. Among those present was Charley Langdon, who invited Twain to accompany him and his family to a reading by Charles Dickens. It was at this reading that Twain met Olivia Langdon, the original for the ivory miniature he had seen on shipboard in the Bay of Smyrna.[2] Whether or not he had fallen in love with the miniature, he certainly lost his heart to the original. Before the evening was over he managed to extract an invitation from Livy, as he would always call her, to visit the Langdons in Elmira. But it was August before he was able to do so.

Earlier in December he had received a letter from Elisha Bliss, president of the American Publishing Company in Hartford, Connecticut, urging him to write a book about his *Quaker City* adventures. On the advice of Henry Ward Beecher, Twain turned down Bliss's offer of a cash payment of $10,000 and accepted, rather, an option of a 5 percent royalty, a decision that ultimately paid off handsomely. So that he could concentrate on the book he began refusing lecture invitations and cutting back severely on his newspaper commitments. He even turned down a chance of being appointed postmaster at San Francisco. Instead he holed up in a Washington rooming house where he nervously paced back and forth, smoked, swore, drank—and wrote. Then came devastating news: the *Alta* owners had copyrighted his letters and planned to publish them in book form themselves. When telegrams failed to provide the clearance he needed, Twain hurried out to San Francisco, this time by way of the Isthmus of Panama, to plead with the *Alta* "thieves" face to face. Fortunately, the encounter turned out to be friendly, and the matter was quickly resolved in Mark Twain's favor. Again it was full steam ahead. A repetition of his earlier lecture tour in California and Nevada provided the pocket money he needed, but otherwise he worked on the book unremittingly both while in California and on the trip home. As a result, he was able to present Elisha Bliss with a completed manuscript on 30 July 1868.

Bliss's American Publishing Company was a subscription house that hired agents across the country to peddle its books from door to door. The system, though elaborate, was profitable. Especially in the depression just after the Civil War, subscription publishers could offer an author substantially higher royalties than conventional publishers, who depended upon bookstores to sell their products. The major drawback was that the Eastern literary establishment sniffed at the subscription method as being too crassly commercial and, consciously or not, downgraded their authors. Thus at the outset of his publishing career Mark Twain impaled himself on the horns of a dilemma that over the years became increasingly painful. Always he wanted *both* money and prestige. If he almost invariably opted for money, he just as invariably further lacerated an ego already wounded by the tendency of the literati to view him as simply a humorist and therefore not as a writer to be taken seriously. In 1868, however, he was still ingenuous enough to be thrilled by the thought of having a publisher—any publisher—and the prospect of prodigious earnings (to use his favorite adjective).

In late August Mark Twain visited Olivia Langdon in Elmira. The Langdons were the epitome of upper New York genteel society: rich, conservative, Protestant, "respectable." Jervis Langdon had made a fortune in coal and lumber and had built a mansion on grounds covering a city block. Theirs was the gracious life that John Marshall Clemens had dreamed of and the genteel Christian home that Jane Lampton Clemens had tried to create in the little clapboard house in Hannibal. Far from breaking with his past, Sam Clemens was returning to the world of his parents' aspirations. At sixteen Olivia, the darling of the family, had hurt her back while skating and had spent two years in bed in a darkened room. No physician seemed to be able to help her until Langdon in desperation called in a mind healer who promptly threw up the shades and told Livy to get up and walk. And she did. She was twenty-two when she met Twain, ten years younger than he. She was slight in build, had smooth white skin, and wore her black hair combed back from her forehead. She had the poise, the moral principle, and the refinement that as a closet Victorian Mark Twain had always dreamed of in a wife. What he was to discover was that her cool and prim exterior hid an almost fiery passion. Impetuously, before he left Elmira on the first visit Twain proposed to Livy and was promptly turned down. Proper courtship in polite society did not move that fast, but she permitted him to write her as a sister, and she promised to pray for him. Soon he was invited back for a short visit—that was extended after he fell from the carriage that was to take him to the railroad station.

On 17 November, under the auspices of James Redpath of the Boston Lyceum Bureau, he began in Cleveland a series of lectures on "The American Vandal Abroad" that eventually totaled forty-two engagements. As he wrote Mrs. Fairbanks, he "smouched" the lecture from the manuscript of *Innocents Abroad,* and added that it included not only preposterous yarns but also "high-toned" glimpses of such places as the Coliseum, the Parthenon, and the pyramids. It ended with the moral that vandals should continue to travel because it liberalized them. Obviously he wrote the lecture not only to satisfy the general public but also to please "Mother" Fairbanks—and Livy. In both respects it was a huge success. Mrs. Fairbanks was probably responsible for the statement next morning in the *Cleveland Herald* that Twain had proved that a man "may be a humorist without being a clown."[3] After Cleveland, Twain lectured in Pittsburgh where he outdrew the actress Fanny Kemble, and then headed for a performance in Elmira. He stayed with the Langdons for about a week, and this time Livy gave in. Twain thought the lecture helped, and probably it did. He promised to give up liquor and become a Christian. Mr. and Mrs. Langdon, however, were not so impressed as Livy by this sudden conversion, and asked that the engagement be kept secret until they could find out more about the humorist's prospects and character. Mr. Langdon wanted references, and Twain for some perverse reason gave the names of persons in the West who hardly knew him. The replies, therefore, were hardly encouraging. Nevertheless, in a few weeks Langdon capitulated, and Mrs. Langdon after corresponding with Mrs. Fairbanks followed suit with reluctant approval. The engagement was announced in early February. In March after he had completed the lecture tour Twain hurried to Elmira to be with Livy and to have her help him with the last proofs of *The Innocents Abroad.*

When Mark Twain sat down in late January of 1868 to put the story of the *Quaker City* expedition into book form, his main purpose was to create a book that would sell. But for the book to sell, as he well knew, the writing had to appeal to a far more general audience than the one to which he had addressed the *Alta* letters. Even though the American Publishing Company targeted their books primarily at those living on farms and in small towns, there were many whose literary taste was a cut higher than what he was accustomed to, and their tolerance for impropriety several cuts lower. That he succeeded with *The Innocents Abroad* as well as he did is a tribute to his judgment and craftsmanship.

Fortunately for Mark Twain, Bliss did not ask for a tightly structured narrative. Twain, therefore, simply used the itinerary of the

Quaker City as a clothesline, as it were, on which to hang a variety of short sketches, the literary form at which he excelled. Most of the episodes, of course, he took from the *Alta* letters. In fact, he used all of the letters in part though none as a whole. Unfortunately, the letters did not cover the entire trip. The first dealt with the adventures in the Azores, and the last (except for two general summations) with the departure form Palestine. Moreover, because fourteen letters had gone astray, only twelve treated the happenings in France and Italy whereas twenty-eight, a disproportionate number, described those in Palestine. None mentioned the Atlantic crossings in detail or the experiences in Egypt. To fill out his narrative and to create the "big book" Elisha Bliss wanted, Twain consequently had to forage for other material. To jog his memory he borrowed accounts of the trip written by Mrs. Fairbanks for the *Cleveland Herald,* those of Colonel J. Herron Foster that had appeared in the *Pittsburgh Dispatch,* and those of Dr. Jackson that had been published in the *Monroe County* (Pennsylvania) *Democrat.* In addition, he filled out the narrative with freshly devised descriptions and adventures, with factual material lifted from other travel accounts, and with burlesques and anecdotes that sometimes had only a dubious relevance. What finally emerged was a surprisingly well-balanced treatment of the trip in its entirety. A survey of the sixty numbered chapters shows two each focusing primarily on preparations, the Atlantic crossing, and the Azores; one on Gibraltar, two on Tangier, seven on France, fifteen on Italy, and one on Greece, two on Turkey, three on the expedition to Odessa to meet the czar, eight on the Levant, eleven on Palestine, two on Egypt, and two on the voyage home. The narrative begins in New York with the narrator's ridiculous expectations for the trip and ends in New York with his equally ridiculous criticisms of it. In between come the events that account for the change. The middle of the book almost exactly divides the experiences in western Europe from those in Russia and the Near East. By good fortune the trip itself provided built-in suspense because the visit to Palestine, the place of most interest to contemporary readers, came toward the end of the cruise and hence toward the close of the narrative.

Within this overall pattern Mark Twain labored to tie the *Alta* material together. As Leon T. Dickinson in a useful article points out, he inserted passages, often long ones, to achieve continuity and carry the reader from place to place. Moreover, he shifted blocks of material to give the narrative tighter construction, and reorganized details within episodes so that the reader could follow the happenings more easily. Finally, to maintain interest he eliminated many repetitions and constantly alternated the writing between the serious and the comic.[4] What he wrote later about the structure of his lectures explains the alteration of material in *Innocents*: "*Any* lecture of mine ought to be a running narrative-plank, with square holes in it, six inches apart, all the length of it, & then in my mental shop I ought to have plugs (half marked 'serious' & the other marked 'humorous') to select from & jam into these holes according to the temper of the audience."[5] Thus the "plugs" of statistics, exposition, description, history, social criticism, and rhapsodic sentimentalizing alternate with plugs involving comic characterizations, Washoe jokes, farce, burlesque, and idiocies resulting from the use of comic masks. Since the serious and the comic jostle each other in constantly varying combinations and permutations, the alternation is not so mechanical as the metaphor of the narrative plank would suggest. Toward the end of the book as he tired and leaned more heavily on guidebooks, the holes in the narrative-plank move farther apart. But he never fully gave up alternating the serious and the comic as an organizing principle. The final form of the book owed something, maybe a great deal, to Bret Harte, who edited the manuscript when Twain was in San Francisco. In *Roughing It,* his next travel book, Twain achieved a more tightly structured narrative, but *The Innocents Abroad* is far from formless. It may resemble a vaudeville show more than a sustained dramatic production, but it is still one show with a discernible beginning, middle, and end.

For today's reader, however, the most fascinating achievement in *The Innocents Abroad* is not the narrative but the narrator. Because of the epistolary style carried over from the *Alta* letters, and the extraordinary clarity of that style, one feels the presence of a single narrator even though he operates in four different ways. He is a reporter, a humorist, a social critic, and a Victorian Man of Feeling. These roles are not wholly discrete, but they are different enough to be distinguishable, and they account for the book's frequent and often sudden shifts in tone and style.

In the preface Mark Twain introduces himself not as a scholar or as an experienced traveler but simply as a writer who proposes to picture Europe and the Holy Land as his readers would find them were they to duplicate his journey. In effect, then, he introduces himself as a reporter. For such a role his credentials turn out to be admirable. He is inquisitive, impressionable, articulate, conscientious about his obligation to inform his readers, and detached in the sense that he represents no geographical region, political party, or religious denomination (though he admits to being a Protestant). But he makes little attempt to be objective as that term is now used in modern journalism. Quite the contrary, he lets it be unmistakably known what he likes (the Milan cathedral, Genoese women) and what he dislikes (hotels that provide no soap). Ugliness evokes his most vivid descriptions: the alleys of Civita Vecchia "carpeted" with dead cats and decayed rags, Palestinian babies with their eyes ringed by flies, and a long-dead monk in a Capuchin monastery with his brown and shrunken skin, crisp dead eyes deep in their sockets, and lips shriveled away from yellow teeth.

A reader must be wary, however, because Mark Twain the reporter invariably and without warning gives way to Mark Twain the humorist, "straight" writing to the bizarre. The book is a compendium of comic modes and devices. But as one would expect of a writer steeped in the Western tradition, most of the fun depends upon exaggeration which makes up in exuberance what it lacks in subtlety: exaggeration of incident (his horse jumps over eighteen hundred donkeys on the road to Nazareth), exaggeration of detail (Michael Angelo created not only St. Peter's but also the Pantheon, the Coliseum, the Vatican, the Tarpian Rock, the Tiber, the pope, and the entire Eternal City), exaggeration in figures of speech (the Coliseum is a band-box with a side bitten out). The best humor, however, results from the exaggerated roles Twain assumes. These are of two kinds: roles in which as an *alazon* he pretends to be greatly superior to others, and roles in which as an *eiron* he pretends to be lamentably inferior. As a socially superior person, for example, he plays the part of a highly cultured gentleman, just as he had in the *Alta* letters when chiding Mr. Brown. Presumably to make *Innocents* more acceptable to the fastidious, he banishes Brown from its pages and lords it over Blucher and Jack Von Nostrand instead. In the role of the intellectually superior instructor he sets us straight on Old World legends, and as an emotionally superior sentimentalist he displays a sensitivity presumably denied us more cloddish morals. At the tomb of Adam, for instance, the fountain of his filial affection is "stirred to its profoundest depths." Through his tears he confides, "I deem it no shame to have wept over the grave of my poor dead relative" (vol. 2, chap. 26).

On the whole, though, the poses of inferiority are the more comic. As the sufferer Mark Twain is physically inferior, sometimes responding vindictively and sometimes stoically. As the stoic, for example, he remains incredibly composed while being "polished" by the attendant in a Turkish bath. After having a layer of skin rubbed off he calmly suggests that the attendant use a jack plane to get the job done more quickly. As the simpleton, Twain is the sublime idiot who believes everything he is told, no matter how absurd. At one point he becomes persuaded that a certain column in Palestine marks the center of the earth and that Adam was made from the dust beneath it. Of all the poses of inferiority, however, that of the tenderfoot is the most appealing because it mirrors in exaggerated form experiences common to all travelers. As the tenderfoot Twain portrays himself as the dupe of romantic preconceptions about Europe and the Holy Land. On each occasion reality shatters the preconception. Storms and seasickness destroy the dream of romantic shipboard life; the Parisian barbershop that Twain expected to be redolent with the perfumes of Araby turns out to be a torture chamber; fabled Arabian horses prove to be ordinary nags; and visions of the glory of the streets where Jesus walked quickly fade before the reality of hot dry alleys jammed with vermin-infested beggars. In fact, one might say that the entire cruise involves the collapse of misconceptions about cruises.

Despite such high jinks, the Mark Twain of the *Innocents* is still the moralist, for as often as not the humor slips into satire and reporting into social criticism. It is not easy to pin down the central principles of Twain's criticism. He is so often ambivalent on issues and so contradictory in his statements that one sometimes wonders if there is any centrality to him. He has no overriding ideology, and is by turns a realist and a romanticist, an idealist and a materialist, an admirer of aristocracy and a Western democrat, a person enamored by the European pastoral life and an enthusiast for technical progress. The list can go on. Despite this assemblage of contradictions, however, two attitudes persist unalloyed; one might almost call them gut reactions. Pretension or hypocrisy always annoys him, and injustice or cruelty always outrages him. Both of these characteristics surfaced in earlier writings, but in *Innocents Abroad* they appear insistently and dramatically enough to stamp Mark Twain indelibly as being both honest and humane.

Pretension, hypocrisy, and other forms of deception he finds everywhere on the journey. Special targets of his satire include Americans who sign hotel registers in French after being abroad only a few days, old travelers who brag about their exploits, tourists who drool over the beauty of Leonardo Da Vinci's *The Last Supper* though it is clearly faded and chipped, cathedral officials who for a gratuity display fragments of the "true cross," and impostors who pose as cripples to win pennies from the sympathetic. Twain reserves his most barbed remarks, however, for the excessively pious among the *Quaker City* passengers. Instead of their being the Christians they profess to be, he finds them mean, hypocritical, stingy, and even wanton in their chipping "specimen" from ancient structures they pretend to venerate. As the book proceeds, Twain establishes a cleavage between these self-annointed "saints" and his own little coterie whom he calls "sinners." As he develops it, the distinction becomes a parody of the Calvinist dichotomy between the Elect and the Damned—a parody because Twain's "saints," despite their outward piety, are really the sinners; and his sinners, despite their drinking and smoking, are really the saints. Specifically the "sinners" are Twain, Dan Slote, Dr. Jackson, Jack Van Nostrand, with Charles Langdon as a junior member. The "saints" are all the others except for Mrs. Fairbanks and the Severances whom he likes and respects.

Although Mark Twain plays no favorites in his attacks on pretension, he clearly favors America over the Old World in attacking those guilty of the more serious crime of injustice to the common man. In the only sustained piece of social criticism in the work (vol. 1, chap. 26), he tells what an Italian might say to his countrymen just after returning from a trip to the United States. Although the Italian pokes fun at American dress and houses, he dwells chiefly on the astonishing (to him) rights enjoyed by ordinary men and women in America. They are allowed, even encouraged, to read; they can own their own land; and, amazingly, they can complain if they do not like the way they are governed. What also surprises this fictional Italian is the relative scarcity on the streets of clergymen and soldiers, and the lack of church taxes and controls. The passage reveals not an abstract theory of equalitarianism so much as Twain's humanitarian concern for the welfare of the common people. It is this concern that prompts the biting remarks throughout the book about those in power who exploit the poor; special targets are the Catholic authorities who turn cathedrals into vast depositories of ostentatious wealth while people starve just outside the doors.

Mark Twain's letters and notes indicate that he became apprehensive about overdoing the satire and thus laying himself open to charges of coarseness and blasphemy. The cautions of Elisha Bliss and Mrs. Fairbanks may have contributed to his uneasiness, but the fear of losing sales among "respectable" readers was undoubtedly a stronger force.

Whatever the reasons, in revising the *Alta* letters for *Innocents Abroad* he toned down the gaudiest of his ridicule. He dropped such words as "stink" and "jackass," and sliced some of the passages that the pious might think especially irreverent. The most arresting cut of this kind occurs in an *Alta* letter where he describes the monks in the Duomo in Florence. The *Alta* version reads: "It takes three hundred flabby, greasy vagabonds in holy orders to run this awful ecclesiastical swindle. And they don't stand a watch worth twenty dollars a month. They begin dinner at noon and gorge till 3; then they smoke, and swill, and sleep till 5, and then they come on watch for just two hours."[6]

In *The Innocents Abroad,* although he does suggest that the poor should rob the Duomo, he reduces this passage to "Three hundred happy, comfortable priests are employed in that cathedral" (vol. 1 chap. 25). Finally, as we already know, in an apparent concession to fastidious readers, Twain banishes the cynical and vulgar Mr. Brown, though he retains the simple-minded Blucher. To conclude from such changes, however, that Mark Twain seriously emasculated the style in the *Alta* is to jump ahead of the evidence. The alterations, taken as a whole, are not so numerous or so radical as to turn *The Innocents* into Sunday School reading. Moreover, he left untouched, or even added, much that Victorian readers might—and did—find displeasing. Both Mrs. Severance and Mrs. Fairbanks let him know in no uncertain terms that there were passages that they wished he had omitted. The truth is that while Mark Twain did make adjustments in his social criticism with such readers in mind, he stopped far short of surrendering to their strictest notions of propriety.

Yet in at least one respect *The Innocents Abroad* turns out to be typically Victorian. For if Mark Twain uses the work to satirize the ostentatious morality of the dominant culture, he shows himself to be a product of that culture by being a Man of Feeling. Added often at the beginnings and endings of chapters are passages of inflated rhetoric that are just as romantic—and empty—as those of William Prime, whom Twain in his sarcastic moments lampoons as "Mr. Grimes." Sometimes Twain softens a harsh description of a hallowed place by shifting the illumination from the glare of daylight to the shadows of twilight or the dimness of starlight. Thus after finding the Sea of Galilee wretchedly disappointing during the day, he tells how in the starlight it becomes a place "meet for the birth of a religion able to save a world. . . . One can comprehend it only when night has hidden all incongruities and created a theater proper for so grand a drama" (vol. 2, chap. 21). On other occasions he invokes history in order to suffuse present reality with the romance of the past. His long and dreamy apostrophe to the Sphinx is the most lyrical of these. It begins: "The great face was so sad, so earnest, so longing, so patient. There was a dignity not of earth in its mien, and in its countenance a benignity such as never anything human wore" (vol. 2, chap. 31). There is not a hint, as one might expect, that Napoleon's cannon had smashed the Sphinx's nose. His romantic picture of the Acropolis in moonlight thrilled not only Victorian readers but listeners as well when Twain gave it a climactic position in his lectures on the trip. One may well ask why Mark Twain after ridiculing the purple rhetoric of others should indulge in it himself. The easy answer would be that he was trimming his sails to the winds of the time. He knew that sentimental novels were the best-sellers, and he had discovered that sentimental set-pieces in his lectures brought enthusiastic applause and often won top acclaim in reviews. The fact that purple writing in *Innocents* appears in set pieces rather than permeating the book as a whole suggests that he added it deliberately. But before accusing him of being a callous opportunist we should remember that such writing had also interrupted the realism of his letters from the Sandwich Islands. Like his contemporaries, Mark Twain could be moved by natural grandeur and ancient ruins, spectacles that passed for the sublime in the nineteenth century. Such spectacles almost invariably smothered his comic imagination. There is little question that he was genuinely moved by the Acropolis and the Sphinx, and that in describing his feelings he fell back upon the clichés by which emotion was popularly conveyed and enjoyed.

Innocents Abroad is not a great book. Its perceptions play along the surface, and there is too much maneuvering and straining for effect. Twain has not yet found a way to achieve a subtle blend of humor and morality—each stands out too obviously from the other—and his people remain two-dimensional. There is no vernacular "character" to provide both charm and an ethical yardstick. Even Mr. Brown might have helped. But it was an immensely popular book because it provided the combination, blended or not, of information, overblown humor, "sublimity," and bedrock morality that was especially congenial to the readers of its time. Moreover, it offered a narrator who in his realism, biases, ignorances, and outspokenness was quintessentially the American common man. As he had hoped, Twain did see Europe and the Holy Land as most Americans would have seen it. What is more, he

was not cowed by the experience, and thus bolstered the American ego,
which typically shriveled when confronted by the riches of European
culture. Whatever the work's immediate effects, its humor was what
most readers remembered. As a result of *The Innocents Abroad,* Mark
Twain became universally recognized as America's premier humorist.
No matter how hard he later tried, he was never able completely to
destroy that image in order to become known as a premier literary
artist.

Innocents Abroad sold well. Bliss backed up his army of salesmen with
an advertising blitz, especially in small-town newspapers, and Mark
Twain himself publicized the volume by his lectures on "The American
Vandal Abroad." By the end of 1869, thirty thousand copies had been
sold. The price of the most inexpensive copy—black cloth with gold
stamping—was $3.50; Twain's share of this was twelve cents. Gener-
ally, papers in the smaller cities and towns reviewed the work favora-
bly, and so did such friendly metropolitan dailies as the *New York
Tribune* and the *Cleveland Herald.* Most of the literary journals, as was
their wont with subscription books, ignored the work. But to Twain's
great delight, the *Atlantic Monthly* broke its rule against reviewing
subscription books to report that "there is an amount of human nature
in the book that rarely gets into literature." Since the review was un-
signed, Mark Twain did not know until later that the reviewer was
William Dean Howells, who was destined to be his best friend and
most influential literary advisor.

Chapter Three
Roughing It

In his second travel book, *Roughing It,* Mark Twain turns to his 1861–66 experience in the West, including the Sandwich Islands. To call *Roughing It* a travel book, though, is to diminish it. For it is also a fictionalized autobiography, an extended tall story, a sketch book of people and places, and at least in the first half, a picaresque novel. It is the best picture we have of the glory days in the Comstock Lode country, and one of the better portrayals of San Francisco before it became tamed and of the Islands before they became an appendage of the United States. Moreover, its final admonition to the reader not to travel suggests that it may even be an apologia, a commitment to his bride that he was putting such youthful rowdiness behind him and accepting the ways of Victorian respectability. Structurally the book has its flaws, but it is more confidently written than *Innocents Abroad* and it carries more conviction. Twain is not dealing in it with a tour he has just taken, but with a substantial portion of his life. Everything considered, *Roughing It* is the best of the five books based on his travels.

On and off, Mark Twain pegged away on the manuscript of *Roughing It* in what for him were the best of times and the worst of times. There were good reasons for his ebullience in the latter half of 1869 and the first half of 1870. His income was ample for his needs; *The Innocents Abroad* was selling "right along with the Bible"; Jervis Langdon lent him $25,000 so that he could buy a third share in the *Buffalo Express;* and a lecture tour in New England and New York proved to be unusually successful. In Boston, that citadel of Eastern Culture, four thousand turned out to hear him, a timely triumph just before he married an Eastern woman. While in Boston, too, he met William Dean Howells, whose praise gave him the strongest intimation yet that he might be capable of something more than journalistic humor. But of course the crowning event of the period was his marriage on 2 February 1870 to Olivia Langdon. The day afterward, the wedding party traveled by private railroad coach from Elmira to Buffalo where Langdon presented the newlyweds with a deed for a house on fashionable Delaware Avenue together with a check to cover the expenses of three servants and a horse and carriage. It was a royal beginning for the grave, proper Eastern bride and the irrepressible Western groom (who sang an off-color ballad for the wedding party). Against all the signs the marriage "took." Much later, when Twain became so irascible that he was almost impossible to endure, Livy still called him "Youth," and for him she was always "the best girl in the world." At first she tried to reform him, and for a few months he did give up liquor and tobacco, and even began reading the Bible aloud and saying grace at the table. But soon he eliminated the grace and the Bible reading, and about the time he began writing in earnest on *Roughing It* he turned to his cigars and ale. Livy came to accept him for what he was. To ease her conscience she used to "dust him off" after he had been particularly outrageous among their friends, but neither of them took such reprimands to heart. In the end it was Livy who changed. In later life she admitted that she did not want to go to heaven if her husband would not be there.

After the marriage he settled down to write for the *Express*. In addition, he contracted to write a regular ten-page section called "Memoranda" for the *Galaxy*, a New York literary monthly. For both publications he turned out an array of sketches, social criticism, and satire, writings that offer little evidence that marriage tamed his style. An attack in the *Galaxy* on a Reverend Mr. Sabine of New York for refusing to read the burial service for the actor George Holland is as vitriolic a piece as he ever devised.

In mid-July Twain signed a contract with Elisha Bliss of the American Publishing Company to produce a book of six hundred pages on his Western experiences and to have it finished by 1 January. His royalty rate was to be 7.5 percent. He began with a rush. Because he had kept no notes of his own on the overland trip to Nevada, he sent for the notebook that Orion had kept. Also, he began assembling potentially helpful works such as Thomas J. Dimsdale's *The Vigilantes of Montana* (1866) and Catherine V. Waite's *The Mormon Prophet and His Harem* (1866). The first four chapters of the book took only a week to write. But then family tragedies undercut the lightheartedness of the young couple and seriously interfered with the process of composition. First, Livy's father died, then a guest in their home contracted typhoid fever and died, and finally Livy, weak and overwrought, delivered her first baby prematurely on 7 November. For weeks both Livy and the little Langdon remained so frail that Twain was beside himself with anxiety. Worse, debts began to accumulate. He failed three times, once seriously, to turn out the requisite ten pages for the *Galaxy,* and he had to watch the deadline for his Western book come and go with only a small fraction of the six hundred pages written. To appease Bliss he offered to prepare a collection of his sketches for immediate publication, and to write a book on diamond mining from notes to be taken by an old friend, J. H. Riley. The plan was that Riley would go to South Africa and gather as many impressions as he could if Bliss would put up the money. Surprisingly, Bliss agreed to both ideas. But neither book substituted for *Roughing It.* The collection of sketches did not appear until 1875, and the volume on diamond mining never appeared because Riley died before Twain began to work with him.

By March 1871 Twain had had enough of Buffalo. In April he sold the house and, at considerable loss, his interest in the *Express,* and moved the family to Quarry Farm, the home of Theodore Crane, Livy's brother-in-law. Situated high on a hill just east of Elmira, Quarry Farm was an ideal spot for a writer. There, he could finally concentrate on *Roughing It,* and his spirits began to rise. He had about a fourth of the book completed when he began to work at Quarry Farm, but he was not pleased with what he had done. He wrote to Orion, who was then working for Bliss, "Just as soon as ever I can, I will send some of the book M.S. but right in the first chapter I have got to alter the whole style of one of my characters and re-write him clear through to where I am now. It is no fool of a job, I can tell you, but the book will be greatly bettered by it."[1] By 8 April he was up to manuscript page 570. Oddly, though, the first chapter still bothered him, and he wished that he had time to revise it again.

In mid-April Joe Goodman, his old boss on the *Territorial Enterprise,* came for a visit that lasted two months. Since Goodman was able to reinforce Twain's memories with his own, the visit was as much a spur as a distraction. By mid-May Twain reported to Bliss that he would soon be done. But as always there were interruptions. Twain himself broke off composition to work on three lectures he hoped would pull him out of debt. Moreover, at Bliss's insistence he took time out to prepare material for the prospectus and for Bliss's journal, the *American Publisher.* It was not until August, therefore, that he could present the publisher with what he thought was a finished manuscript. But to his dismay he found that he had not only to "cut and slash & trim & revamp" what he had already done but also to add new material because he had miscalculated the number of manuscript pages he needed. Worst of all, one chapter was totally missing. He wrote Bliss with fervor, "I remember the heavy work it was to write it before and I wish that man had the M.S. stuffed into his bowels that lost it."[2] To be closer to his editors while making the changes they required, he rented the Hooker house on Forest Avenue in Hartford. (He eventually built his own house close by.) Even after he delivered the manuscript in October he was apparently not through because a comparison of the American, English, and Canadian pirated editions suggests that parts of the book were reshuffled at the last moment for the American edition. At long last, the American edition appeared in early March 1872, a few days after the English edition. Sales in the first two years ran behind those of *Innocents Abroad* for the same length of time, 73,207 to approximately 90,000, but *Roughing It* has always been one of Mark Twain's four or five most popular books.

Despite the fact that *Roughing It* follows the route of Mark Twain's actual travels in the West, the very first paragraph lets the reader know that this is to be an imaginative autobiography, not a factual one. In it Twain says that he was "young and ignorant" and that he had never been away from home before—hardly a description of a man who was twenty-five years old and who had been a journeyman printer in the East and Midwest as well as a pilot on a Mississippi River steamboat. Obviously, the adventurer here is another innocent—and much younger than the one who went to the Holy Land on the *Quaker City*.

Chapters 1–20 of *Roughing It* deal with the trip from St. Louis to Carson City, with a four-chapter pause to observe the Mormons in Salt Lake City. No sooner are they started on their overland trek than Mark Twain as a young tenderfoot begins to discover that his romantic dreams of the West have little basis in fact. The stagecoach breaks down. At the stagecoach stations the combs are revolting and the tea undrinkable. The outlaw Slade, who had reportedly killed twenty-six human beings, proves to be friendly and gentle-spoken, and a Mormon Destroying Angel nothing more than a profane old blackguard. Even more dismaying, the stalwart Westerner of dime thrillers turns out more often than not to be a slovenly dispirited drunkard, and the Noble Red Man to be a filthy Goshoot. But there are surprises such as the coyote, the jackass rabbit, and the alkali desert; and the pony express comes up to all expectations. Chapters 21–41 tell of attempts, all of them unsuccessful, to make a quick fortune in the silver region of Nevada. Shortly after arriving in Carson City, Twain with a Johnny Kinney of Cincinnati tramps over to Lake Tahoe where after posting a claim to about three hundred acres of timber land they build a brush lean-to and settle back to laze away a fortnight or more. Ever afterward, Lake Tahoe for Twain represented the ultimate in beauty and quiet and ease. Ironically, it is Twain who brings this idyll to an end by accidentally setting fire to the timber on their claim. Back in Carson City he is smitten with "silver fever." With three companions he pushes a wagon—the horses are too weak to help—to the Humboldt River region. But there he finds nothing but mica. When drilling brings no better luck, he and two other companions, Ballou and Ollendorf, head back toward Carson only to have a flood force them to hole up for eight days in an inn with a number of other marooned miners. When the flood recedes, they start out again but this time are caught in a snowstorm. As night comes on they try, like heroes in Western stories, to light a fire by shooting at a pile of shavings. Unhappily, the explosion blows the shavings away. Convinced that they will freeze to death, they say their farewells and, in a fit of repentance for their evil ways, throw away their cards, liquor, and pipes. Then they lie down in the snow to await oblivion. Oblivion comes but only in the form of a sound sleep. When morning arrives they awake to discover that they are only fifteen steps from a stagecoach station. Sheepishly they retrieve their possessions and agree to say no more about repentance. Then follow exhausting days of prospecting and near poverty until Twain and a miner named Higbie find a blind lead (a vein that does not crop out above the surface). Wealth is within their grasp. They neglect, however, to work the site within the necessary ten days and lose title to it. The biggest balloon of all—silver and gold for the taking—has finally burst.

In chapters 42–55 (chapters 1–14 of volume 2 in some editions) Twain tries to give a sense for his early days as a reporter on the *Virginia City Territorial Enterprise* and for the flush times in the mother lode (Comstock) region in and around Virginia City. Among much else he tells about the town itself perching on a steep mountainside, the newspapers, the speculation in mining stocks, the loads of silver bricks taken from the town, and a literary magazine called the *Occidental*. In addition, he describes the newspapermen, the rich "nabobs" and the Chinese, the drunkards and outlaws and murderers. But his list is selective, for he says little about the shopkeepers and nothing about the prostitutes except to mention that there were brothels.

In chapters 56–61 he skates rather quickly over his experiences in and around San Francisco, first as a social butterfly when he assumes that the mining stocks he brought from Virginia City are valuable and

second as a "slinker" after he discovers they are not. Perhaps the best
reporting in these chapters centers on "the great earthquake" in San
Francisco and on pocket mining in the Tuolumne Hills. He mentions
visiting Angel's Camp but says nothing about a jumping frog. Chapters 62–77 are a rewriting (and sometimes a copying verbatim) of about
a fifth of the letters he had written in the Sandwich Islands in 1865
for the *Sacramento Union*. Like the letters, these chapters are a hodge-
podge of descriptions of native costumes and customs, reports of shipping costs and other business items, lyrical apostrophes to the natural
scenery (especially volcanoes), and tall tales. Chapters 78–79 briefly
tell of his return to San Francisco, his first lecture there, and his departure by sea for the East. He ends the story with the astonishing
admonition to the reader that anyone of any account should stay at
home and work hard. Then he concludes the volume with three appendixes: "Brief Sketch of Mormon History," "The Mountain Meadows
Massacre," and "Concerning a Frightful Assassination that was never
Consummated."

Since both Mark Twain and Elisha Bliss wanted to capitalize on the
popularity of *The Innocents Abroad,* it is not surprising that *Roughing It*
resembles the earlier book in several important respects. It is a big
book—seventy-nine chapters—designed to impress prospective buyers. Again Twain selects his material for its novelty, and again serious
passages alternate throughout with comic ones. Especially in the first
half, a naive narrator repeatedly confronts situations that are new to
him and for which he is unprepared. And once more the author is both
the Wild Humorist of the Pacific Slope as well as the Moralist of the
Main. As much as *Roughing It* resembles *Innocents Abroad,* however, it
differs significantly in the handling of the point of view and in its
overall coherence and stability. In both of these regards, *Roughing It* is
a superior literary achievement.

To understand the complexity of the book's point of view, one must
recall that for the first half (chapters 1–41) Twain had no travel letters
to depend upon; in the second half, however, he was able to lean heavily on those he had written for Nevada and California newspapers. As
a result, the first half is primarily fresh invention, the second primarily
rewriting. The main element holding the two together is "Mark
Twain," the persona selected to be the chief narrator. He is middle-
aged and knowledgeable; he has had time to reflect on the adventures
of his younger years and to add information gathered from reading as
well as experience. He has a penchant for the incongruous in both

material and language, and his reactions are both human and laudable. All of this may make him sound like the real Mark Twain. But he is not the actual man, for his activities are not precisely those of Mark Twain himself; his reasons for moving from one place to another are clear fabrications, and perhaps most important, his story has a controlled sequence about it that Mark Twain's chaotic movements never had. This basic persona gives *Roughing It* an authority and stability that *Innocents Abroad* does not possess.

This is not to say, however, that Mark Twain handles his basic persona the same way in all parts of the book. In the first half of the volume, for instance, the "I" who tells the story holds together two points of view: that of the middle-aged narrator just described and that of the naive greenhorn he pretends that he was when he was having the adventures. These points of view, or roles of the old-timer and the tenderfoot, have two quite different functions. The narrator as old-timer provides factual contexts that give the adventures a modicum of credibility. This factual information bears so directly on the adventures that it reinforces the narrative rather than interrupting it. Thus the account of the stagecoach system supplies an apt context for the narrator's trials with a particular stagecoach and particular stagecoach stations. Sometimes Twain makes the shift from the humorous to the serious disarmingly obvious, as he does when he writes: "I do not remember where we first came across 'sage-brush,' but as I have been speaking of it I may was well describe it." At other times he blends exposition and narration so adroitly that the information becomes an integral part of the narrative. At Big Sandy, the narrator and his companions on the stagecoach see their first jackass rabbit. Before going on with the story Twain offers a description of jackass rabbits in general, what they do when they are frightened, and what they do when they are shot at. Then, climactically, he tells what a particular "specimen" did when the narrator and two others simultaneously shot at it: "He dropped his ears, set up his tail, and left for San Francisco at a speed which can only be described as a flash and a vanish! Long after he was out of sight we could hear him whiz." Perhaps his handling of the pony express is the best example of the blending of exposition and narration. For two pages the older narrator reports on the pony express system, what the riders wear, how far they ride without stopping, how fast they go, and so on. Then he slips back into the role of the younger man. The driver exclaims:

"HERE HE COMES!"

Every neck is stretched further, and every eye strained wider. Away across the endless dead level of the prairie a black speck appears against the sky, and it is plain that it moves. Well, I should think so! In a second or two it becomes a horse and rider, rising and falling, rising and falling—sweeping toward us nearer and nearer—growing more and more distinct, more and more sharply defined—nearer and still nearer, and the flutter of the hoofs comes faintly to the ear—another instant a whoop and a hurrah from our upper deck, a wave of the rider's hand, but no reply, and man and horse burst past our excited faces, and go winging away like a belated fragment of a storm! (chap. 8)

Mark Twain thought this description the best writing he had yet done. Its effectiveness, he might have added, is due in no small degree to the information that sets the stage.

Besides being incredibly naive, the tenderfoot is adventurous, ambitious, well-read in romantic fiction, sentimental, and ingenious enough to get others to do his share of the work. Often he is silly enough to win the scorn of the author as old-timer. But does this alert and excitable novice learn anything from his experiences and end up being an old-timer? If he does, Twain almost in spite of himself has produced an elementary *bildungsroman* and has begun his career as a novelist. Readers disagree. Some argue that he does change. Henry Nash Smith suggests that he not only advances in know-how but also that he experiences a change in moral values as well. In the chaos of frontier conditions, Smith argues, the values that the tenderfoot brings from home become irrelevant for him, witness what happens when he and Ballou and Ollendorff are lost in the snowstorm. When they think they are going to die, they revert to conventional piety, regretting their evil lives and throwing away their cards, liquor, and pipes. But the next morning when they realize that they will survive, they quietly retrieve their possessions. From the vernacular society of the West the young narrator has learned that what are taken as vices in the East often prove to be virtues in the West.[3] Other readers find no such basic intellectual or moral change. They contend that the tenderfoot is simply a pose that Twain adopts whenever he sees the possibility for humor in doing so. The young adventurer is just as much the simpleton in chapter 41 when he fails to establish ownership of a blind lead as he is in chapter 1 in dreaming of silver bars to be had for the taking. These readers admit that as the first half of the book proceeds the young adventurer comes to be accepted as an equal by his fellow prospectors, but they point out that such acceptance signals no particular maturation because the fellow prospectors are themselves simpletons. All readers agree, however, that whether or not he matures, the tenderfoot is an appealing character that gives focus to Mark Twain's first attempt at sustained narration.

From the outset, the second half of *Roughing It* shows the effects of the reworking of earlier travel accounts. Exposition and description predominate over narration. The point of view of the tenderfoot disappears rather quickly, and with its disappearance the older writer loses his special role as old-timer. He is now simply a restless reporter. In adapting the style to the farm wives who might buy the book, Twain tones down the personal attacks that featured his Nevada and California work. But entertaining exaggerations remain in both details and language. In chapters 62–77 on the Sandwich Island trip, which Twain added at the last minute to fill out the book, he selects his material even more carefully for the prospective reader. Much of the factual material about costumes and customs remains and enough of the original high jinks to provide leavening. He allows his narrator to adopt a few comic roles, especially the role of the sufferer in riding the horse Oahu or submitting to the rats and bugs on board the interisland boat the *Boomerang*. Excised, however, is that irrepressible realist Mr. Brown with his bad breath and his habit of vomiting when the narrator becomes too lofty. In both the Mainland and Island sections, there are memorable vignettes, such as those of the flag flying atop of Mt. Davidson, the San Francisco earthquake of 1865, and the Hawaiian volcanoes Kilauea and Haleakala. Comic anecdotes are carefully scattered throughout. One thinks, for example, of Scotty Briggs trying desperately to communicate in his Western vernacular with the new minister from the East (chap. 47) and of Jim Blaine, who always gets so entangled in side issues that he can never finish the story of his grandfather's old ram (chap. 53). Toward the end is the wild burlesque of Horace Greeley's handwriting (chap. 70). Without question, the second half of the book is good reading, but one misses the sustained invention of the first half.

Too much, however, can be made of the differences between the two halves of the book because they have much in common. In content they both follow Mark Twain's Western experiences during the 1860s, and in form they are both episodic as they alternate between the factual and the comic. Moreover, whatever his point of view of the moment, Twain writes as though he were speaking to the reader. To enhance this sense of intimacy he asks the reader a question, points out why he is changing the subject, admits that a chapter has become too long, and moralizes in a folksy way. He is careful to distribute comic anecdotes and tall stories between the two halves, and to do the same with evidences of the "sublime" in nature. Most important for the book's coherence, perhaps, is that the narrator as the older and wiser man remains clearly in control—even when giving way temporarily to a comic pose. Throughout he wins and retains the reader's confidence because he carries authority (he has been there) and because he avoids making the narrative sound self-serving. Quite the contrary, he is willing to make himself as a younger man seem ridiculous. The tenderfoot may be the focus of interest in the first half, but the book as a whole belongs to the older author who is looking back on a segment of his life with amusement and considerable insight.

Apart from *Huckleberry Finn, Roughing It* is Mark Twain's best compendium of well-crafted comic styles and devices. Appropriately, given its Western setting, its chief stock in trade is overstatement. Exaggerations abound in words, figures of speech, details, and whole episodes. Anecdotes that interrupt the narrative are tall tales, and the narrative as a whole suggests a life that is a step beyond reality. Examples of anticlimax are not wholly lacking. Probably the best is the remark of the Indian whose stove has just exploded and disappeared through the walls: "Mph! Dam stove heap gone!" Typical of Western humor, too, are the use of vernacular characters and the juxtaposition of vernacular and well-educated characters. On the other hand, there are frequent evidences of the literary comedy that Twain wrote for such journals as the *Golden Era* and the *Californian* when he lived in San Francisco. These include malapropisms (in the speech of Mr. Ballou), silly plays on words ("the precious ottar of roses out of the otter"), false references, misquotations, correct quotations in incongruous contexts, parodies, and burlesques. Franklin Rogers calls attention to the fact that the Mexican plug incident burlesques serious accounts of Mexican and Californian horsemanship, and that Bemis's encounter with the buffalo is a takeoff on the buffalo hunt that was a stock fixture in both factual and fictional accounts of the West. Moreover, attempting to make a fire by shooting into a pile of shavings ridicules Western romances in which lost hunters stay alive by making fires without matches.

The handling of comic poses in the first half of the book shows a similar advance. In *The Innocents Abroad* Mark Twain employed such poses for the immediate comic effect and with little or no regard for consistency in characterization. Thus the narrator may appear in one paragraph as a superior personage and in the very next as an inferior one. In *Roughing It,* however, Twain with few exceptions keeps the tenderfoot an inferior. By exaggerating his naiveté he turns him into a simpleton, or by stressing the effects of his stupidity he makes him a sufferer, but these are only excesses of his tenderfootedness. The basic character remains intact. On the rare occasion when he frees the tenderfoot to be a man of feeling, as he does in making him moist-eyed when viewing the homeliness of Mormon women, the strain on characterization is so great that the incident is not only implausible but unfunny (chap. 14). In effect, in the first half of *Roughing It* Twain is practicing with a narrative persona that he eventually modifies and brings to perfection in *Huckleberry Finn.*

Even though *Roughing It* is not a literal autobiography it reveals much of its author's inner urges and ideas—probably more than Mark Twain himself realized. There is much of the sensual man in it, his love of ease, for example. He writes with obvious satisfaction of stretching out on the mailbags in the stagecoach or of lazy days on the shore of Lake Tahoe. Whenever he can, he "superintends" rather than chopping trees or digging a mine shaft. As in *Innocents Abroad* he shows that he hates filth and that he enjoys natural beauty of a massive kind—though still unable to describe such beauty without dropping into Victorian sentimental cant. He prefers the company of men and is apparently still squeamish about sex. His women are "characters" who talk interminably or put down a drunken bully with scissors. As in *Innocents* he is the humanitarian—except where Indians are concerned. He has little to say for Indians here or any place else, a phobia probably instilled in him in his early years by old Indian fighters or by farmers who told stories handed down by their parents of Indian raids on their homes. But he hotly defends the downtrodden Chinese. Anticipating his attack in *The Gilded Age* on government bureaucracy, he also blisters those in Washington who cheat his brother, the secretary of the territory, by paying his expenses without taking into account the inflation of the dollar in Western communities (chap. 25). More profoundly, some of his deep inner contradictions are beginning to become more obvious. He attacks sharp business practices but is willing to take advantage of them when he can; he shows the local or vernacular characters to be more impressive than Eastern "emigrants," but he tires of one Western community after another and at the end of the book is returning East; and his optimism about the future of the West is undercut by a pervasive pessimism. In reviewing the book in the *At-*

lantic in 1872, William Dean Howells also called attention to this dark side: "The grotesque exaggeration and broad irony with which the life is described are conjecturably the truest colors that could have been used, for all existence there must have looked like an extravagant joke, the humor of which was only deepened by its nether-side of tragedy."[4] Howells's point, however, must not be the last word. For *Roughing It* offers abundant evidence that in 1872 Mark Twain could still see the nether side of tragedy too: the rollicking idiocies that make life not only tolerable but something of a lark.

Chapter Four
The Gilded Age

The Gilded Age was a direct result of the move to Hartford in 1871. The presence of the American Publishing Company was an important reason for selecting Hartford, but not the only one. In January 1868, when Twain was there consulting Elisha Bliss about the publication of *The Innocents Abroad,* he had stayed with John and Isabella Hooker in Nook Farm, a suburb just west of the city. It was then that he first became attracted to the region. Moreover, Isabella's brother, Thomas K. Beecher, had been pastor of the Park Church of Elmira, Livy's parents' church, and Livy and Isabella's daughter Alice were close friends. So when the Hookers offered to rent their house while they were traveling in Europe, the Clemenses quickly accepted. It was not a minor decision in their lives. They soon built their own home in Nook Farm and lived there until 1891.

When the Clemenses arrived, Nook Farm was a closely knit colony of writers and reformers who were as receptive to Mark Twain's unbuttoned views as Victorian Americans dared to be and still retain their claims to respectability and Christian faith. Among the residents were Charles Dudley Warner, the essayist and publisher of the *Hartford Courant*; Harriet Beecher Stowe, whose recently published story of Lord Byron's incest had set off a furor second only to that created by her *Uncle Tom's Cabin*; Joseph Hopkins Twichell, the handsome and vigorous pastor of the Asylum Hill Congregational Church (the Church of the Holy Speculators, Twain called it); and, of course, Isabella Hooker, famous for her suffragette activities. Some critics have labeled Mark Twain's move to Nook Farm as his final surrender to the Eastern establishment. Twain would never have considered it a surrender. Nook Farm offered the comfort and security Livy was accustomed to and that he had always aspired to. Moreover, the people there offered just enough of the friction he needed to set his mind going without imposing smug restrictions that would have closed it down in fury. The Nook Farmers changed few of his eccentric habits or basic attitudes, but their interest in literature may well have fed his desire to become more than a humorist. Moreover, it was useful to be so close to Boston that he and William Dean Howells could frequently visit each other. One can argue, therefore, that instead of caging him, Hartford better than most cities offered rich opportunity for development.

Misfortune, however, continued to dog the family. Hardly had they had time to rejoice in the birth of Olivia Susan (Susy) in March, 1872, when Langdon died in early June. Mark Twain was sure that he had killed the baby by neglecting to keep him covered while out in the carriage—just as he was sure that he was responsible for his brother Henry's death, and as later he would torture himself for Susy's death. He seemed to invite the pain of guilt whether or not it was justified. Langdon actually died of diphtheria, but throughout his life Twain persisted in believing his carelessness was responsible. As so often happened, though, he soon shot from the depths to the heights. After an early summer on Long Island for the sake of Livy's health, Twain sailed alone for England on 21 August 1872. Primarily he wanted to pin down arrangements for authorized publications of his books by George Routledge & Company, thereby circumventing the notorious pirate John Camden Hotton who had pirated *The Innocents Abroad* and was currently publishing collections of Mark Twain's short works with such jazzy titles as *Eye Openers* and *Screamers*. Twain had confided to his friends, too, that he hoped to collect material for a companion volume to *The Innocents Abroad* in which he would satirize the English. He could not have arrived in England at a better time. Having taken to their hearts such American writers as Artemus Ward, Bret Harte, and Joaquin Miller, the English were all set to do the same for the next American literary oddity. In Twain they found a dazzler. He quickly established himself as an extraordinarily funny after-dinner speaker and so became the number one catch for those planning major social events. He was a guest at the House of Commons and at a lord mayor's dinner at the Guildhall. Best of all, from his point of view, he was sought out by such literary lions as Robert Browning, Charles Kingsley, Charles Reade, and Anthony Trollope. Nor did he lose any of his popularity by attacking Hotton in the pages of the *Spectator* as John Camden Hottentot, the "sinful aborigine" whose brain he felt like knocking out with a broomstraw. Literary London howled with delight, and Twain had little trouble thereafter with unauthorized English publications. Eventually he grew homesick for his family, and when Livy refused to risk a sea voyage in late fall he returned to Nook Farm in November, promising to be back in England before long for a series of lectures.

He never wrote the companion volume to *The Innocents Abroad*. He had developed such a love affair with the English that he found it distasteful to satirize them. Moreover, he had been too busy in London to take a journey throughout the island and hence could not offer a travel narrative worthy of the subject. What he did gain from the trip was something more important: a heightened sense of his own literary abilities as well as a deep admiration for a country ruled by a responsible educated class. He returned to the United States a rabid anglophile and an equally rabid critic of America's raucous and, so it seemed to him, corrupt and irresponsible democracy. He was eager to satirize America rather than England, and he was eager to try a more challenging literary form such as the novel. The chance to do both came more quickly then he would have guessed.

One February evening in 1873, so the story goes, the Clemenses and the Charles Dudley Warners were dining together when the men began deriding the popular novels their wives had been enjoying. Mildly irked, the wives taunted their husbands into writing one of their own, and the men took up the challenge. That evening they began to block out a book-length story intended to burlesque not only sentimental novels but life as a whole in the United States. By 5 May they had the narrative written and all sixty-three chapters assembled. Twain wrote the first eleven, and Warner the next twelve. Thereafter they alternated in shorter units, small groups of chapters, single chapters, and even parts of chapters. In the evening they read aloud what they had done during the day and asked their wives for suggestions. Both authors wrote a final chapter and had their wives select the one to use. (Warner's won.) Twain frequently maintained that there was scarcely a chapter that did not show the marks of both men, but the manuscript indicates that the "marks" made by one author in a chapter by another are mainly short, almost inconsequential interpolations. The book is primarily a paste-up job with minimal transitions between parts. Twain himself undercut the notion of close collaboration when he wrote to Mrs. Fairbanks, "I think you don't like the Gilded Age,—but that's because you've been reading *Warner's* chapters."[1] Then he listed the thirty-three chapters he had written along with portions of three others. To ridicule the "motto business" the authors persuaded a neighbor, the scholarly James Hammond Trumbull, to supply chapter headings in a variety of foreign languages. Trumbull included such exotic tongues as Sindhi, Choctaw, Ethiopic, and Eskimo. Working more rapidly than usual, the American Publishing Company got out the book in time for the Christmas Trade in 1873.

Not surprisingly, the sixty-three chapters that the authors managed to assemble are a welter of loosely connected episodes. Basically the story concerns two sets of characters—backwoods Midwesterners created by Mark Twain and middle-class Easterners created by Warner—who come together because of a common passion for speculation. A summary of just the major strands of the action requires considerable space. In the opening eleven chapters Mark Twain turns to his family history for both characters and events. Squire and Nancy Hawkins (John Marshall and Jane Clemens) and their children Washington and Emily (Orion and Pamela) have been living in Obedstown (Jamestown) in east Tennessee. One of their two slaves is an Uncle Dan'l (the middle-aged black who used to fascinate the young Sam Clemens when he visited the farm of his Uncle John Quarles). In the hope that it will eventually result in untold wealth, Squire Hawkins has bought 75,000 acres of scrub land (the 70,000 acres of Tennessee Land bought by John Marshall Clemens). When the story opens, the Hawkinses are so poor that a letter from a friend Beriah Sellers (James Lampton, a cousin of Jane Clemens) easily persuades them to move to a tiny frontier town in Missouri (Florida, where Sam Clemens was born). On the way they adopt an orphan named Clay (no clear counterpart) and subsequently a girl named Laura (probably Laura M. Wright, whom Twain later called his first sweetheart, though a Laura Hawkins lived across Hill Street from the Clemenses; Twain later used her as the model for Becky Thatcher in *Tom Sawyer*). Laura has been left homeless as the result of a steamboat explosion (the explosion of the *Pennsylvania* that caused the death of Henry Clemens). Unfortunately for the Hawkinses, "Colonel Sellers" turns out to be an affable but wholly untrustworthy visionary who dreams of millions while providing only turnips and water for the family dinner. After years of ups and downs because of Seller's wild schemes, the Hawkins family is again destitute. Even then Squire Hawkins refuses to sell the Tennessee land, and dies convinced that it will still yield a fortune.

At this point in the story Warner introduces a clutch of characters living in the East: the dependable Philip Sterling, the fop Harry Brierly, Philip's rather headstrong sweetheart Ruth Bolton, and sundry others who would feel right at home in the sentimental novels the authors are trying to ridicule. To establish a connection between the

Eastern and Western groups, the authors have Sterling and Brierly journey to Missouri posing as construction engineers. There they encounter Sellers, whose newest venture is to convert Stone's Landing on Goose Creek into a great river-rail metropolis (the same plan Twain's father had for Florida on the banks of Salt Creek). Enchanted by the Colonel's dreams of millions, Brierly teams up with him, but the steadier Sterling returns east to study engineering. Brierly, it should be added, finds Laura an additional reason for remaining in Missouri. To obtain a federal appropriation Sellers and Brierly enlist the support of Abner Dilworthy, a United States senator who cares little about the future of Stone's Landing but sees the project as a way of looting the public till. In the meantime Laura, now a beautiful Southern belle, marries George Selby, a Confederate colonel, who quickly deserts her after admitting that he is already married. Laura is left with "a devil in her heart."

The scene now shifts to Washington where Senator Dilworthy with no little chicanery succeeds in having Congress pass an appropriation bill to dredge Goose Creek, but Sellers and Brierly discover to their dismay that after the appropriate lobbyists and congressmen have been paid off there is no money left for workmen. Subsequently, with Laura as a lobbyist and with Washington Hawkins's consent, Senator Dilworthy tries to buy sufficient votes to ram another appropriation bill through Congress, this one to create a Knobs Industrial University for blacks on the Hawkins Tennessee land. This time Dilworthy's corruption is exposed. But the Senate with its customary delicate sense for what is right and wrong exonerates Dilworthy and expels Senator Noble, the exposer. While all this is going on, Laura once more meets Colonel Selby, and the two are reconciled. When he leaves her again, however, she follows and kills him. After a jury acquits her of murder on the grounds of insanity, she tries to lecture about her experiences but is hooted off the stage and shortly dies of a broken heart. Washington Hawkins, finally deciding that the Tennessee land is a curse, sells it for taxes and returns to a sweetheart resurrected for the purpose. The last we see of Colonel Sellers he is dreaming of taking up law and becoming Chief Justice of the Supreme Court. Love among the Easterners concludes happily when Ruth Bolton, who has been giving Philip Sterling a rough time, finally accepts his proposal after he (a) strikes it rich in coal, (b) saves her father from financial ruin, and (c) nurses her devotedly through a severe illness. As a final touch of poignancy, Alice Montague, a friend of Ruth's who has all along been secretly in love with Sterling, handsomely resolves never to disclose her passion.

Not even the authors claim much cohesion for the work. Mark Twain said that it had been written in the "superstition that we were writing one coherent yarn, when I suppose, as a matter of fact, we were writing two *in*coherent ones."[2] Without exaggeration he might have said they were writing five yarns: the domestic comedy of the Hawkins family, the Laura Hawkins melodrama, a burlesque featuring Colonel Sellers, the love story of Ruth Bolton and Philip Sterling, and a satire on the jousting for cash and power in the nation's capital. In trying to weave these strands together the authors forget about Clay Hawkins for fifty-five chapters though Clay supports the family from the time his stepfather dies, neglect Harry Brierly when Laura needs him most, and completely lose Laura's real father, a fact that they admit in an appendix. The structure suffers, too, from the overload of stock situations and characters: the loyal father who sacrifices himself for his children even unto death, the adopted son who is more attentive to his parents than the natural children, the despicable seducer who loves and leaves, the too-beautiful daughter who has been wronged and becomes revengeful, the lazy and the industrious apprentice, the shady politician, death by a broken heart, the heroine who is nursed back from the brink of death, the loyal and stalwart hero who ends up a rich man, and, of course, the happy but poignant ending. There is a nice question as to whether Twain and Warner leaned so heavily on stock situations and characters because they were new to novel writing or whether they piled them up as a way of burlesquing the popular sentimental novel. If it was the latter, the device does not wholly succeed because many of the situations that might add to the burlesque detract from it by giving the impression the authors genuinely share the sorrows of their characters. Being products as well as critics of their age, both Twain and Warner possessed a good measure of Victorian "softness," especially about women. As a result, a scene such as that depicting the death of Laura may play along the edge of burlesque for modern readers but for most readers in the 1870s, including the authors' wives, it must have seemed an occasion for genuine tears. Burlesque or not, the plethora of stock situations and characters make a jumble of the structure. Style does little to improve the situation. Although the authors maintained that they both participated in the writing of every chapter, their styles are a dead giveaway as to who wrote what. Warner's writing is carefully crafted but dull. Much too often he drops into the clichés of the books the authors were supposed to be deriding. Twain, also, frequently falls back on tired locutions, especially in scenes of melancholy or grief. But his tritenesses are less anaesthetizing because he intermixes them with phrasing that is both fresh and colorful. In his satire especially, Twain achieves a vigor of language that Warner never matches. Moreover, Twain's backwoods dialogue is an achievement far beyond Warner's powers.

However confused (and confusing) in structure and style, *The Gilded Age* is not a negligible literary accomplishment, and for two reasons: the character of Colonel Sellers and the social criticism. Along with Simon Wheeler, Colonel Sellers ranks as one of Mark Twain's classic windbags. Twain always maintained that the character was an accurate picture of his wife's cousin, James Lampton, "a man with a big, foolish, unselfish heart in his bosom, a man born to be loved; and he was loved by all his friends, and by his family worshiped."[3] When Washington Hawkins first visits the Sellerses, he finds them penniless but serenely happy in the cloudland of the Colonel's talk. As the evening wears on, Washington, blue from the chill in the house, discovers by accident that the glow in the stove comes from a pitiful tallow candle. The Colonel is disconcerted for only a moment. Then he explains to Washington that only the *appearance* of heat is needed, not the heat itself. Later the Colonel lets Washington in on additional fantasies: an "operation" in corn, another in hogs, one in wildcat banks, and, the most fabulous of all, "Beriah Sellers' Infallible Imperial Oriental Optic Liniment and Salvation for Sore Eyes," to be distributed not only in the United States but also in such exotic places as Delhi, Constantinople, Cairo, Jerusalem, Peking, Bangkok, Yedo, and Ispahan—with a resulting income of, well, millions and millions. Some days later the Colonel dreams up the plans for making Stone's Landing a midwest metropolis—just as John Marshall Clemens had supported plans for improving Florida on the Salt River. This scheme is a device of the authors for bringing Sellers together with Sterling and Brierly—and eventually with Senator Dilworthy. As Colonel Sellers begins to mix with real speculators (and scoundrels) he begins to fade as a character, though there is one hilarious scene in Washington in which, appearing as a witness at the trial of Laura Hawkins Selby, he bemuses both the judge and the jury with his magnificent irrelevancies. But it is his talk in the early chapters that one never forgets. Incidentally, Twain at Warner's suggestion originally called him Eschol Sellers but hurriedly changed the name to Beriah after some of the copies of the novel had been distributed and a real Eschol Sellers appeared and threatened to sue.

Primarily, *The Gilded Age* has been famous for its widespread attack on corruption in post–Civil War America. The authors may have differed in their backgrounds and styles, but they were one in their condemnation of the age. Their targets include both city and small-town life, political fraud, swindling in business and finance, speculation in real estate, the perversion of the jury system and the insanity plea, and the antiques and parvenus in Washington society, the first represented by the Fulke-Fulkersons and the second by the Oreilles (pronounced O-*relays*) and the Gashlys. Readers of the book in the mid-1870s could easily recognize, for example, the Salt Lick Extension of the Pacific Railroad as the Atchison Branch of the Union Pacific, the National Internal Improvement Directors' Relief Measure as the so-called Credit Mobilier scheme, the *Daily Love-Feast* as the Washington *Chronicle*, Laura Hawkins as Laura Fair, the adventuress who was acquitted of murder on the grounds of insanity, and Senator Abner Dilworthy as Senator Samuel C. Pomeroy, a notorious vote-buyer from Kansas whose attempts at bribery caught headlines during the months that Twain and Warner were writing their book. Dilworthy and Sellers make a fascinating contrast. Both want to make millions, both are willing to use and misuse the political system to achieve their ends; both are speculators, hypocrites, and con men par excellence. The difference is that Dilworthy is practical, powerful, and a threat to the nation's institutions, whereas Sellers is impractical, powerless, and a threat to no one unless it is his immediate family. Dilworthy, consequently, is a totally unsympathetic character whereas Sellers retains throughout something of his original appeal as an ineffectual clown.

Vigorous as it was, the satire in *The Gilded Age* did not precipitate social reform. It was too diffuse; there were too many targets. It undoubtedly appalled its readers by demonstrating the extent of corruption in the 1870s, but it did not document any particular corruption sufficiently to stir up a popular outcry (as Upton Sinclair's *The Jungle* later stirred up resentment against the meatpackers). Its major public accomplishment was to provide a permanent name for the post–Civil War period: the Gilded Age.

For Mark Twain's development as a writer, however, the book was by no means inconsequential. Even though it shows little mastery over the novel form, it forced him for the first time to grapple with the complex problems of unity, coherence, proportion, and suspense in a long piece of fiction. Achieving such qualities in a short yarn was one thing; collaborating on *The Gilded Age* taught him that achieving them in a novel was quite another. It taught him also that the novel offered possibilities for social criticism not afforded by travel accounts. For one thing, the long narrative form provided greater aesthetic distance—and Twain, as he himself realized, needed such distance in order to keep his personal feelings from flaring up so violently that they called attention to the author rather than to the object being satirized. For another thing, the long narrative form enabled him both to sustain and to vary a satirical attack. In *The Gilded Age,* to be specific, he was able throughout the length of a book to expose facet after facet of the ugliness he found in America—physically, socially, and morally—after his trip to England. In immeasurable ways the book thus provided practice in exploiting the novel for social criticism, practice that paid off especially in *Huckleberry Finn* and *A Connecticut Yankee in King Arthur's Court.* Finally, working on *The Gilded Age* enhanced his notion of himself as a writer. By doing so he was demonstrating that he was no longer a "mere" humorist. He was edging into the company of Dickens and Trollope, and thus becoming what both he and Livy dearly wanted him to be, "a literary figure."

As might be expected, American reviewers differed according to their prejudices, some finding it "puerile" and even "vicious," others praising it for its "pungency" and "accuracy of aim." English reviewers, almost to a person, greeted it with delight, glorying in the fact that such an exposé of America should be written by an American. American sales started out well enough: approximately 35,000 copies in the first two months. But only 15,000 were sold in the next ten months, and the figures tapered off even more rapidly after that. Mark Twain believed that over twice as many copies would have been sold had it not been for the Panic of 1873—a panic, ironically, triggered by the very speculation that Twain and Warner had decried.

Fortunately for Twain a dramatization centering on Colonel Sellers proved to be more profitable than the book. In May 1874 Twain learned that the popular comic actor John T. Raymond was performing in San Francisco in a dramatization of the Sellers story written by a Gilbert Desmond. Since Warner and he had shrewdly reserved dramatic rights on the book they quickly put a stop to this unauthorized production. Furthermore, since Warner had turned over to Twain the right to use his own characters in a play, Twain was free to arrange with Raymond to perform in a version that Twain himself authored (with generous assists from Raymond and the Desmond scenario). By today's standards *Colonel Sellers* (for a while called *The Gilded Age*) was an artistic disaster, but it was performed 119 times. The only explanation for its popularity is that Raymond, a talented comic actor, hammed up the role of Sellers sufficiently to turn the production into undiluted farce. In three years, Twain estimated, the combined royalties of book and play came to $100,000, the play accounting for at least half of this figure.

Chapter Five

"A True Story" and "Old Times on the Mississippi"

After finishing the manuscript of *The Gilded Age* Twain returned to England as he had promised to do, this time with Mrs. Clemens and Susy. If possible, the English received him more enthusiastically than on his previous trip. He lectured regularly and submitted (quite willingly) to unceasing luncheons, dinners, and soirées in his honor. Eventually, though, the strain of public appearances told on Livy, and for the sake of her health they left London for Edinburgh where they met Dr. John Brown, author of *Rab and His Friends*. Then they journeyed to Ireland and Paris, to London for another week of lectures, and finally back to Hartford. Once Livy and Susy were again comfortable in the Hooker house, Twain returned to London, where for two months he packed auditoriums for lectures based on *Roughing It*. By February 1874 he was back in the United States. His reputation as the premier humorist of his time was well established before he had written any of his major novels.

In the spring the family went to Quarry Farm where Clara was born in June and where Twain settled down to daily writing in an octagonal outdoor study built for him by his sister-in-law, Sue Crane. It was one of his most productive summers, for among other manuscripts he turned out "A True Story" and part of *Tom Sawyer*. In the fall the family returned to Hartford where in October they moved into their new home at 531 Farmington Avenue in the Nook Farm section. If an objective correlative is needed for the enthusiasms, quirks, and tastes of the author, the Hartford house is it. Designed by a New York architect Edward Tuckerman Potter from designs sketched out by Twain and Livy, the house in Twain's words is "part cathedral, part cuckoo clock." Three turrets, five balconies, and seemingly innumerable gables and chimneys cut up the three stories of red brick in a manner that still boggles the minds of viewers. Inside there were originally

61

nineteen rooms and five baths with a magnificent hall and staircase, carved wood panels, a conservatory, and a window surmounting a fireplace so that Twain could see the snow seemingly fall into the fire. As the family grew, Twain's second-floor study had to be turned into a nursery and he had to move his working space to the billiard room on the third floor with its ceiling decorated with pipes, cigars, and crossed billiard cues. Not fully content with this display, Twain in 1881 added a servants' wing and employed Louis Comfort Tiffany and his "Associated Artists" of New York to redecorate the major rooms of the original building. To run such an establishment the Clemenses employed six servants: a Negro butler and an Irish coachman, a Negro cook, an Irish housemaid, a German housemaid, and an Irish laundress. Entertainment was on the same scale: the best of food, drink, and tobacco—and Mark Twain's one man show as he interrupted dinner to pace around the table pontificating. After the meal he would often sing Negro spirituals or spin out yarns until long after midnight. As William Dean Howells wrote to his father, "The Clemenses are whole-souled hosts, with inextinguishable money, and a palace of a house."[1] In time, of course, the money would not be inextinguishable, but in the mid-seventies, when the royalties from books and plays continued to pour in and when the interest on Livy's inheritance continued to be substantial, Mark Twain could spread himself. Not even Horatio Alger, Jr., could dream up a better rags-to-riches story. John Marshall Clemens would have felt his dream of gracious living finally realized. Had Mark Twain been able to curb his excesses, he might have lived out his days as the squire of Farmington Avenue. But then he would not have been Mark Twain.

"A True Story"

Not until the early 1870s did Mark Twain discover that his earlier life in the antebellum South offered the combination of fond memories, vivid evidences of human suffering and idiocy, and the aesthetic distance that his imagination needed for its best efforts. In the twelve years between 1872 and 1884 he produced "A True Story," "Old Times on the Mississippi," *The Adventures of Tom Sawyer, Life on the Mississippi,* and *Adventures of Huckleberry Finn,* all of them based on Southern life and all of them with persisting appeal.

"A True Story, Repeated Word for Word as I Heard It" is a short tale presumably provoked by Mark Twain when he asks Aunt Rachel, a cheerful ex-slave, how it is she has lived for sixty years without seeming to have any troubles. Startled, she wants to know if "Misto C——" is in "'arnest." Assured that he is, she launches into her story. Back in the 1850s she was separated from her husband and seven children at a slave auction in Richmond. Thirteen years later she is cooking for Union officers in a Southern mansion when a platoon of black soldiers join in the "sojer ball" being held there. When the blacks begin making fun of her red turban, Aunt Rachel lights into them: "'Look-a-heah! I want you niggers to understan' dat I wa'nt bawn in de mash to be fool' by trash! I's one o' de old Blue Hen's Chickens, I is!'" The chicken phrase (meaning a Marylander) rings a bell with one of the soldiers because it is a phrase both his mother and grandmother had used. The next morning early he appears in the kitchen when Aunt Rachel is lifting a pan of biscuits out of the oven.

De pan drop' on de flo' an' I grab his lef' han' an' shove back his sleeve,—jist so, as I's doin' to you,—an' den I goes for his forehead an' push de hair back, so, an' "Boy!" I says, "if you an't my Henry, what is you doin' wid dis welt on yo' wris' an' dat sk-yar on yo' forehead? De Lord God ob heaven be praise', I got my own ag'in!"

Oh, no, Misto C——, I hain't had no trouble. An' no *joy*!

"A True Story" was Mark Twain's first attempt to capture blacks truly and sympathetically. His model was Aunty Cord, a cook at Quarry Farm whom he greatly admired. As was so often true, he did not realize the value of what he had done until others began telling him. In fact, he offered the story to Howells apologetically, saying that he was sending him "A Fable for Old Boys & Girls" for the *Atlantic* and then added, "I enclose also a 'True Story' which has no humor in it . . . it is rather out of my line."[2] With his impeccable taste Howells accepted "A True Story" and not the "Fable," and printed it in the *Atlantic* for November 1874. Still praising it a year later Howells wrote in the *Atlantic* for December 1875 that "the rugged truth of the sketch leaves all other stories of slave life far behind and reveals a gift in the author for the simple, dramatic report of reality which we have seen equalled in no other American writer." One of the greater ironies of his literary career is that Mark Twain should break into the bastion of the Eastern literary establishment with a sketch that he felt out of his line.

What Twain wrote Howells about his handling of Aunt Rachel's dialect anticipates his problems with dialect in *Huckleberry Finn:* I amend dialect stuff by talking & talking & *talking* it till it sounds right—& I had difficulty with this negro talk because a negro sometimes (rarely) says 'goin'' & sometimes 'gwyne', & they make just some discrepancies in other words—& when you come to reproduce them on paper they look as if the variation resulted from the writer's carelessness."[3]

"Old Times on the Mississippi"

Howells was so enchanted by "A True Story" that he kept badgering Twain for more of the same. Twain, however, failed to think of anything more to write about until one day he got to telling Joseph Twichell about the days of glory and grandeur on the river as he had seen them from the pilot house, and Twichell had said, "What a virgin subject to hurl into a magazine!" Incredibly, though Twain for years had dallied with the idea of a book describing travel on the Mississippi, he had never thought of writing up his personal experiences. After the conversation with Twichell he immediately got in touch with Howells, offering him a series of papers on the subject to "run through 3 months or 6 or 9?—or about 4 months, say?"[4] Howells was delighted, and the result was seven papers that appeared in the *Atlantic* January through June plus August 1875. Entitled "Old Times on the Mississippi" the seven installments eventually became chapters 4–17 in *Life on the Mississippi.* After reading the first installment, Howells wrote that "it almost made the water in our ice-pitcher muddy as I read it."[5]

Based on the facts but certainly not confined to them, "Old Times" tells chiefly of Mark Twain's experiences, largely fictionalized, during the months he was learning to be a pilot. The first five installments tell of his adventures while a cub pilot under the tutelage of Horace Bixby, a master pilot, and the next two of more general matters such as the qualifications of good pilots, their rank and dignity, and the monopoly they commanded. The episodes dealing with Twain as cub pilot are the ones best remembered. In them the "I" of the narrator is ambivalent, as it is in the first half of *Roughing It,* for it may stand for either the mature author of thirty-nine or the naive tenderfoot of about sixteen that the author pretends to have been. Typically Twain introduces an incident as the mature author, then slides into the role of the tenderfoot, and finally returns to the adult point of view in order to comment on the incident. The pose of the tenderfoot, therefore, is not steadily maintained but is assumed and discarded so adroitly that the reader is hardly conscious of the change.

For the sake of the humor Twain makes the cub much younger and far more of a greenhorn then he actually was. As a matter of record, he was going on twenty-two when he apprenticed himself to Bixby, and he had already knocked about a good part of the country as a tramp printer. Moreover, having grown up along the river, he undoubtedly knew more about piloting than most beginners. But he pretends in "Old Times" that he was so green that he did not realize he would have to stand regular watches or memorize landmarks. In contrast to Bixby he seems a complete ignoramus. But because he seems so young and so anxious he comes off as a delightfully sympathetic character. Had Twain stuck to the facts of his age and experience, he would have appeared as an absurd dolt. Slowly the cub—and the reader—learn the river by day and by night, heading north and south in various kinds of weather. For whatever reasons, Twain does not follow the cub until he becomes an experienced old-timer eligible for a pilot's license. Even in the last episode the boy still loses his nerve when Bixby tricks him into believing that a bottomless crossing endangers the boat. Hysterically he shouts into the speaking-tube to the engineer, "Oh, Ben, if you love me, *back* her! Quick, Ben! Oh, back the immortal *soul* out of her!" It was months before he stopped being kidded about that one.

From the beginning of "Old Times" it is obvious that Twain again found the point of view of the greenhorn congenial. He is at great pains to see the events as the greenhorn might, and the results appear in sharply pictorial detailing, breathless crises, colorful rendering of river talk, and a combination of wonderment and anxiety—sometimes fear—in the cub's attitude toward the river. Moreover, the viewpoint of the boy discourages Twain—as it will in *Huckleberry Finn*—from parading his personal prejudices. There is in "Old Times" none of the emotional rhetoric he used when inveighing against the wealth of the church in *Innocents Abroad* or against United States senators in *The Gilded Age*. Even when he writes as the adult author he keeps himself under wraps, looking back on his years as a cub pilot with amusement and affection. In the most frequently quoted passage, he movingly contrasts the beauty of the river before he mastered its "language," and its practical realities after he had mastered it, when its beauties had been transformed into mundane signs of safety and danger. This passage (in the section on "Continued Perplexities") has been cited many times as the perfect metaphor for distinguishing between the poetic and the practical. Walter Blair believes that "Old Times" is Mark Twain's finest autobiographical narrative, and few would disagree.[6]

Chapter Six
The Adventures of Tom Sawyer

Mark Twain started *The Adventures of Tom Sawyer* in the winter of 1872–73, possibly just before he and Warner began *The Gilded Age,* dropped it and picked it up again at Quarry Farm in the spring and summer of 1874, and finished it in Hartford in the spring and summer of 1875 just after completing the last installment of "Old Times on the Mississippi." Until the very end he seems not to have known how to end the book or whether he was writing for children or adults. Apparently he originally intended to carry Tom from boyhood into middle age because a short outline on the first page of the manuscript indicates that Tom is to engage in "the battle of Life in many lands" and return home after many years to find his childhood sweetheart full of "rasping, puritanical, vinegar piety." As late as 21 June 1875, he wrote William Dean Howells that "since there is no plot to the thing, it is likely to follow its own drift, & so is as likely to drift into manhood as anywhere—I won't interpose."[1] Just two weeks later, however, he wrote that he had finished the story and did not take the chap beyond boyhood. To do so, he argued, would make Tom "like all the one-horse men in literature & the reader would conceive a hearty contempt for him."[2] In the same letter he maintained—not very perceptively—that "it is *not* a boy's book, at all. It will only be read by adults. It is only written for adults." But in November, obviously after discussions with Howells and Mrs. Clemens, he changed his tune: "Mrs. Clemens decides with you that the book should issue as a book for boys, pure & simple—& so do I. It is surely the correct idea."[3] In the preface, written the following April, he tried to have it both ways: "Although my book is intended mainly for the entertainment of boys and girls, I hope it will not be shunned by men and women on that account." After all the waffling, he had finally hit on the truth. *Tom Sawyer* is one of the few literary works that appeal to readers of eight and eighty, and of every age in between.

The action of the story takes place in or near St. Petersburg, a small Missouri town on the west bank of the Mississippi River (really Han-

nibal) during a spring and summer in the 1840s. The hero, Tom Sawyer, is a lively, imaginative, mischievous boy of twelve or thirteen who
lives with his Aunt Polly, his very proper but sneaky half-brother Sid,
and his gentle cousin Mary. Aunt Polly tries to be strict with Tom but
he knows and takes advantage of the fact that she is basically quite
sentimental. At the opening of the story Tom goes swimming after
being told not to, and is sentenced by Aunt Polly to spend the next
day whitewashing their nine-foot-high board fence. With a little ap-
plied psychology, however, Tom persuades the other boys in the neighborhood to do the whitewashing—and to reward him for the privilege
of doing it. Late in the same day he catches a glimpse of Becky
Thatcher, a new girl in town, and immediately begins to show off.
That night, in true romantic fashion, he lies under her window, or
does until a maidservant opens the window and tosses a pail of water
out of it. The next day Tom attends Sunday School and claims a Bible
by presenting the proper number of tickets he has amassed, not by
memorizing Bible verses as he was supposed to but by trading marbles
and fishhooks and other valuables for the tickets of other boys. Unhappily, right in front of Becky and her parents, when asked to name the
first two disciples Tom can come up only with the names of David and
Goliath. The next hour he suffers through the church service until a
dog relieves the tedium by sitting on his pinch bug and has to be flung
out a window because of its yelping. In school the next morning Tom
shrewdly explains his tardiness by admitting he stopped to talk with
Huckleberry Finn, the town pariah who lives in a hogshead down by
the river. Tom is whipped and further punished by being made to sit
among the girls—right beside Becky Thatcher where he wants to be.
He persuades Becky to meet him in the empty school room at lunch
time and there succeeds in getting her to exchange vows of love. Everything is blissful until he lets out that Becky is not his first conquest.

That night, Tom and Huck in order to cure their warts take a dead
cat to the cemetery where to their horror they see Dr. Robinson, Muff
Potter, and Injun Joe get into a fight while digging up a recently
buried corpse. Injun Joe kills the doctor and plants the murder weapon
on Potter who has been knocked senseless in the melee. The boys slip
away and speed back to the town tannery where they take a mighty
oath to keep mum about what they have seen. In the next days, for
reasons unknown to Aunt Polly, Tom seems listless, thus giving the
old lady a wonderful opportunity to experiment with all of her patent
medicines. When she discovers that Tom has been feeding the pain

killer to the cat, however, she sends him back to school where more trouble awaits: Becky cuts him cold.

With his world in pieces, Tom persuades Huck and Joe Harper to become pirates and "sail" to Jackson's Island aboard a small raft. The next day, when a ferry boat steams past firing a cannon over the water, the boys realize that the townspeople believe that they have drowned. That night Tom slips back into town to leave a note telling Aunt Polly that they are safe, but while hiding under her bed he learns from her conversation with Mrs. Harper that memorial services for the boys will be held the next Sunday. Instead of leaving the note, he returns to Jackson's Island, tells the others the glorious news, and on Sunday the boys appear in church while their own memorial services are in progress.

Once again in school Tom recaptures Becky's love by taking the paddling due her for tearing the picture of a nude figure in the schoolmaster's "Anatomy." "Tom," Becky says to him adoringly, "How *could* you be so noble?" Vacation approaches and with it Examination Day when the pupils offer patriotic and sentimental recitations for the benefit of their parents and friends. Tom, of course, flubs his performance. The triumph of the evening comes, however, when a cat let down by a string from a hatch overhead claws off the schoolmaster's wig and reveals that the signpainter's son has managed to gild the teacher's bald dome.

When Muff Potter is put on trial for the murder of Dr. Robinson, Tom appears as a surprise witness to give the true facts. Injun Joe bounds through an open window and escapes. Later, while Tom and Huck are treasure hunting in an abandoned house, they are trapped upstairs while Injun Joe and an accomplice enter the building and uncover real treasure in the form of gold coins. Fortunately the boys are not caught. Then, a few days later, on a picnic south of town Tom and Becky become lost in McDougal's cave. The other picnickers, not knowing that Tom and Becky are missing, return home. That evening Huck follows two sinister men up Cardiff Hill where the Widow Douglas lives. To his horror he discovers that one of the men is Injun Joe and that the half-breed intends to mutilate the widow because her husband had once had him horsewhipped. Huck speeds to the nearby house of a Welshman, who with his sons intercepts the blackguards before they do any damage. But Injun Joe again escapes. Meanwhile Tom and Becky are still trying to find a way out of the cave. Their candles die out and Becky, especially, becomes exhausted. Tom keeps

exploring the cave as far as a kite string tied to a rock projection near
Becky will let him go. Once in rounding a turn he sees—who else?—
Injun Joe. Fortunately, Joe does not see him. At long last Tom catches
sight of a speck of sunlight, and the two emerge from the cave at a
point five miles south of where they entered it. After two weeks back
in St. Petersburg Tom learns that the city fathers have sealed up the
cave. When he reports having seen Injun Joe there, the cave is immediately reopened, and Joe is found dead with his face close to the
crack under the door. To end the story Twain has Huck and Tom discover and divide the treasure—$12,000 in gold. The Widow takes
Huck to her house to civilize him, but Huck rebels and sneaks back
to his hogshead. At the end, Tom persuades Huck to return to the
Widow's on the grounds that he cannot belong to Tom Sawyer's gang
unless he is respectable.

The principal sources for the material in *Tom Sawyer* are Mark
Twain's own experiences as a boy in Hannibal, his reading, and several
of his earlier fictions. The book is first of all a reminiscence. The
school, the church, the slaughterhouse, the creek, and the cemetery
appear in the narrative just as they were in fact. So do the homes of
Tom and Becky (the Clemens and Hawkins houses on Hill Street),
McDougal's cave south of town (really McDowell's cave), Cardiff Hill
north of town where the Widow Douglas lives (Holliday Hill where
Mrs. Richard Holliday lived), and Jackson's Island (Glasscock's Island,
since washed away). For the characters in the story Twain used Hannibal people he had known: himself and two friends for Tom, his
mother in part for Aunt Polly, his sister Pamela for Mary, his younger
brother Henry for Sid, Laura Hawkins who lived across the street for
Becky, and Tom Blankenship for Huck. To be sure, Twain modified
some of the characters to make the story funnier and more dramatic.
His mother, for example, was not so sentimental and ineffective as
Aunt Polly, and Henry was a much more likable lad than Sid. The real
Injun Joe was not a villain but simply a village good-for-nothing whose
worst habit was getting drunk. Even with the modifications, though,
the story reflects the life of young Sam Clemens sufficiently to merit
its being called at least semiautibiographical.

Yet a surprising amount of material stems from Mark Twain's reading. The relation between Tom and Huck, for example, probably owes
as much to Cervantes' *Don Quixote* as it does to Sam Clemens's friend-
ship with Tom Blankenship. Like Don Quixote, Tom is romantic,
imaginative, and well-read, and like Sancho Panza Huck is uneducated

and matter-of-fact. Even Tom's relationship with Aunt Polly depends as much upon a fictional Mrs. Partington and her son Ike as it does upon Mrs. Clemens and young Sam. Twain undoubtedly got the details of the grave-robbing scene from Dickens's *Tale of Two Cities*; the treasure-hunting episodes have much in common with Poe's "The Gold Bug"; and other episodes call to mind sketches by earlier humorists such as A. B. Longstreet and George Washington Harris.[4] The Robin Hood talk, as Alan Gribben discovered, comes word for word from Joseph Cundall's *Robin Hood and His Merry Foresters*.[5]

Tom Sawyer is not Mark Twain's initial attempt at writing about boys. He had burlesqued Sunday School fiction, for example, in "The Story of the Bad Little Boy Who Did Come to Grief" (1865) and "The Story of the Good Little Boy Who Did Not Prosper" (1870). In *The Gilded Age* he had tried to report some of the action through the eyes of young Washington Hawkins, and his imagination had particularly flourished in "Old Times on the Mississippi," when he assumed the point of view of the cub pilot. The fullest rehearsal for *Tom Sawyer*, however, was an unfinished manuscript found by Albert Bigelow Paine, Twain's literary executor, after Twain had died. Paine gave it the title "Boy's Manuscript." Written about 1870, it is suggestive of such works as Thomas B. Aldrich's *The Story of a Bad Boy* and Charles Dickens's *David Copperfield*. Among other events, the "Manuscript" describes the schoolroom antics of a Billy Rogers and tells about his idiotic courtship of an Amy Lawrence. Although these characters play only minor roles in the novel, Twain transfers some of their activities almost verbatim to the major characters in *Tom Sawyer*. In the form of a diary kept by Billy, "Boy's Manuscript," was clearly going nowhere. Twain was wise to drop it, but it served him well when he came to write *Tom Sawyer*.

Tom Sawyer is structurally much tighter than the episodic nature of its composition and Mark Twain's comments on how to write a narrative would lead one to expect. "Narrative," as he wrote in his autobiography, "should flow as flows the brook down through the hills and the leafy woodlands, its course changed by every bowlder it comes across and by every grass-clad gravelly spur that projects into its path . . . but always *going*, and always following at least one law, always loyal to that law, the law of *narrative*, which *has no law*."[6] To this astonishing dictum he added the more personal confession that "as long as a book would write itself I was a faithful and interested amanuensis and my industry did not flag, but the minute that the book tried to shift to *my* head the labor of contriving its situations, inventing its adventures and conducting its conversations, I put it away and dropped it out of my mind."[7] Such statements explain why Mark Twain was more comfortable composing short stories than novels. Writing short pieces came to him easily because he had learned how to mold them for unity and climax on the lecture platform and in telling anecdotes to whoever would listen. But a book-length narrative, unless it was simply a series of anecdotes, as his travel books tended to be, required careful planning, a process against which his mind rebelled. Once he got an idea for a book, he started writing instead of planning—unless one calls the brief and rather silly little outline at the beginning of *Tom Sawyer* a plan. As a result, when his imagination flagged, he had no notes or outline to fall back on, and had to pigeonhole the manuscript until, as he said, his tank filled up again. Fortunately, he had an intuitive sense for literary form and movement, and could recognize when a story needed to be pigeonholed. One can argue that given Mark Twain's temperament his major works benefited from layoffs in composition. He worked on them only when his tank was full and he felt his narrative move.

On the surface the organization of *Tom Sawyer* seems relatively simple; actually, it is a complex blend of four structural patterns, each taken from a popular literary genre of the 1870s. (1) the episodical structure of local color writing: this pattern appears particularly in the first five chapters in which Twain reports and romanticizes boy-life in St. Petersburg. (2) The cause and result pattern common to juvenile fiction: in such works the superior behavior of the Good Boy, or Model Boy, results invariably in both praise and prosperity. On the other hand, the shocking lapses of the Bad Boy just as surely result in physical as well as spiritual punishment. Although Twain borrows this tight cause-and-result pattern, he reverses the sequence and thereby in effect turns *Tom Sawyer* into a genial burlesque of juvenile fiction, not an imitation of it. Tom has most of the traits of the Bad Boy: he deceives and disobeys his elders, runs away from home, fights and dirties his clothes, smokes, steals, plays hooky, and associates with a ragamuffin who has not had a Christian upbringing. Yet such Bad Boy behavior in Tom's case results in the rewards usually reserved for the Good Boy. Tom succeeds in every one of his undertakings, and ends up with general acclaim, wealth, and a beautiful little maiden. Sid, the conventional Good Boy, gets clodded for his efforts. (3) The pattern of the sentimental romance: boy meets girl, boy loses girl, boy gets girl. Here, too, Mark Twain in borrowing a popular pattern succeeds in ridiculing the genre from which he takes it. The puppy-love affair of Tom and Becky underscores the silliness of the adult courtships in the soupy romances of the day (and our day, too, for that matter). (4) The suspense plot of the dime thrillers in which a heartless villain threatens the happiness and even the life of the hero until by great good fortune the hero escapes form the villain's toils and the villain, of course, gets his just deserts.

Blending such diverse structural patterns was an architectural triumph for Mark Twain. The manuscript shows that Twain after he had finished most of the first draft moved some of the parts of the story around so that Tom would seem steadily to mature as the narrative proceeds: a silly showoff at the beginning, he acts far more like the adults in St. Petersburg at the end. The manuscript also reveals Twain's concern for structural details.[8] Marginal notes, such as "Learning to Smoke" and "T takes B's whipping," are reminders to himself of episodes that might be introduced into the story when the context is appropriate. Originally Muff Potter was Pap Finn, Huck's father, but once Twain got into his narrative he must have realized that the presence of the old reprobate would shift the reader's attention from Tom and Huck to Huck and Pap, and thereby push the story off-center. So he eliminated Pap in favor of Muff Potter, who had no close ties to either Tom or Huck. Apparently to tighten the manuscript further, he deleted part of chapter 18 and all of an original chapter 19. Moreover, at Howells's suggestion he lopped off a final chapter that would have been anticlimactic. One final point about the structure: it has not only coherence and movement but one dramatic climax after another. Closing each of the major episodes is a Big Scene with, seemingly, the whole town present: Tom's disgrace in Sunday School, the appearance of the boys at their own funeral service, Tom's testimony in court against Injun Joe, the rejoicing when Tom and Becky are found, and the display of the treasure at the Widow Douglas's. If it was not so before *Tom Sawyer,* certainly after it the Big Scene becomes a trademark for most of Mark Twain's fiction.

Stylistic alterations in the manuscript show Twain changing words and phrases to improve transitions, to make the writing more descriptive ("snowbanks of girls" in the graduation scene instead of "rows of girls"), and to soften the wording for Victorian readers. For example, in the revision he has the Thatcher maid throw water on Tom instead of slops. Of all these alterations the most curious are those in numbers indicating the extent of time, space, and size. Some of these, though certainly not all, can be justified as making a detail more dramatic or more comic. After gulping the pain-killer, for example, the cat in the revised phrasing jumps two yards into the air instead of two feet; the fence that Tom must whitewash is nine feet in height instead of the original five feet.

After he had completed the manuscript Twain sent a secretarial copy to Howells for criticism. Although Howells was thoroughly delighted with the story as a whole, he did suggest over thirty changes he believed would make the phrasing still more precise or less offensive ("off-key" was the term he used).[9] Twain accepted most but not all of Howells's suggestions. Ordinarily Twain slips from one perspective to the other without jarring the reader, even though the writing from the boy's point of view is invariably more pictorial and less "literary" than that from the author's viewpoint. Note the change in style in the following passage as Twain shifts from the author's viewpoint in the first sentence to the boy's in the second: "The marvel of Nature shaking off sleep and going to work unfolded itself to the musing boy. A little green worm came crawling over a dewy leaf, lifting two-thirds of his body into the air from time to time and 'sniffing around,' then proceeding again—for he was measuring, Tom said . . ." (chap. 14). Sometimes the author intrudes in the story too obviously, as he does in explaining the difference between "work" and "play" at the end of the whitewashing scene (chap. 2) or when he sentimentalizes about the drops of water that have been falling in McDougal's cave since the time the pyramids were new (chap. 33) or especially when he tells of the "sappy women" who urge the Governor to pardon Injun Joe (chap. 33). Such passages are few in number, however. Ordinarily Mark Twain uses the authorial viewpoint to enlarge the reader's perception of Tom, not to offer distractions.

In *Tom Sawyer* Twain escapes from his own "gilded age" back into what he considered to be the golden age, the age of boyhood. The picture he develops is more invented than actual. Although he exploits the real Hannibal for places and persons, by careful selection of material he turns the real town into St. Petersburg, that is, St. Peter's town or heaven. Summer never ceases, though if one were to add up all the comments about the passing of time the last events should occur in November. It is a tight little world circumscribed by Tom's concerns.

The adults, it would seem, do little but wait for Tom to create excitement, and are inordinately grateful when he does it.

Like so many heroes in the boys' books of the time, Tom is an orphan. Indeed, most of the facts about the family are blurry. Who was Tom's father and what happened to him? Who was his mother other than being the sister of Aunt Polly? How did Sid come to be a half brother and Mary a cousin? And why are they living with Aunt Polly? The lack of close family ties makes Tom's aggressiveness understandable. He has to fend for himself. He may not be a wholly lovable character, but given his need to make his own way he is an admirable one. His worst trait is that he insists on dominating everyone, and this he can do because he is better read than most and, especially, because he is more articulate than most. He talks his way into jams, but he can usually talk his way out of them. He may behave like the Bad Boy in juvenile fiction, but he is a Good Bad Boy because he is mischievous rather than evil. He may con others into doing what he wants, but he is never consciously cruel, except possibly when he clods Sid, who really deserves more than he gets. Tom is a juvenile rebel who for the time being resists the forms of middle-class society, but we all know that he is too much a part of that society to be a real revolutionary. Sure enough, at the end of the book he is insisting that even the boys in his gang must be "respectable." Victorians, including Mrs. Clemens and the other residents of Nook Farm, could take Tom to their hearts.

The other characters appear in the book only in their relations to Tom, and are therefore thinly developed. Becky is the brave, pretty, adorable Good Girl from juvenile fiction. Aunt Polly with her crochets and sentimentality and moral preoccupations is almost as much a creature of New England humor as was Mrs. Partington, on whom she was partly modeled. Even Huck in this book is an uncomplicated character. Both he and Sid operate as foils for Tom: Sid's priggish espousal of middle-class ways and Huck's strong rebellion against them dramatize by contrast Tom's mid-position of the temporary rebel who really wants to make it within the system. Injun Joe is the standard villain, Twain even following the popular myth that a half-breed is the most unscrupulous of scoundrels. None of these characters is real in the sense that they are as complicated as actual people, but they are realistic in the sense that their simple motives and emotions are ones that readers can recognize and share.

Since in writing *Tom Sawyer* Mark Twain was nostalgically recalling his own boyhood, the humor is much more genial than it was even in "Old Times." When Tom shows off or causes Aunt Polly grief Twain seems to be chuckling indulgently. Yet this indulgence toward Tom and the other youngsters does not mask Twain's customary irritation with middle-class adults. Although he shows them on occasion to be kind and thoughtful, he also paints them as normally vain, fickle, provincial, and culturally deprived. They read their Bibles and go to church, but their basic values are material. Their highest desires are prosperity and a reputation for respectability. St. Petersburg may be heaven for boys, but it is a good deal less than that for grownups. Artistically, Twain had to make the town seem dull so that it could serve as a foil for Tom's superactivities, but there seems no doubt that he believed it was, in fact, dull. As an older man, he returned to Hannibal for only three brief visits. Perhaps the most depressing aspect of the book is the realization that Tom as he grows older will become as conventional and uninteresting as his fellow townsmen. We can see the change coming. At the beginning of the book, it will be recalled, Tom wants nothing so much as the freedom from convention enjoyed by Huckleberry Finn. At the end, after many indications that he is becoming more responsible, he not only has given up his own desire for freedom but is forcing Huck to give up his also. Tom, in short, does not really mature; he simply becomes more like St. Petersburg adults, who themselves are not mature in any fine sense. Thus the golden age of boyhood begins inexorably to give way to the gilded age of adulthood.[10]

Still, the central interest of the book is about boys as they are and not about what they will become. Twain maintains enough distance from his characters to keep *Tom Sawyer* an essentially comic book. Its pessimism is well masked by its humor. Like every real boy Tom is a dreamer. He becomes a comic legend in that in wild and wonderful ways he realizes all of his dreams. He gets the better of adults, becomes the leader of his gang, suffers and sacrifices for his loved one and finally wins her, has a Jackson's Island to which he can escape when the going gets tough, becomes an instrument of justice, and ends up with a pile of gold and the unstinting praise of the community. Moreover, what could possibly better satisfy boyish paranoia than to attend one's own funeral service and have the entire congregation burst into "Old Hundred" from sheer joy over one's existence? *Tom Sawyer* may not have the art or the profundity of *Huckleberry Finn,* but as an idyll of boyhood it has no peer anywhere. Mark Twain was not far wrong when he called it "simply a hymn, put into prose form to give it a worldly air."[11] It has been translated into over two dozen foreign languages and its sales, domestic and foreign, extend into the millions. Among Mark Twain's books only *Adventures of Huckleberry Finn* has proved more popular.

Chapter Seven

Three Works of the Early 1880s

Between *Tom Sawyer* and *Huckleberry Finn* Mark Twain published three major works: a travel book (*A Tramp Abroad*), a children's book (*The Prince and the Pauper*), and another travel book focusing on the great river (*Life on the Mississippi*). The first two are relatively unimportant in the Mark Twain canon and the third is badly flawed, but none should be dismissed as a potboiler. The first contains several sparkling cameos, the second still entertains youngsters, and the third is an essential part of Mark Twain's total picture of the Mississippi Valley.

A Tramp Abroad

A Tramp Abroad is Mark Twain's third travel book, and by no means his best. He wrote it in the interval after his tank ran dry on *Huckleberry Finn* and before he tapped a full tank for *The Prince and the Pauper*. His purpose for *A Tramp Abroad,* he says, in the first paragraph of the book, is to furnish the "spectacle" of a man going on a journey through Europe on foot. He might have added, had he wished to be candid, that the underlying purpose was to make money because his expenses were beginning to mount up in frightening fashion. With sales in mind he was determined that the book should be both light and comic. Unfortunately, in 1878–79 he was in a mood that was neither light nor comic, and the style as a whole turns out to be unusually stiff for him and the comedy often only silliness. Nevertheless, the book contains several episodes that rank with his funniest, and "Jim Baker's Blue-Jay Yarn" in chapters 2–3, many believe, is the finest piece of Western yarn-spinning to be found anywhere.

To get away from the pressures in Hartford so that he could concentrate on his writing, Mark Twain in April 1878 took his family to Europe, presumably for a short stay. The trip, however, ultimately extended to September 1879 and included Germany, Switzerland, Italy, and France, with shorter visits to Belgium, Holland, and England. In Heidelberg they were joined by Joseph Twichell. An earlier walking trip in Bermuda with Twichell had so delighted Twain that he willingly paid the minister's expenses for a longer walk through the Black Forest and into the Alpine region of Switzerland. As he had hoped, the "tramp" was thoroughly enjoyable. Once Twichell left for home, however, the trip for Twain turned into a nightmare. He came to hate all aspects of it: the railroads, the hotels, the food, and especially the weather, which for eleven months remained wet and chilly. Most of the time, moreover, at least one member of the family was ill. The lowest point came in Paris where in addition to all of the other irritants the easy attitude of the Parisians toward sexual matters grated on his puritanical sensibilities.

What bedevilled him most during the trip as a whole, however, was his inability to get a handle on his book. In Munich he tore up what he had written and started over. Thereafter he discarded at least as many pages as he kept. When he finally landed in New York, he glumly confessed to a reporter that months of work would still be necessary. Even at Quarry Farm and in Hartford he continued to have trouble fashioning the narrative. Except for several episodes, in short, he seems to have had to fight the book from beginning to end. Not until early March 1880 could he rejoice that "that most infernally troublesome book is at last hidden from my sight & mind in the jaws of three steam presses."[1] The American Publishing Company issued it later that month.

Though it suggests the entire trip taken by the Clemenses in 1878–79, *A Tramp Abroad* concentrates on the five weeks in which Twichell (called Harris) and Twain took their walking trip through parts of Germany and Switzerland. The major segments of the narrative deal with Heidelberg, especially the bloody duels fought by the students; the Neckar valley; Baden Baden and the Black Forest; Lucerne and the ascent of Mount Riga; the Interlaken area; Zermatt and the expedition up the Riffelberg; Chamonix and the beauties and terrors of Mount Blanc; and the art and architecture of Milan, Venice, and Florence. In the segment on Italy Twain continues to use the plural "we" although Harris is never mentioned (Twichell had gone home before the Clemenses reached Italy). Ending the volume are six appendixes, the best known being "The Awful German Language."

It was inevitable that signs of his disgruntlement in 1878–79 should
surface in *A Tramp*. Examples of human pretentions he has to strain to
make funny. He is more revolted than amused by the violence of stu-
dent duels in Heidelberg. His disgust with the French comes out in
an attack on Louis XVI and Marie Antoinette, and his abhorrence for
nudity in art breaks through in an attack on Titian's *Venus*, which he
castigates as the foulest picture the world possesses. He suspects that
it was rejected by a brothel because it is too strong for any place except
a public art gallery, a remark that strikes out at public taste as well as
the *Venus*. Taken as a whole, however, *A Tramp Abroad* is not a major
assault on the human race. Though the attempt is sometimes painful
to behold, Twain does try to produce an amusing spectacle. When
writing as a reporter he seeks out not only the colorful and informative
detail but also the comic one: the huge piles of manure on the farms
in the Black Forest, the allegations that the Protestants whitewash
glaciers that over the years have become dirty. Sometimes he ends even
his most sensitively wrought descriptions with a snapper, as though
the description exists only for the concluding joke. For example, a
description of Mount Blanc concludes with an elderly English gentleman saying that now he can go home because he has seen the principal
features of Swiss scenery: Mount Blanc and the goiter, a common af-
fliction of Swiss women.

At least a third of the time Twain is back at his old tricks of burlesquing his material by viewing it through a comic mask. He is the
gentleman, for instance, in reproving Harris for using pretentious
words in a report on the Furka region. He is the instructor in sum-
marizing medieval legends, in providing "helpful" drawings, and in
telling how they harness horses on the continent (about which he obviously knows nothing). He is the sufferer in attempting to get dressed
in a dark hotel room. And he is the simpleton in burlesquing such
diverse matters as guidebooks, art criticism, and the German language. As might be expected, such an outpouring of tomfoolery plays
havoc with the character of the narrator. As the book proceeds "Mark
Twain" becomes less credible and for most readers less interesting. But,
again, by playing the role of the semi-idiot, Twain trivializes reality
and makes it more tolerable. Paradoxically, the clowning in *A Tramp
Abroad* is perhaps the best evidence of Twain's increasing disgust with
the human race.

The point of view of the idiot, however, never results in Twain's best
imaginative efforts. It makes humorous perceptions possible but not

perceptions that are at once humorous and intensely human. For these Twain always had to adopt the persona of a character that is identifiable in place and time, preferably the persona of a rural character who speaks in the vernacular. Simon Wheeler is such a persona, and so is Huckleberry Finn. In *A Tramp Abroad* it is Jim Baker, who in chapters 2 and 3 spins the "Blue-Jay Yarn." A middle-aged, simple-hearted California miner, Baker tells of the lamentable experiences of a blue-jay that makes a fool of himself in the jay world by trying to fill with acorns what he thinks to be a knothole. The knothole is in fact a chimney in a deserted house. Given the distance provided by a tale completely removed from actuality, Twain's imagination soars. Besides possessing an easy and colorful style, the sketch creates two characters not easily forgotten, Baker and the blue-jay. Baker is right in saying that the jay is just as real and as ornery "as you may be." The sketch is a gem in a so-so context.

The Prince and the Pauper

Since Mark Twain had such a difficult time keeping the lid on his growing disgruntlement with life while writing *A Tramp Abroad,* he might understandably let the lid blow off in his next volume. But Mark Twain was rarely logical. His next book—*The Prince and the Pauper*—turned out to be the most conventional and the blandest that he ever wrote. We can only guess at his motives. Besides wanting a commercial success he apparently hoped for a story that would entertain his daughters. He regularly read to them from the manuscript and he dedicated the book to "Those good-mannered and agreeable children, Susie and Clara Clemens." Apparently, too, he was so tired of being called a "mere humorist" that he wanted to prove that he could compete successfully with the more serious writers by tackling one of their favorite genres, the historical romance. And probably after reading so much English history while abroad he wanted to exploit the English past. As in *Huckleberry Finn,* he selected two boys and an older man as his major characters. He has the boys change clothes and tries to imagine what would happen. Plenty happens because one boy is a London ragamuffin and the other is the heir apparent to the English throne. Rolled into one, *The Prince and the Pauper* is a tall tale, an historical romance, and a story designed to entertain and ennoble juvenile readers. When he read it, Joe Goodman, Twain's former boss on the *Territorial Enterprise,* thought Twain had lost his senses, but Twain's family and Hartford friends believed that he had finally brought out the best in him.

To give his narrative the aura of legend, Mark Twain in a preface calls it a tale that has been passed down from generation to generation. It is the story of two fourteen-year-old look-alikes, Tom Canty of Offal Court in London and the young prince soon to be Edward VI of England. It opens at 9:00 A.M. on 27 January 1547—seventeen-and-a-half hours before Henry VIII dies—and covers the period between then and the crowning of Edward VI on 20 February. In the first three chapters Twain introduces the boys and their contrasting backgrounds. Seeing the Pauper manhandled by one of his guards, the Prince invites him into the palace where as a jest they exchange clothes. It is not so much of a jest, though, when the Prince in rags gets thrown out of the palace grounds. In chapter 4 John Canty, Tom's father, collars the Prince, mistaking him for Tom, and drags him off to the human sty that the Cantys call home. Chapters 5–9 switch the story to Tom and his perplexing problems as prince. Despite his ingenuity and the bits and pieces of information he had picked up about court life, his behavior appears so strange that word gets out that the Prince has lost his mind. In chapter 9, though, Tom, "magnificently habited," stands forth as the commanding figure in a fantastic river pageant—one of Mark Twain's great scenes.

In chapters 10–13 the real prince also gives the impression that he has lost his mind when he issues orders in regal language to the inhabitants of Offal Court. Only his "mother" and twin "sisters" are kind to him, his mother suspecting that all is not right because he does not, when startled, cast his hand before his eyes as Tom had habitually done. Escaping Canty the next day, the Prince tries to break into the Guildhall, where a royal banquet is in progress. He well might have been trampled to death by the jeering mob had he not been befriended by an ex-soldier named Miles Hendon. The two repair for the night to Hendon's room in a little inn on London Bridge. When he awakes the next morning, Hendon finds the Prince has gone. Chapters 14–16 shift the story back to Tom, who must now with the help of the whipping boy adjust to being king. Though Tom rapidly begins to feel a captive of the stuffy palace routine, he wins general admiration for his compassion in dealing with persons unfairly accused of crime.

The next thirteen chapters, 17–29, describe the continuing troubles of the Prince as he falls into the hands of a band of outlaws and probably would be put to death except that once more Miles Hendon rescues him. The two set out for Hendon Hall, where Miles discovers that all of his family have died except an evil brother, who has taken over the estate and married Hendon's former sweetheart. Miles and the Prince are thrown into jail as vagabonds. There the Prince has a chance to observe firsthand the horrors of English prison life. When free again, the two set off for London.

In chapter 30 the tale turns once more to the court where preparations are under way for the coronation. By this time Tom has begun to adjust to court life—and to like its ease and splendor. But during the great procession from the palace to Westminster Abbey for the crowning he sees his mother and "up flew his hand, palm outward, before his eyes." Recognizing the old involuntary gesture, his mother struggles up to the horse on which Tom is riding but is rudely snatched away by an officer of the king's guard. Although the encounter pricks Tom's conscience, he nevertheless enters the Abbey and is about to allow himself to be crowned when suddenly the real prince, who has been hiding in the Abbey all night, strides up the aisle to the throne. The guards would arrest him, but Tom intervenes and in a burst of natural goodness announces that the tattered intruder is the real king. Appropriately the final chapter of the book is entitled "Justice and Retribution." The new Edward VI makes Tom Canty the head of Christ's Hospital and Miles Hendon the Earl of Kent. Hendon's evil brother flees to the Continent where he dies, thus leaving his wife free to marry Miles, whom she has loved all along. The last sentence wraps fact and story together: "The reign of Edward VI was a singularly merciful one for those harsh times. Now that we are taking leave of him, let us try to keep this in our minds, to his credit."

Mark Twain said that the idea for the story came from Charlotte M. Yonge's *Little Duke,* a copy of which he discovered in the mid-1870s in his sister-in-law's house at Quarry Farm. Yonge's little Duke, Richard of Normandy, escapes from bondage at the court of King Louis IV and returns to Normandy where he is a much more compassionate ruler because of what he has endured. Apart from suggesting a line of action the Yonge book undoubtedly appealed to Twain because it shows how he might use the historical novel form to dramatize the moral development of a young boy, a subject he had already introduced in *Tom Sawyer* and later developed more fully in *Huckleberry Finn.* To turn his prince into a pauper he conjured up the idea of look-alikes whose stations in life become reversed when in jest they exchange clothes. After trying contemporary possibilities he selected Edward VI, the Tudor boy king who lived from 1537 to 1553 and Tom Canty of Offal Court out of Pudding Lane in London. To familiarize himself with the setting he began in the summer of 1876 to steep himself in the history and language of Tudor England. That he enjoyed the task hugely seems certain from the fact that its first literary consequence was the hilariously bawdy *1601* or *Conversation as It Was by the Fireside in the Time of the Tudors,* written to amuse Joseph Twichell, his minister. He continued his research in the summer of 1877 and by November, as an entry in his notebook indicates, he had the plan of the book well in mind. Then he put the partly written manuscript aside in order to prepare for the 1878–79 trip to Europe. It was not until he had finished *A Tramp Abroad* in January 1880 that he got back to *The Prince and the Pauper.* When he resumed work, he was more than ever convinced that he should use the book to show the need for compassionate rulers. So he dropped the idea of alternating more of less equally between the two boys, and began to concentrate on the Prince whose misfortunes offered a better chance to point out the cruelty of English laws and customs— and hence the need for reform.

Mark Twain finished the first draft of the work in September 1880, but spent the next four months enlarging and revising it. For advice and encouragement he turned to his family and to such friends as Howells, Twichell, Warner, Mrs. Fairbanks, and the young ladies of the Saturday Morning Club in Hartford, all of whom, as might be expected, enthusiastically approved not only of the book itself but also of Mark Twain's new interest in conventional and hence "respectable" fiction.

Finally satisfied, he gave the manuscript to James R. Osgood, a Boston publisher who had already brought out his small volume entitled *A True Story and the Recent Carnival of Crime* in 1877. He dropped the American Publishing Company, which had brought out his earlier books, because he was convinced that the company had been cheating him—and there is evidence to indicate that it had been. Osgood was a trade publisher, but for Twain he agreed to sell the book by the subscription method and to retain only a 7 1/2 percent commission for himself. In effect, the arrangement made Twain his own publisher. Much care was taken with the illustrations, Twain insisting that the costumes and settings be accurate, and that the boys seem thirteen or fourteen years of age. Production proceeded with surprisingly few delays: the American edition appeared in December 1881, shortly after the English and Canadian editions. The sales, however, were disappointing, Twain blaming Osgood's inexperience as a subscription publisher.

His research for the book was surprisingly extensive. He investigated not only general histories of England but also works dealing more narrowly with English laws, customs, and life among the rogues and outlaws. For the language he relied upon specialized dictionaries as well as works by such writers as Shakespeare and Sir Walter Scott.[2] As he found words that might be useful, he jotted them down in his notebook. He wanted, he said, to saturate himself in archaic English to a degree that would enable him "to do plausible imitations of it in a fairly easy and unlabored way."[3]

As in previous books, his use of sources varied from copying a passage verbatim (without acknowledgment) to changing the facts to suit the fiction (also without acknowledgment). The description of Tom Canty's progression to Westminster Abbey to be crowned, for example, is largely Holinshed's description of the progress of Elizabeth. On the other hand, to make Edward a more credible character he changes his age from ten to about fourteen, and to make his moral improvement more striking he says nothing of the real Edward's religious intolerance. The book's chief contribution to our understanding of English history, however, is not factual information, but a sense of the extremes of life in Tudor England, the wealth and pageantry on the one hand and the poverty and suffering on the other.

With young readers especially in mind, Twain tells a lively story. He packs it with action, keeps the adventures of both boys moving at a rapid pace, and fashions a smashing climax in which everything hinges on the Prince's being able to remember where he cached the Great Seal. For readers thrilled by dime novels there are villains aplenty and one last-minute rescue after another. For those charmed by sentimental fiction there are tender scenes of youthful virtue and mother love. The story never slows down. Its steady pace is all the more remarkable because the basic design of shifting attention back and forth between the boys created at least three major problems for the author. The first was that the book could easily have broken into two stories unrelated except at beginning and end.

Though he makes the adventures of the two boys strikingly different, Twain holds them together with considerable skill. Tom Canty's miscues serve as constant reminders of how the Prince would have behaved, and many of the Prince's blunders bring to mind how much more easily Tom Canty could have gotten along. Additionally, Twain keeps the reader anxious about the fates of both boys even when concentrating on only one. He does this by breaking from the Prince to the Pauper (or vice versa) when events become ominous. The technique resembles that used today in multiplotted soap operas that leave television viewers worried about the fate of one heroine while watching the catastrophes befalling another. A second problem for Twain was that each boy when placed in an alien environment had to have information and protection in order to survive. Tom manages because he has learned to read while still in Offal Court, and has played at being a prince. Once in the palace he finds a book on court etiquette and is befriended by the Earl of Hertford and his whipping boy. The Prince, of course, is befriended by Miles Hendon. Finally, Twain encounters the problem faced by the author of every historical novel: how to adapt history to the story but yet in the end seem to leave history undisturbed. In the instance of *The Prince and the Pauper,* no matter how he alters the details of the life of Edward VI, Twain has to get him crowned on 20 February 1547. What Twain does is to use the fact of Edward's coronation to build suspense. Until the crown is about to be placed on Tom Canty's head he conceals from the reader the information that Edward is in Westminster Abbey. Even when he finally produces the Prince he intensifies the suspense by making it difficult for the Prince to prove his identity. At the last moment, however, everything gets resolved—just as it should in historical novels of the kind written by Charlotte Yonge and Sir Walter Scott.

Intentionally or not, some of Twain's more serious themes of the 1880s slip in. Several of these reveal him as the sentimentalist who accepts as articles of faith the miracles of mother love, the almost preternatural perception of young children, and the spirit of compassion that persists in individuals who have had at least a modicum of Christian nurture. Moreover, as a typical Victorian he suggests that goodness pays off both spiritually and materially. Yet for a work intended for young readers the book contains astonishing evidences of his growing cynicism. Mark Twain is not yet the mechanical determinist, but the doctrine is clearly taking hold of him. The characters are what they are principally because of their time and station in life. He shows himself, moreover, increasingly sour about the fickleness and cowardliness of crowds, and about the pervasiveness of human injustice, both legal and economic. Granted that Twain wanted to show how Edward VI learned through contact with the worst elements in English society, his rendering of those elements is at times so biting as to suggest that he was drawing on the "damned human race" theme that already lay at the heart of the half-completed *Huckleberry Finn.*

If *The Prince and the Pauper* contains hints of Mark Twain's more mature ideas, however, they remain shadows in the background. Up front the book is neither dark nor profound. Rather, it is what Twain meant it to be: a lively story for young readers fitted into the form of the conventional historical romance. Its action is engrossing, its fatherly tone is reassuring, and its language, liberally besprinkled with words such as "prithee" and "mayhap," suggests the atmosphere of ye olde time. The humor is definitely muted. Only once does the Western spirit erupt: when told that Henry VIII will not be buried for almost twenty days after his death, Tom Canty as the fake heir apparent asks, "Will he keep?" For his own generation Twain probably did prove with this work that he could be more than a humorist. But tastes have changed. Modern adults prefer the humorist. Many believe that, for an author who could write a *Tom Sawyer* and a *Huckleberry Finn, The Prince and the Pauper* was a waste of time.

Life on the Mississippi

Taken together, *Tom Sawyer, Life on the Mississippi,* and *Huckleberry Finn* compose Mark Twain's celebration of the great river and the people living along its banks from the 1830s to the 1880s. *Life on the Mississippi* differs from the other two in that it makes the region the center of attention, whereas the other two make it the background for fiction. Apparently, Twain wanted to make the book a definitive treatment of the subject. In preparation for writing it he not only engaged in extensive reading but also took a "field trip" down and up the river to add to the fund of information gained during the years he was a pilot. As informative as it is, though, the book is no documentary. It is too casually organized, too personal, too stuffed with irrelevancies, too humorous and satiric, in short, too Mark Twainish to be that. Nevertheless, it is a readable account of "life on the Mississippi."

The idea for a book about the Mississippi was not something Twain dreamed up after finishing *The Prince and the Pauper.* As early as January 1866 he wrote his mother and sister from San Francisco that he was planning such a work, and after finishing *Roughing It* in 1871 he mapped out for Livy the procedure he would ultimately follow: "When I come to write the Mississippi book, *then* look out! I will spend 2 months on the river & take notes, & I bet you I will make a standard work."[4] By "standard work" he must have meant a comprehensive factual account rather than a personal narrative, because three years later he confessed to Howells that he had never thought of writing up his own experiences as a pilot until Twichell suggested the idea.[5] In 1875, after he had finished the seven installments of "Old Times on the Mississippi" for the *Atlantic,* Twain intended to return as quickly as possible to the river to gather the material necessary for expanding those installments into a book, but he was not able to break himself loose for such an expedition until April 1882. Then, with Osgood, his publisher, and Roswell Phelps, a stenographer, he boarded the *Gold Dust* in St. Louis for the trip to New Orleans. Phelps was along to take down Twain's spoken impressions of the trip and, as it turned out, to handle Twain's business correspondence. The trip down, as his notes show, was for Twain a combination of surprise and nostalgia: surprise because of the new developments along the river and nostalgia for the glory days. Once in New Orleans, he plunged into a "whirlwind of hospitality." He stayed there with Osgood and Phelps until 6 May, when they were able to board the magnificent *City of Baton Rouge* piloted by Twain's former mentor, Horace Bixby. The trip north to St. Louis was all too short for the reminiscing of the two men. At St. Louis Twain and his companions boarded a smaller packet for Hannibal, where Twain spent three days examining old localities and talking with gray-heads who had been boys and girls with him. The stenographer apparently left the expedition in Hannibal, but Twain and Osgood continued on to St. Paul, where they disembarked in a snowstorm. As soon as possible, they took the train for home, arriving there in mid-May.

Although he returned east with voluminous notes—his own and the stenographer's—and even with part of the book written, composition on *Life on the Mississippi* proved bothersome. As usual the book had to be a large one to attract subscription buyers and, again as usual, Twain tired of the task before completing it. The contract called for him to finish the manuscript in time for the Christmas sales, but he came nowhere near meeting such a deadline, partly because of business ventures and partly because of a rash of illnesses in the family that kept them from moving to Quarry Farm until July. When they returned to Hartford in October Twain was still 30,000 words short of the number called for by the contract. To make matters worse, Osgood asked that certain sections—some 15,000 words—be deleted because the material might give offense, especially to Southern readers. Swearing fulsomely at the book and everything connected with it, Twain finished the last chapters by stuffing them with Indian legends and quotations taken from other travel works. Then, to Osgood's consternation, he insisted that Livy have the last say on its contents. Osgood's fears were justified. After 50,000 copies had been printed and 40,000 bound, Livy asked that two illustration be removed, one showing Mark Twain's head in flames and another displaying a rather grisly corpse in grave clothes. Osgood deleted the plates but let the illustrations stand in the pages already printed. Somewhat uncertainly, therefore, the book finally appeared on the market in May 1882, the American edition a few days after the English.

The book shows signs of the up-and-down enthusiasms of its author. The first three chapters introduce the river, its geography and history and a sample of the talk and behavior of the rowdies who manned the huge lumber rafts in the middle of the nineteenth century. This last, chapter 3, Twain swiped from the partly completed *Huckleberry Finn* manuscript and did not reinsert it. Chapters 4–17 reprint in their entirety the installments of "Old Times on the Mississippi" that had appeared in the *Atlantic Monthly* eight years before. To them chapters 18–20 add, as a sad postscript, the story of the explosion of the *Pennsylvania* that resulted in the death of Henry Clemens. Then, in chapter 21, Twain summarizes in a single page the next twenty-one "slow drifting" years of his life and thus comes finally to the main part of the book, the narrative built around the trip he and Osgood and the stenographer had just taken. Characteristically, he never calls his companions by their real names.

In the selection and manipulation of material, the main part of the book recalls Twain's earlier travel works. The narrative follows the itinerary of the actual trip down and up the river, with frequent interruptions for reminiscences, anecdotes, folk tales, and quotations from the works of earlier travelers. A marked difference is that the proportion of factual information is much greater—understandably since this is supposed to be a more definitive and hence more impersonal account than those of the three previous travel books. The first segment, chapters 22–40, deals with the trip from St. Louis to New Orleans. Throughout, the narrator is excited about what is new for him (e.g., spotlights on the boats) and saddened by what has passed (e.g., the lines of steamboats at the levees, the "acres of lumber-rafts and dozens of big coal-barges; also occasional little trading-scows, peddling along from farm to farm, with the peddler's family on board" [chap. 28]). Quotations from such early travelers as Captain Marryat and Frances Trollope provide an historical context, but a long Gothic murder story and a tale of professional gamblers simply interrupt it. Two items are reworkings of passages already written for *Huckleberry Finn*: "The House Beautiful" recalls the Grangerford home in *Huckleberry Finn* and the Watson-Darnell feud the Grangerford-Shepherdson feud. Both of these later treatments are more factual and less colorful than the earlier ones, especially "The House Beautiful," which incorporates many details from Charles C. Cook's *The House Beautiful* (1877). Chapters 41–52 capture much of the color of New Orleans without the usual moonlight-and-magnolia clichés. Especially interesting to current readers are the descriptions of visits with George Washington Cable and Joel Chandler Harris, and vignettes of the Mardi Gras, New Orleans cemeteries, cock fights and mule races, and the inevitable conversations about the Civil War. It is in chapter 20 that Twain gives the strange (and false) account, already mentioned, of how he selected his pseudonym as a way of making amends for once ridiculing Captain Isaiah Sellers.

Chapters 53–60 tell of the trip from New Orleans to St. Paul. Since he had already written about the river south of St. Louis, Twain now gives this stretch short shrift. One could wish for snatches of his conversations with Horace Bixby. But the account of his three-day stay in Hannibal is vintage Twain. He woke up every morning, he says, with the impression he was a boy again—and went to bed every night feeling a hundred years old. In twenty-nine years, everyone, of course, had changed—or died. The greatest changes, he reports, were in the women: "These were good women; it is very wearing to be good" (chap. 55). North of Hannibal he finds the towns clean and orderly and apparently prosperous. There is little nostalgic reminiscence now since, except for the stretch from Hannibal to Muscatine, this part of the river is unfamiliar to him. One gets the feeling that he had collected too little material for this segment, or that he was enormously tired of the book, or both. Whatever the reasons, the work ends anticlimactically with unassimilated chunks of factual information, the hyperbole of a travel brochure put into the mouth of an elderly gentleman who comes on board at LaCrosse, and Indian legends that are only vaguely relevant. There are four appendixes, none of them of transcendent importance.

As must be apparent, the book is a blend of personal reminiscence, reading (Horst H. Kruse lists forty-seven books Twain consulted, along with eighteen other sources),[6] the notes he and his secretary kept on the trip (Kruse counts 450 of them), and passages lifted from works he had written for other purposes. Not all of the notes or the printed materials he consulted, of course, proved helpful. "I drudged through all of those old books mainly to find out what the procession of tourists thought of the river towns of the Mississippi. But as a general thing, they forgot to say."[7] Nevertheless he generously salted his text with material from such works as Basil Hall's *Travels in North America in the Years 1827 and 1828* (1829), Thomas Hulme's *A Year of Residence in the United States of America* (1816–17), Alexis de Tocqueville's *Democracy in America* (1862), Frances Trollope's *Domestic Manners of the Americans* (1832), and Francis Parkman's *LaSalle and the Discovery of the Great West* (1879).

It is easy to downgrade a book so loosely constructed as *Life on the Mississippi*. Even Kruse, who argues that Twain in this book does what he had planned to do, has to admit that in its last fourth, at least, Twain seems more of an improviser than a planner. Most critics agree that the work is the most disorganized of Twain's travel books. But no one contends it is the least interesting. Its appeal obviously transcends its casual structure, and we need to examine the work more carefully. What elements in it have continued to attract and delight readers for more than a hundred years? Most would probably agree that three stand out particularly: the river, the narrator, and the combination of humor and satire.

The great river is undoubtedly the most compelling force in the book: the huge, dangerous, lonesome, beautiful Mississippi that T. S. Eliot called a great brown god. Twain's other travel books may achieve greater unity of action, but none of them has so gripping a focus. The trip holds the narrator to or near the river and constantly opens up fresh areas for his consideration. Moreover, Twain is eager to have the reader experience the river in a variety of ways. He presents it not only through his own eyes but also through the eyes of other travelers, apprentice and licensed pilots, business men, historians, yarnspinners, and even Huckleberry Finn. He alternates passages of factual material with personal reminiscences. He contrasts the romance and excitement of the river during its heyday in the 1850s with its relative emptiness and melancholy during the 1880s. He sets off the activities of the river against those of the shore. And scattered throughout he offers such marvelous vignettes as the phony fighting of the loudmouthed rafts-men, the terror of a wind reef for a cub pilot, Horace Bixby's mastering the dangerous and intricate Hat Island Crossing at night, the storm below Memphis when the pilot has to tie up to the bank, the blacks dragging their dogs aboard a steamboat, and the tension and excite-ment of a steamboat race.

The basic point of view, or voice, in the narrative is an unusual blend of authority and informality. Since he wanted the book to be accepted as a serious treatment of life on and along the Mississippi, Twain had to present himself as being informed and reliable. On the other hand, since he wanted the book to sell he knew that he had to be informal and entertaining. The result is a narrator who, though he may not be so amusing as the madcap that narrates *Innocents Abroad* or so likeable as the tenderfoot in *Roughing It,* is nevertheless altogether appropriate for the purposes of narrating *Life on the Mississippi.* In fact, this "Mark Twain" comes closest to being the actual author.

Although his desire to be taken as an authority discourages Twain from adopting a variety of comic poses and thereby losing credibility, the informality of the style allows him to slide easily back and forth between reporting and humor or satire. Thus, while the main part of *Life on the Mississippi* is not sidesplitting comedy, it is often amusing. Exaggerations abound. He describes a boat, for example, so slow "that we used to forget what year it was when we left port," and he declares that every tumblerful of Missouri River water holds nearly an acre of land in solution. Occasionally he assumes a mild superiority to those about him, once even trying his old trick of turning his companions into oafs so that he can pose as a high-toned gentleman. But the at-tempt is halfhearted, and he does not repeat it.

Often the humor takes on a critical edge and turns into satire. When it does, we recognize a Mark Twain we already know: the realist who abhors pretense and the humanitarian who hates injustice. He finds sham particularly in the South: sham castles that dot the landscape, sham chivalries, jejune romanticism, and absurd feuds kept going through the years in the name of honor. Twain is sure he knows the cause of all this "humbug": Sir Walter Scott. "Sir Walter," he charges, "had so large a hand in making Southern character, as it existed before the war, that he is in great measure responsible for the war" (chap.

46). "The first [*Don Quixote*]," he added about his favorite book, "swept the world's admiration for the medieval chivalry silliness out of existence and the other [*Ivanhoe*] restored it." As a former newspaperman he is especially revolted by the flowery language in Southern newspapers. He quotes a report of the women at a mule race as being "a sea of foamlike loveliness" (chap. 45).

Yet he is still nostalgic about the South, the region of his youth. Everything considered, he lets it off rather lightly. He provides examples of business corruption, but there is little about political corruption or the baleful effects of Reconstruction. This is by no means another *Gilded Age*. Yet the book might have had much more of a bite had he not softened or removed his sharpest remarks. The notebooks contain many comments that a modern reader would enjoy. To take two rather well-known examples: he tells in his notebook of an "old bitch" who had the biggest whorehouse in St. Louis, and he calls the St. Louis hotel in New Orleans "a vast privy"; in the book he rejects the first and bowdlerizes the second into "if a broom or a shovel has ever been used in it there is no circumstantial evidence to back up the fact" (chap. 44). Much of the sharpest satire, however, occurs in the passages he dropped, mostly because Osgood warned him that they would interfere with sales in the South. There are some two dozen of these passages, totaling about fifteen thousand words. They vary in length from a single sentence to an entire chapter, and in intensity from mild irreverence to downright vitriol. The most arresting of these attacks the dreadful condition in American cities forty years before, the outrageous abuse of passes on American railroads, and the continuing enslavement of Southern whites by political and social customs. Osgood was probably right that these "suppressed passages," especially the one on the enslavers (white Southerners), might have offended enough readers to cut into sales.[8] He might on aesthetic grounds have contended also that the aggressive tone of most of them would have been foreign to a book that on the whole is good natured.

Despite its freight of historical and social and economic fact the *Life* is not a documentary of the Mississippi Valley in the 1880s. It is too personal and impressionistic, and it lacks a clear social purpose. At best it simply reflects the ambivalences of its time. Twain oscillates between sentimentality and antisentimentality, romance and realism, pessimism and optimism, nostalgia and pride in new developments along the river, social stasis and industrial progress. As Guy A. Cardwell points out, these were popular oppositions that "flooded the mag-

azines in Britain and in American, were prominent in the English
travel books about America that Clemens read and borrowed from,
were suggested by the life he observed in the course of his actual return
to the Mississippi, and almost necessarily found their places in the
book during composition."[9] Twain needed the focus that Huckleberry
Finn would provide him to eliminate the scattershot satire in *Life on
the Mississippi*.

Chapter Eight
Adventures of Huckleberry Finn

Besides being Mark Twain's masterpiece, *Adventures of Huckleberry Finn* is one of the most popular and respected works of fiction ever written. Since the first American edition, published in 1885 by Charles L. Webster and Company, Mark Twain's own publishing house, over 150 American editions have come on the market. Abroad it has appeared in roughly 700 editions and has been translated into over fifty languages.[1] Every year, approximately two hundred thousand copies are sold by American publishers. The response to it by scholars and critics has been equally amazing. In the English language alone there have been four books and well over six hundred and fifty articles written about it, not to mention the countless discussions of it in works on broader topics. Among nineteenth-century American novels it is second only to *Uncle Tom's Cabin* in provoking controversy, originally on the grounds of coarseness and more recently on the grounds of racism. Like *Moby-Dick*, *Huckleberry Finn* defies classification. Critics have variously called it local color, a romance, a picaresque novel, a comic novel, an historical novel, a gothic novel, a tall tale, an allegory, a satire on American civilization, a satire on humanity, and even "the" American epic. Whatever it is—and the category does not really matter—the work shows the Wild Humorist of the Pacific Slope as well as the Moralist of the Main at the peak of his literary power.

Mark Twain began writing the book at Quarry Farm in the summer of 1876, the season when he was reading proof on *Tom Sawyer*. Both the place and time were advantageous. Quarry Farm always offered the relaxation he needed for his best efforts, and *Tom Sawyer* provided a ready-made setting and cast of characters. Moreover, he had already determined that he would tell the story in the first person. A year before, he had written William Dean Howells that "by & by I shall take a boy of twelve [actually he makes him fourteen] & run him on through life (in the first person) but not Tom Sawyer—he would not be a good character for it."[2] The selection of Huck as narrator and main character was sheer inspiration. Huck's point of view so energized and focused Twain's imagination that for a time characters and events came, as Henry James would say, with a rush. Before the summer was over he had written the first sixteen chapters of the book, with the exception of part of chapter 12 and all of chapters 13 and 14.

The title page identifies Huck as "Tom Sawyer's Comrade" and Huck offers this further explanation: "You don't know about me, without you have read a book by the name of 'The Adventures of Tom Sawyer,' but that ain't no matter. That book was made by Mr. Mark Twain, and he told the truth, mainly. There was things which he stretched, but mainly he told the truth." Thus having established his own identity and disposed of Mark Twain, Huck begins his narrative. It opens in St. Petersburg with a series of genial local color sketches involving Tom Sawyer's Gang and Huck's life with the Widow Douglas and her sister Miss Watson. In chapter 6 Huck's Pap appears and forces Huck to accompany him to a shack on the Illinois shore. Huck soon begins to enjoy his release from being "sivilized" by the Widow Douglas and her sister, Miss Watson—or does until Pap in one of his drunken rages threatens to kill him. Shortly, with considerable ingenuity he manages to escape and leave behind him evidence suggesting that he has been murdered. He paddles down to Jackson's Island in a canoe he had previously found and there discovers Miss Watson's slave Jim, who has run away after overhearing Miss Watson saying she might sell him down river. Four incidents on the Island (chaps. 8–10) have significance for later parts of the book: Huck and Jim snare a raft and hide it for future use; Huck agrees not to inform on Jim; they explore an old frame house that comes floating by (Jim will not let Huck look at a dead man in the house because, as he tells him long afterward, he recognizes the body as that of Huck's Pap); and Jim gets bitten by the mate of a dead snake that Huck has coiled at the bottom of his blanket. Although Jim suffers for four days, Huck avoids admitting his responsibility.

When they grow curious about what is happening in St. Petersburg, Huck puts on a girl's dress and sunbonnet they had cadged from the floating house, and paddles over to the Missouri shore. There he stops at the cabin of a Mrs. Loftus, and although she sees through his masquerade he manages to worm out of her the information that Jackson's Island is to be searched for Jim. He paddles back as quickly as he can, and he and Jim throw their traps on the raft and push out into the main channel. Thus begins the famous flight down the river.

To avoid detection they tie up under overhanging tree limbs during the day and travel only at night. Also at night, Huck forages for food, "borrowing" he calls it, and Jim builds a wooden wigwam on the raft to protect them from the weather. On the fifth night, below St. Louis, they board a sinking steamboat named the *Walter Scott,* and narrowly avoid being captured by two cutthroats who are threatening to kill a third. Because the raft breaks loose while they are on the derelict, they make off in a skiff that belongs to the scoundrels, and thus capture all manner of loot, including books that make it possible for Huck later to read to Jim about kings and dukes. In one of the funniest sections of the narrative they dispute about the ways of kings, the wisdom of Solomon, and why Frenchmen do not speak like men.

They plan to float as far as Cairo and there leave the raft and paddle up the Ohio to a state that will be safe for Jim. (Illinois though nominally a free state was really unsafe because there were too many bounty hunters there looking for escaped slaves.) Just before they reach Cairo, however, a thick fog closes in and separates them, Huck in the canoe and Jim on the raft. Not until hours later when the fog lifts does Huck sight the raft and rejoin Jim, who has fallen asleep from fright and exhaustion. Again Huck tries to fool Jim, this time by telling him that he must have dreamed they were separated in the fog. But seeing the leaves that have been deposited on the raft when it hit towheads in the fog Jim realizes Huck is having sport with him. "Trash," he says, "is what people is dat puts dirt on de head er dey fren's en makes 'em ashamed" (chap. 15). This time Huck apologizes, his first acknowledgment that Jim is something more than property. Soon afterward he makes further amends by giving two bounty-hunters the impression that he has a father in the wigwam ill with smallpox. Each man puts a twenty-dollar gold piece on a board and floats it toward Huck, and the two row away as fast as they can. Before too long Huck and Jim realize that they have passed Cairo in the fog, and they glumly agree that they must sell the raft and begin paddling back to Cairo. But the next night, before they can put their plan into operation, a huge steamboat looms unexpectedly out of the dark and smashes into the raft (chap. 16).

At this point Mark Twain stopped writing on *Huckleberry Finn.* The smashing of the raft suggests his frustration with the story. In the course of composition he had, probably unconsciously, altered the tone and nature of the book by introducing serious moral considerations into

what he had intended to be a lighthearted boys' book. The story had
turned from fun and games into a flight for freedom for both Jim and
Huck. So what to do? As an author he could not successfully have the
fugitives paddle up the Ohio River because he did not know that country well. On the other hand, he could not plausibly have them seek
freedom in the deep South, at least not Jim. Stymied, he put the manuscript aside, presumably hoping that his tank would fill up again
some time in the future. He wrote to Howells that he liked the story
"only tolerably well" and might burn the manuscript when it was
done.[3] He did not return to it until the winter of 1879–80. In the
meantime, he experienced one depressing incident after another. His
collaboration with Bret Harte on *Ah Sin* was a failure. He disgraced
himself, or so he thought, by burlesquing Emerson, Longfellow, and
Holmes at a birthday celebration for John Greenleaf Whittier in December 1877. Business obligations continued to harrass him. To escape
from it all, he took his family to Europe in 1878–79, only to have the
trip turn into a fiasco. Back home again, Dion Boucicault would not
produce his new play *Simon Wheeler, Amateur Detective,* and Twain failed
in an attempt to turn it into a novel. And, as it may be recalled, *A
Tramp Abroad* proved to be a miserably troublesome book to write.
More fundamentally, perhaps, Twain's reading of French and English
history continued to nourish his growing conviction that the human
race, especially its aristocratic classes, is fundamentally cruel. It is not
surprising, therefore, that when he turned again to the *Huckleberry Finn*
manuscript in the winter of 1879–80 he changed his picaresque tale of
Huck and Jim on the raft into a satirical attack on Southern aristocrats.
Since there is no role for Jim in such an attack, he is put aside for two
chapters. So is the decision about how to resolve the flight southward.

Huck survives the crash with the steamboat by diving under its
paddle-wheels. When he surfaces he calls for Jim several times, but
getting no reply he strikes out for the left-hand or Kentucky shore.
There he comes upon an old-fashioned double log house inhabited by
the high-toned Grangerford family. It soon becomes apparent from
their formal behavior and the tasteless decorations of their house that
the Grangerfords value appearance more than genuine feeling. A high
spot in the book is Huck's report of the lugubrious "crayons" and "po-
etry" of Emmeline Grangerford, who had died at the age of fifteen
(chap. 17). Victims of their own tradition, the Grangerfords have been
engaging in a feud with a rival clan, the Shepherdsons, for so long that

no one can remember how it started. In chapter 18 the feud reaches a wild climax just after both families attend church on Sunday morning to hear a sermon on brotherly love. That afternoon the younger Grangerford daughter elopes with a Shepherdson, and the men in both families take to their horses and guns. Before the day is over, two or three of the Shepherdsons and all of the Grangerford males have been wiped out. Huck, who views much of the carnage from a perch in a tree, is so sickened by it all that he cannot describe it.

Gradually the idea was taking shape in Twain's mind of enlarging *Huckleberry Finn* into an exposé of life along the Mississippi. For such a purpose the feud of the plantation owners was an arresting beginning. But how to continue? Obviously, to report on the life and the customs of the region Huck would have to travel about more than the raft would allow. Twain's working notes of the time show him dallying with various possibilities, including having Huck join a circus. But when no idea struck fire, he again pigeonholed his manuscript and did not go back to it until the summer of 1880, when he apparently wrote chapters 19, 20, and the first half of 21. The idea that finally got him going again was to put Huck and Jim back on the raft and have them be joined by two con men whose "business" ashore would require Huck to describe a fair cross-section of Mississippi valley life. The trip for Huck would no longer be a flight, although Jim's status as a slave would continue to raise practical as well as moral problems. The narrative thus takes on a symbolic dimension in offering a contrast between the beauty and peace that are possible on the river and the invariable nastiness and cruelty of life on shore.

When the story resumes at the end of chapter 18, Huck slops into a swamp near the Grangerfords where he has learned that Jim, while hiding, has repaired the raft. The two shove off into the river as fast as they can. After the horrors of the feud the raft is a place where "you feel mighty free and easy and comfortable" (chap. 18). But even on the raft such bliss is transitory, for one morning two Southern con men climb aboard. The younger, who is about thirty, announces that he is a printer by trade but by rights is the Duke of Bridgewater. Not to be outdone, the older, who is about seventy, claims that he is "the pore disappeared Dauphin, Looy the Seventeen." Previously unknown to each other, they work out a *modus vivendi* that includes taking over the wigwam and treating Huck and Jim as their retainers. Although he quickly sees through the two frauds, Huck as schooled by Pap is willing to go along with them. Soon the frauds go to work. For entertainment designed to milk the yokels in towns along the shore they rehearse their own version of *Romeo and Juliet* with the King floundering about in the role of Juliet. Their first stop is Pokeville, where the Duke steals $9.50 from a print shop and the King nets $87.75 by taking up a camp-meeting collection to be used to reform the pirates in the Indian Ocean. The next stop is Bricksville.

At this point (halfway through chapter 21) Twain put aside the manuscript for the third and last time, and did not begin writing on it again until the summer of 1883, when in a great burst of energy he finished the book. In the interim of three years he finished and published *The Prince and the Pauper* (1882), took the trip on the Mississippi with Osgood (April–May 1882), published a collection of short pieces called *The Stolen White Elephant* (1882), and completed and published *Life on the Mississippi* (1883). Although these tasks diverted him from working on *Huckleberry Finn,* they helped to prepare him for the book as he now conceived it: a satire on nothing less than the "damned human race."

When they land at Bricksville, the King and the Duke put up handbills for their "Shakespearean Revival" and Huck lounges about the town, observing its squalor and the indolence of its scruffy inhabitants. Shortly a drunkard named Boggs so persistently taunts old Colonel Sherburn, the town's aristocrat, that Sherburn shoots and kills him. The crowd swarms up to the Sherburn house to lynch him, but Sherburn, holding a gun, steps out on his porch roof and delivers a philippic about the cowardliness of mobs. As if to prove Sherburn's contention, the crowd "washes back sudden." Huck says he could have stayed if he had wanted to, but he did not want to. Instead he goes to a circus where he naively thinks the ringmaster is terribly embarrassed when a drunkard turns out to be a superb equestrian. The "Shakespearean Revival" bombs, but the King and the Duke advertise "The Royal Nonesuch . . . Ladies and Children Not Admitted," a sure fire come-on for the male inhabitants of Bricksville. The first-night audience realizes that they are sold by the short sleazy performance but keep mum so their neighbors can be similarly cheated the second night. Then they all arrive, armed with dead cats and such, the third night. But the King and Duke high-tail it for the raft as soon as they collect the admission fees.

At a town farther down the river they impersonate two English brothers of Peter Wilkes, who has just died. Their purpose is to share in the inheritance—and steal the shares of three nieces as well. The two frauds hoodwink the nieces and most of the townspeople so successfully that they would have made off with all the money had not Huck, moved by the charms of Mary Jane Wilkes, hidden it, and had not the real brothers suddenly appeared. As it is, to settle a matter of tattoo marks on Peter Wilkes after he has been buried, the townspeople dig up the coffin and discover the gold where Huck had placed it. Again the two scoundrels escape.

In Pikesville, a town still farther south, the King sells Jim. Thus, Huck is finally confronted with the moral problem that has been nagging him all the way down the river: should he inform Miss Watson about Jim's whereabouts as his conscience, schooled by his society, urges him to do? At first he surrenders to his conscience, and writes Miss Watson a note. Immediately, he feels washed clean. But then he begins to think how helpful and decent Jim has been to him. So, following his heart, he says to himself, "All right, then, I'll *go* to hell"—and tears up the note (chap. 31). The act is the emotional climax of the book.

Mark Twain, however, continues the narrative for twelve more chapters, bringing back Tom Sawyer to direct activities. Seeking Jim, Huck walks inland to the farm of the Reverend Silas Phelps, arriving there the day when the Phelpses are expecting their nephew Tom Sawyer—probably the most amazing coincidence in a major American novel. Tom himself soon arrives, and since the Phelpses think Huck is Tom, Tom pretends he is his half-brother Sid. At supper that evening the boys learn that the King and the Duke may be driven from Pikesville before they can stage another performance of the Royal Nonesuch. To warn the rascals the two boys slip away in the Phelps wagon, but get to Pikesville only in time to see the two frauds, tarred and feathered, being ridden out of town on a rail. Sickened that even scoundrels should suffer so, Huck mourns, "Human beings *can* be awful cruel to one another" (chap. 33).

When the two boys discover that Jim is being held prisoner in a shed on the Phelps farm, Tom insists that they free him as though he were the Count of Monte Cristo. The silly and, for Jim, painful burlesques of gothic romances that follow come to a head when fifteen local farmers with their guns and dogs arrive to take a hand. Tom and Huck quickly pull Jim out of a hole they have dug under the shed, and attempt to run off with him. But Tom is shot in the leg, and Jim is recaptured when he insists on staying with him until a doctor can be obtained. At this point Tom's Aunt Polly arrives from St. Petersburg and exposes Tom's charade. He in turn reveals that Miss Watson has died and in her will has freed Jim. Jim reveals that the dead man in the floating house opposite Jackson's Island was Huck's Pap. Aunt Sally says that she wants to adopt Huck, but he allows as how he'll not go through that again, and he reckons he's got to light out for the territory (Oklahoma) ahead of the rest: "so there ain't nothing more to write about, and I am rotten glad of it, because if I'd a knowed what a trouble it was to make a book I wouldn't a tackled it and ain't agoing to no more."

Mark Twain finished the first draft of the manuscript of *Huckleberry Finn* late in August 1883, but did not sent an edited version to the publisher for over seven months. The wonder is that he got it there that soon. He worked over the text with unusual care, making almost a thousand changes, inserting some passages and rewriting others. The book, however, was only one of Twain's interests at the time. He and Howells worked on an incredibly bad play about Colonel Sellers, and by himself he tried to dramatize *The Prince and the Pauper* and, for the second time, *Tom Sawyer.* He began collecting material for a book about a Bill Ragsdale, a leper in the Sandwich Islands. He spent time on such inventions as grape shears, a clamp to hold bedclothes over restless children, and a typesetting machine about which more will be said later. In addition, he campaigned for Grover Cleveland for the presidency and, convinced that Osgood could not market his books satisfactorily, organized his own subscription house, calling it the Charles L. Webster Company after the nephew he put in charge. Although Webster hurried the publication process along by writing the running heads and the picture captions, and the ever-helpful Howells and Mrs. Clemens aided with the editing and Howells with the proofreading, Twain himself caused delays by interrupting E. W. Kemble, the illustrator, when he did not like a picture, and by insisting as late as 13 September that an engraving of a bust of himself by his protégé, Karl Gerhardt, be tipped in as a second frontispiece. Yet the worst was to come. Late in November, while Twain was on a lecture tour with George Washington Cable, someone discovered that a jokester had so altered the illustration on page 283 that mild, well-meaning Uncle Silas was turned into an exhibitionist with his fly open. The book missed the Christmas trade, of course, because a new leaf had to be printed and tipped into each of the forty thousand copies already bound and whole signatures reprinted for unbound copies. The printer did such a thorough job of correction before distributing the books to the buyers that no copy of *Huckleberry Finn* with the defaced illustration has been found. We know what the illustration looks like, however, because one copy of the canvasser's prospectus in which it appeared escaped the company's stern order that all such prospectuses be turned in. At long last, the book appeared in the United States on 18 February 1885. The English and Canadian editions, experiencing no unusual misadventures, came out for the Christmas trade on 10 December 1884, thus creating the continuing quandary over the book's real birth year, 1884 or 1885.

As with his other major works, Mark Twain in the course of composing *Huckleberry Finn* drew on his memory, his reading, and on his own earlier writings. Since the book starts out as a continuation of *Tom Sawyer* (and probably makes use of the last chapter of the earlier book that W. D. Howells had persuaded the author to drop), it is hardly surprising to encounter Tom, Huck, Huck's Pap, the Widow Douglas, and Aunt Polly once more. New characters drawn from his boyhood are Miss Watson, a character based on a teacher in Hannibal and a pious Calvinist, and Miss Watson's Jim, whose prototype was Uncle Dan'l, a slave on the farm of Sam Clemens's uncle, John Quarles. (This Jim should not be confused with the young black boy named Jim in *Tom Sawyer*.) From both Uncle Dan'l and Aunty Cord at Quarry Farm Twain picked up many of the character traits and superstitions he ascribes to Jim. Twain's later experiences along the Mississippi provided him with his vivid impressions of the squalid towns along the Mississippi south of St. Louis, and of the degenerates who peopled them. Finally, his experiences as a pilot packed his memory with information about the river itself.

The book also substantially exploits his reading. The major categories of works he tapped include American humor (especially the tall tales of humorists such as A. B. Longstreet, J. J. Hooper, and G. W. Harris); "befo' de wah" romances; the works of the so-called literary comedians (e.g., Artemus Ward and Petroleum V. Nasby); local color sketches (especially those of his neighbor, Harriet Beecher Stowe); histories of France and England that he used in writing *A Tramp Abroad* and *The Prince and the Pauper;* accounts of early travel on the Mississippi that he read while preparing *Life on the Mississippi*; and moral and philosophical discussions (especially W. E. D. Lecky's *History of European Morals* that began affecting his thinking while he was writing *Tom Sawyer*). What becomes clear is that Twain never had to set the manuscript of *Huckleberry Finn* aside because of lack of material.[4] What failed him on three occasions was his invention: what to do with the material he had.

The structure of the story may be described in a variety of ways. Most simply, for example, it can be seen as a modified frame story with Tom Sawyer as the dominant character in the frame (chapters 1–3, 33–43) and Huck as the dominant character in the inner story. Recognizing the frame structure helps to explain why Mark Twain felt it necessary to reintroduce Tom in the final eleven chapters, though not why there had to be so many of them. Another way of viewing the organization is to note the change, as suggested by the synopsis, in fictional modes. The narrative begins as local color (chapters 1–6), continues as a picaresque adventure story down the river (chapters 7–16), turns into a satire on Southern aristocrats (chapters 17–18), goes on as a picaresque novel interlaced with social satire (chaps. 19–32), and ends as burlesque of gothic fiction (chaps. 33–43). The structure can also be described, oversimply perhaps, as an internal drama with rising tensions in Huck's mind as he contemplates his responsibility for Jim, the climax when he decides he will go to hell if necessary to free Jim, and the falling action from then to the end of the book when he determines to set out for the Territory no longer worrying about Jim.

However one describes the formal structure, though, one must admit that it is flawed. The story of Tom Sawyer's Gang is introduced and dropped; so are Pap and the trip south as a flight from the authorities in St. Petersburg. In chapter 16 Twain deleted a long passage on life on a great raft and inserted it in *Life on the Mississippi* as chapter 3. On the advice of his publisher he did not restore it in *Huckleberry Finn*. The return of Tom in chapter 33 results in an inordinate fall from social satire to literary burlesque. Ernest Hemingway, after saying that "all modern American literature comes from one book by Mark Twain called *Huckleberry Finn*," added, "If you read it you must stop where the Nigger Jim is stolen from the boys. That is the real end. The rest is just cheating."[5] The last eleven chapters, however, do contribute modestly to the formal structure. They achieve artistic completeness by bringing back Tom, and by returning the action to the shore—and to the cruel and absurd events that take place on shore. They satisfy the reader that Jim has achieved freedom, and they show Huck, predictably, preparing to "light out" once more. They underline, as we shall see, important traits of the main characters. Moreover, they do all this without the writing's becoming mawkish or moralistic. Nevertheless, the action in these last chapters is so trivial compared with what has come before that the section does seriously weaken what is already a shaky structure.

To say that *Huckleberry Finn* is loosely constructed in a formal sense, however, is not to say that it is seriously fragmented. It contains many elements that provide both unity and coherence. The river not only gives the narrative a beautiful and powerful setting but also sweeps the action along toward what Jim hopes is his freedom, and creates a mood that lingers long after one has finished the book. Patterns of action, such as Huck's always "lighting out" when a situation becomes intolerable, relate parts of the book. Moreover, the constant alternating between shore and river sets up a strong counter movement to the main journey southward, and in doing so reinforces the central opposition between the depravity of society and the restorative power of life alone on the raft. Superstitions and prophecy help happenings to cohere, as do such recurrent themes as human gullibility, hypocrisy, cruelty, and the loveliness—and rarity—of human affection. Especially effective in binding the book together is Huck's increasing awareness of the selfhood of Jim. Finally, and fundamentally, the narrative gains the cohesion necessary for high art from Huckleberry Finn's language and sensibilities. He is the main participant in the action and as the narrator of the story he determines the nature of its language and the quality of its humor.

The most significant decision Mark Twain made as he approached the writing of *Huckleberry Finn* was to have Huck tell the story, for as narrator Huck has important consequences for the author as well as the book. Almost magically, Huck's point of view concentrates Mark Twain's energies on what he does best: report human life in the vernacular. It provides him with a psychic prop, for it simplifies life for him and holds it at a distance. Without Huck as narrator Twain would have had to confront his material directly, and being the kind of man he was he would have sentimentalized over what he liked and railed at what he disliked. With Huck inserted between him and his material, however, he can be more relaxed and hence more artistically effective. Moreover, while setting bounds for Twain's imagination, Huck's point of view stimulates its operation by breaking up conventional habits of perception and introducing fresh ones. When Twain as Twain describes life in the Mississippi valley in the latter part of *Life on the Mississippi* he writes in what can only be called a pedestrian fashion. But when he writes about the same region as seen through Huck's eyes his writing becomes vibrant with life. Mark Twain must have realized how valuable Huck's point of view was for the narrative, for Huck is the only narrative persona of a major work that Twain does not seriously rupture for the sake of being funny or because he wanted to inject one or more of his own fulminations. The Sherburn episode in chapter 22 shows how he preserves Huck's integrity. While writing that part of the book he had been steaming over the cowardice of men and the ways of mobs. But to put such sentiments into Huck's mouth would have been to destroy his persona. So Twain brings forth Colonel Sherburn to be his spokesman, and has Huck simply report what Sherburn says.

It is Huck who is responsible for the language of the book because it is narrated in his vernacular. Mark Twain worked hard on Huck's speech. What he wanted was language that sounded like real talk but had much of the economy and precision of good writing in standard English. He would speak the lines over and over until they satisfied his ears as well as his eyes. As it finally appears, the writing discriminates among several dialects (three, Mark Twain says, with four modifications of one of the three). It even discriminates among pronunciations of the same word in a single sentence in order to catch subtleties due to stress and sentence position.

Like most vernaculars, Huck's features simple everyday words, local idioms, parallel constructions, and figures of speech involving comparisons with natural phenomena and rural activities. Huck's vernacular is unique, however, in that Mark Twain enriches it for pictorial effects. Sometimes the style changes quite subtly to reflect the material or the mood. In the circus episode (chap. 22), Huck's sentence rhythms reflect the gait of the horses and the number of horses abreast of one another. The sentence elements come in twos, then in threes, then there is a quick acceleration into a climax, followed by a sudden drop to the ending.[6] More obvious is the shift in Huck's style when he undertakes a long description of place, especially of the river. The sentences become longer than ordinarily, the rhythm and tempo slower, and the sounds more subdued. There is an almost magical blend of the casual and the poetic that avoids flatness on the one hand and mannered intensity on the other. In forcing Twain into the vernacular, Huck makes him abandon his bookish expressions. The "pretty" wording of conventional fiction, which weakens even *Tom Sawyer,* now disappears almost completely.

The humor in *Huckleberry Finn* gains its special nature from being filtered through the sensibilities of Huck. What Mark Twain does in this book is what he saw Artemus Ward do in his lectures: maintain a solemn mien no matter how ludicrous the material. It is the manner of telling that creates American humor, Twain argued in "How to Tell a Story," not the matter that is told. Thus Huck tells everything soberly and matter-of-factly, however comic it happens to be. Nor does he ever give any indication that he is aware that what he is saying is comic. The result is that there is little raucous humor in *Huckleberry Finn* and much that is tinged with melancholy. Often, whatever else it does, it ends up characterizing Huck. An obvious example of this is Huck's narration of the ancient joke about Hank Bunker's falling off a shot tower and spreading himself out so that he had to be buried between two barn doors (chap. 10). Huck tells it so that the story characterizes Pap from whom he heard it, and himself because he uses it as a solemn warning of what happens when one looks over his left shoulder at the new moon as Hank Bunker had done. The joke is now no longer a chestnut told to evoke thigh-slapping laughter, but an amusing and poignant story that suggests Huck's fear of the horrible consequence of flouting a superstition.

There are two levels of incongruity, and therefore potential sources of humor, that operate throughout the book. One is the disparity just mentioned between what is told and how it is told, and the other is the disparity between Huck's dialect and standard English. There is no page in the book in which one or both of these potentials for humor are not exploited. In addition, the book is a compendium of the forms of humor that were popular in nineteenth-century America: the lusty farce of the West, the crackerbarrel wit of New England, the parodies and burlesques of the literary comic, the quiet chuckles of the local colorists, and the affectionate fun of those who wrote about blacks and other minorities. There are folktales, old jokes, and satirical jabs without number. There is a panoply of comic types from the coward braggart (especially in the deleted raftsman's passage), to the con man, the drunkard, the spinster and the widow, the sentimental poetess, the pious fraud, and the superstitious black.

At he had in his travel books Mark Twain alternates the comic and

the relatively straight reporting. When the material is intrinsically
funny, as are the harangues of Pap and the conversations of the King
and the Duke, he has Huck report it without comment. When he
believes the material needs touching up for the sake of humor, he has
Huck comment on it in his unaffected and serious way: "Uncle Silas
he asked a pretty long blessing over it, but it was worth it; and it
didn't cool it a bit, neither, the way I've seen them kind of interruptions do, lots of times" (chap. 33). Occasionally Twain even has Huck
play a comic role, not unlike the type, though more muted in language, that "Mark Twain" played in the travel books. (These roles, or
masks, should be distinguished from the impersonations he has Huck
adopt to further the action.) Thus Huck is the instructor in teaching
Jim about French kings, and the simpleton in praying for fishhooks or
rubbing an old lamp to bring forth a genie, or being astonished at the
circus when an apparent drunkard can stand on a galloping horse. Although Twain manipulates his narrator more freely than many readers
suppose, he still honors his narrator's integrity. In every case the role
he has Huck play is an extension of one of Huck's basic traits. Moreover, he never uses a role to make fun of Huck, though he comes
dangerously close to doing so when he has his customarily canny boy
be so obtuse at the circus.

There is much more that accounts for *Huckleberry Finn*'s appeal than
structure, language, and humor. Charles Webb, Mark Twain's first
editor, it will be remembered, called Twain not only the Wild Humorist of the Pacific Slope but also the Moralist of the Main. In his
autobiography Twain stressed the second: "Humor must not professedly teach, and it must not professedly preach, but it must do both
if it would live forever. By forever I mean thirty years. . . . I have
always preached. That is the reason that I have lasted thirty years. If
the humor came of its own accord and uninvited, I have allowed it a
place in my sermon, but I was not writing the sermon for the sake of
humor."[7] It is in *Huckleberry Finn* that Mark Twain best demonstrates
his ability to teach without *professedly* teaching, for in his narrative
persona, Huck, he finds an instrument that enables him powerfully to
communicate his social and moral themes without resorting to
didacticism.

What Twain does, to put it as briefly as possible, is to employ a
narrative persona that is a tenderfoot somewhat like the one he used in
the first part of *Roughing It*. Then, by making it necessary for him to
"light out" from one situation after another, Twain exposes him to an

ample cross-section of the adult life in the Mississippi valley in the 1840s. As this narrator reports his experiences and makes his boyish judgments about them, the reader gains the evidence for more sophisticated judgments—and more damning ones. Two theses emerge strongly: (1) that at every social level the white race is corrupt and cruel; there is much that stifles the human spirit, little that nurtures it; (2) that reform is impossible because every class, not just the blacks, is enslaved. This latter position Twain had taken explicitly in the suppressed chapters of *Life on the Mississippi* that he wrote at the same time he was writing part of *Huckleberry Finn*. Here he makes the point implicitly but far more persuasively.

Huck is eminently the narrative persona that the author needs, for he is both naive and perceptive. Twain is at pains to make him as inexperienced in adult society as possible so that he can start off almost as a *tabula rasa*. Huck has grown up in a hogshead without a mother; his father, the town drunkard, appears only when he thinks Huck has a dollar or two, and is finally found dead in chapter 9, though Huck is not told of the fact until much later. In effect, then, Huck is an orphan and a social outcast, and thus is a spokesman for no creed or class. But he is no dummy. He is a highly perceptive boy possessing what Albert E. Stone, Jr., calls the "innocent eye," a combination of youthful naturalness and moral integrity.[8] Moreover, as we already know, he is serious and literal, and is not inclined to doctor his account for laughs or self-aggrandizement, as Tom Sawyer would have done. Finally—and this is especially important—Mark Twain, following the theory of William Lecky, provides Huck with a set of innate values as well as the set he acquires from his environment. Thus his judgments are not all environmentally determined, for many proceed from his "sound heart." Though a boy, he is the "truth carrier" in the book, and for the reader his very presence can serve as a rebuke to less scrupulous characters. Because he has two sets of values, his judgments on occasion may be in conflict, but even on such occasions his voice remains firm and honest. He is, in short, a remarkably trustworthy character to follow as he learns about and reports on the world of his contemporaries.

Huck's report of Mississippi valley life, though often unconsciously funny, is not a pretty one. His general estimate that "human beings can be awful cruel to one another" is well documented at every social level. The aristocrats are the cruelest of the lot, at least as they are represented by the Grangerfords and Shepherdsons, and, possibly, by

old Colonel Sherburn. Although in their stiff way the Grangerfords are
kind to Huck, and young Buck proves to be a good friend, their humanity has been largely drained away by their forms and pretensions.
They try to maintain the graciousness of Virginia plantation life along
the shore of the Mississippi, and overdo their act undoubtedly to convince themselves that they are bringing it off. Their behavior is excessively formal, and their decor in their double log-cabin is tacky, a
quality underlined by Huck's naive admiration for it. Even their grief
for the dead Emmeline has become nothing more than a matter of
forms. They are the worst of hypocrites. Following a sermon on Christian love, they renew their bloody feud with the Shepherdsons, a feud
that got started so far back that no one remembers its cause. Worst,
the Grangerfords and Shepherdsons are wanton killers. They injure
boys by shooting them in the back, and then finish off the job while
shouting "Kill them! kill them!" as the boys attempt to swim away
downstream. Huck's good heart cannot take it. He is so sickened that,
for the first and only time, he cannot continue his narrative. Colonel
Sherburn, an aristocrat in the eyes of Bricksville, kills wantonly, too,
striking down a crazy drunkard because the drunkard has injured his
pride. What becomes evident to the reader is that the aristocrats, with
all their money and social standing, are slaves to their fierce pride,
their institutions, and their absurd sense of honor. Mark Twain will
have much more to say on this theme ten years later in *Pudd'nhead
Wilson.*

The middle class is a more complicated group. They include the
Widow Douglas and her sister Miss Watson, Tom Sawyer and Aunt
Polly, Mary Jane Wilkes, and Aunt Sally and the Reverend Silas
Phelps. At their best Huck finds these people gentle and even affectionate; at their worst they are intolerant and demanding. They insist
on cleanliness, good manners, and "proper" behavior generally. With
equal fervor they oppose tobacco, liquor, profanity, and indolence.
They insist on obedience to one's conscience, which they believe is the
voice of Providence—though there is some division of opinion over the
nature of Providence, since the Widow sees it as kindly and Miss Watson as dictatorial. Generally, seeing these people as his social betters,
Huck hesitates to criticize them severely, though he does realize that
they try to rob him of his liberty and to substitute a life he finds
uncomfortable. He tries to adapt but is not too displeased when his
Pap kidnaps him, and at the end of the book he lights out rather than
have Aunt Sally adopt him.

The reader finds Huck's report more damning than he does. These middle-class people, for the reader, are self-righteous hypocrites. While they prate about Christian love, they own slaves—even Miss Watson, the most pious of them all. Moreover, they seem to believe that they exhaust their Christian duty by having the slaves in each evening for Bible reading and prayers. Their so-called Christian conscience is simply an instrument that has been locally fashioned to keep the dominant social class in control and to help them profit materially. They may not maim or destroy the body, but they brainwash the mind. The ironic aspect of it all is that they have brainwashed their own minds. They are slaves to their conventional consciences, and to the slave economy they have created. The middle-class is the only group that permanently defeats Huck, though he does not know it. When he leaves St. Petersburg in chapter 6, he carries with him for the rest of his life an implacable middle-class conscience. His only defense against it is his innate kindliness, his "heart," but his heart never wholly overcomes the effects of his training in St. Petersburg.

Tom Sawyer demonstrates what middle-class attitudes and values can make of a boy. In him, self-satisfaction balloons into arrogance. He requires that his ideas, picked up from his reading, be accepted if Huck is to be a member of his gang and, later, if Jim is to be rescued "properly" from the shack on the Phelps farm. In a carefully detailed analysis Judith Fetterley shows that aggression, instead of being part of Tom's character, *is* his character.[9] The worst of it is that his aggression always results in cruelty. He organizes games in which everyone except himself is victimized. And in the last chapters he takes inordinate delight in manipulating Jim's escape from his hut as though he were a medieval nobleman attempting to break out of a gothic keep. The fact that Jim suffers both physically and psychologically is a matter of little concern to Tom. He treats it as a commercial deal, and pays off Jim by giving him forty dollars. (Forty dollars seems to be the ultimate expression of benevolence in the Mississippi valley. This is the sum that the two bounty hunters donate to Huck as they paddle away from the raft after Huck gives them the impression that his pap is in the wigwam sick of smallpox.) Although Mark Twain makes Tom into a parody of adult cruelty and pretentiousness, Huck, ever respectful of higher social standing, criticizes him only for his lack of common sense, and continues to admire him for his "style."

Among the members of the lowest class of whites, Huck finds

cupidity and violence unadorned. This is the class of Pap, the King
and the Duke, and those who live along the river in such towns as
Pokeville and Bricksville. It is—or was—the class of Huck himself.
But he views it dispassionately and makes no attempt to identify with
it. Nor does he romanticize it. The lowest class in Huck's eyes are
rascals, not pathetic victims of the inexorable ordering of things. These
people are dirty, untrustworthy, bigoted, and cruel. They take out
their aggressions on the blacks and dogs and such whites as they can
con. They are the ultimate materialists, for they seek nothing more
elevated than whiskey, tobacco, and such cash as they can scrounge or
steal. They are bored with life and are immensely grateful for any event
that breaks the tedium of sitting on a fence rail or leaning against the
front of a store. Only the King and the Duke seem to have a spark of
ingenuity and a smattering of learning, however undigested. Huck
views this group with astonishing dispassion considering the threat to
his life they sometimes pose. And for the reader they offer the best
proof that Twain was fast turning into a determinist—until one remembers that Huck manages to fight free of them. What makes Huck
differ from the other members of his social class is that he is capable of
compassion. Mark Twain had emphasized this quality in him when he
described the original Huck, Tom Blankenship: "He was ignorant, un-
washed, insufficiently fed; but he had as good a heart as ever any boy
had."[10] But Huck aside, it is the lowest socioeconomic class that puts
a capper on Mark Twain's major contention that the human race is a
sorry lot, and that every group, not just the blacks, is enslaved.

There was, of course, one other large socioeconomic class in the Mississippi valley: the blacks. But Mark Twain chooses to have his narrative persona associate with only one of them, and hence there is no
picture of the blacks as a class. As an individual Jim is the exception
to Twain's generalization about the cussedness of human kind. Less
educated and more superstitious than Huck, Jim has just as large a
heart, a fact that it takes Huck the whole trip down the river to realize.
Those who think that in *Huckleberry Finn* Mark Twain debases the
blacks through Jim have not read the book carefully. Given the odds
against him, Jim endures with shrewdness and dignity. For a comparison one can think only of Dilsey in Faulkner's *The Sound and the Fury*.

The last words should be about Huck. For a balanced view, one
should think of him as a hedonist who sees life in terms of pain and
pleasure. Unhappily for him, the scales are tipped heavily on the side

of pain. Because of the nature of his adventures he must endure physical discomfort, anxiety, and frustration. Ironically, though, his sharpest pain results from his most admirable asset, his humanity. It is Huck's heart, his affection and sympathy for others, that hurts so keenly when he sees Buck Grangerford get killed, or when he watches the Wilkes girls about to be cozened by the King and the Duke, or when he sees the King and the Duke—for the heart plays no favorites—being ridden out of town on a rail. Especially he anguishes when he thinks he is responsible for hurting others, as he does after he makes a fool of Jim by pretending they had not been separated in the fog. The crowning injustice of an unjust world, therefore, is that Huck suffers most because of what is finest in him. Even in what seems his moment of greatest moral triumph—the moment when he renounces conventional morality—he achieves only a standoff. His heart triumphs because he decides to treat Jim as a person rather than a piece of property, but his "deformed conscience" triumphs because he continues to believe that "nigger stealing" is a sin, and that blacks generally are not people. A little later when Aunt Sally asks him if anyone was hurt in a steamboat explosion, he says, "No'm. Killed a nigger" (chap. 32). To the end of the book Huck's life continues to be marked by pain: he remains the lonely outsider needing all of his wits just to survive, not to triumph.

Yet in *Huckleberry Finn,* Mark Twain has not reached the depth of despair and cynicism to which he will sink in the 1890s. He allows Huck the pleasures that he himself in the 1880s still managed to extract from human affection, physical comfort, and natural beauty. Before Pap kidnaps him from St. Petersburg, Huck begins to sense the affection in the Widow Douglas and to appreciate it. He responds— excessively for him—to the kindness of Mary Jane Wilkes: "And when it comes to beauty—and goodness too—she lays over them all. . . . I reckon I've thought of her a many and a many a million times, and of her saying she would pray for me . . ." (chap. 28). And, of course, it is the affection of Jim that makes him as much of a social rebel as he ever becomes. He treasures his moments of comfort. He loves his old rags and sugar-hogshead, and his tobacco. He likes being "lazy and jolly" with Pap until Pap gets too handy with the hick'ry. It is "free and easy" on the raft, and it is "nice" being in a cave with Jim at night while the rain pelts down and the thunder goes "rumbling, grumbling, tumbling down the sky towards the under side of the world" (chap. 9). Moreover, the whir of the spinning wheel has a haunting beauty about it that makes him think of death, the final escape. Best of all, however, is sitting in the shallow water with Jim watching the dawn spread over the river (chap. 19). Huck never experiences greater pleasure than that—nor provides greater pleasure for his reader.

Chapter Nine
A Connecticut Yankee in King Arthur's Court

Paradoxically, *A Connecticut Yankee in King Arthur's Court* is one of Mark Twain's most humorous books and one of his most somber. On the surface it is an extended tall tale that lampoons chivalric romances, while underneath it is a compendium of Mark Twain's increasingly gloomy thoughts about human behavior in both the past and the present.

As preparation for such literary schizophrenia one should read the sketch entitled "A Private History of a Campaign That Failed" that Twain published in the *Century Magazine,* December 1885, four years before the *Yankee* was issued. In it Twain attempts to combine the farcical and the serious in describing his experiences as a member of the Marion Rangers, a Confederate volunteer group. He treats the adventures of the volunteers ludicrously until six of them (the narrator included) shoot and kill a man on horseback whom they take to be a Union soldier. Then, suddenly, the piece becomes an apologia for the narrator's subsequent desertion. The killing of the horseman becomes for him "an epitome of war; that all war must be just that—the killing of strangers against whom you feel no personal animosity. . . . It seemed to me that I was not rightly equipped for this awful business; that war was intended for men, and I for a child's nurse."[1] By the end of the sketch, however, the narrator has lost his tenderheartedness, and treats the event as a joke. The volunteers had done their share in the war: they had totally exterminated the enemy that came against them. The episode of the horseman must be taken as having serious purpose, for it is a deliberate invention of the author. The Marion Rangers in reality never killed anyone. What Twain is apparently trying to do is invest a farce with serious purpose—just as he later does with *A Connecticut Yankee.* In neither case does the combination totally jell.

As a tall tale *A Connecticut Yankee* has the characteristic frame structure. One evening Mark Twain meets a feeble old man in Warwick

Castle who gives him a manuscript to read. The main story, then, is what Twain reads that night. It tells how the old man, when younger and a superintendent in the Colt arms factory in Hartford, Connecticut, is knocked out one day by a fellow worker and wakes up in Camelot. Because of his nineteenth-century know-how and abilities he quickly rises to the position of boss over King Arthur's England. For ten years he amazes and delights the ingenuous people of the sixth century with nineteenth-century customs and artifacts. But when he departs for France because of the sickness of his baby daughter, the country erupts in civil war, the Catholic Church invokes the Interdict, and all but a few young knights turn against him. In a final scene he slaughters 25,000 knights with his modern weaponry but is in turn put under a spell by Merlin, the king's wizard, and falls asleep for thirteen centuries. Shortly after Mark Twain finishes reading the manuscript, the old man dies, mourning his sixth-century wife and his "lost land." Some readers view the narrative not only as an extended tall tale but also as the first successful attempt at science fiction involving time travel. Either way, it is a fantasy that has captivated thousands of readers and has served as the scenario for two highly popular films, one with Will Rogers and the other with Bing Crosby in the title role.

It need hardly be said that *A Connecticut Yankee* is far more than a tall tale. Instead of being the main purpose of the book the fantasy more importantly serves as a vehicle for social satire. Twain seems to have worked on the manuscript in three periods: January–February 1886, summer 1887, and from summer 1888 to spring 1889.[2] The narrative deepens with each return to it. In fact, though staying within the context of the fantasy, Twain beginning in chapter 8 frequently takes the story away from his narrator and speaks for himself. This is something he never did with Huckleberry Finn. To see what happens and how it happens we need to trace the course of the book's composition.

Although Twain had read the Arthur story in 1880 in Sidney Lanier's shortened version entitled *The Boy's King Arthur,* he did not begin to see its possibilities for a work of his own until late in the fall of 1884 when George W. Cable, while they were on their lecture tour, gave him a copy of the version written by Sir Thomas Malory. Soon, Twain and Cable in high good humor were talking to each other in Malory's ancient English, and Twain began jotting down ways of burlesquing the legend. In his notebook for December 1884 he wrote:

> Dream of being a knight errant in armor in the middle ages. Have the notions & habits of thought of the present day mixed with the necessities of that. No pockets in the armor. No way to manage certain requirements of nature. Can't scratch. Cold in the head—can't blow—can't get at handkerchief, can't use iron sleeve. Iron gets red hot in the sun—leaks in the rain, gets white with frost & freezes me solid in winter. Suffer from lice & fleas. Make disagreeable clatter when I enter church. Can't dress or undress myself. Always getting struck by lightning. Fall down, can't get up.[3]

The time could not have been better for such a burlesque. Sparked by the enormous popularity of Tennyson's *Idylls of the King* (1859), Arthurian romances were enjoying a strong revival in both England and America. Furthermore, the gothic novels of Sir Walter Scott and others continued to be popular. The romantic flummery of the chivalric tradition offered a perfect target for the humorist. Nevertheless, preoccupied with business affairs, Twain did not begin writing the book until early in 1886.

By February he had written "A Word of Explanation" (the opening part of the frame story) and the first three chapters as we now know them. In these he establishes the basic opposition between the practical nineteenth-century Yankee, Hank Morgan, who narrates the story and the romantic untutored folk of sixth-century England (or what Mark Twain chooses to call the sixth century; there are scores of anomalies). At the outset the underlying assumption is that modern civilization is in almost all ways superior to that of ancient times. Arthur's knights and ladies are ingenuous, coarse, and superstitious. Twain calls them childlike innocents without "brains enough in the entire nursery, so to speak, to bait a fishhook with" (chap. 3). Even Merlin, who is the villain later in the story, is in these chapters nothing more than a bumbling bore who puts the entire court to sleep by repeating for the nth time the story of how Arthur got his sword from the Lady of the Lake. (Merlin's account is taken verbatim from Malory, 1.xxiii.) Yet these early bits of local color are not a complete put-down of the medieval characters. Hank records that there was "a fine manliness observable in almost every face, and in some a certain loftiness and sweetness that rebuked your belittling criticisms, and stilled them" (chap. 3). Sir Galahad exhibits "a most noble benignity and purity," and Sir Launcelot both "majesty and greatness in his giant frame." Clarence, the page who befriends the Yankee and who will throughout the book be his right-hand man, is bright enough to act as the bridge that Twain needs between Hank Morgan and the English.

Something of Twain's early uncertainty about his characters emerges in the statements he made at the time. In November 1886 he appeared before the posh audience of the Military Service Institution on Governor's Island. To them he read the chapters he had already written, and outlined what he intended to do in the remainder of the narrative. The narrator in this outline, called Sir Robert Smith, was with astonishing ferocity to electrocute and mow down with Gatling guns all who oppose King Arthur and then to set up businesslike procedures that would bring nineteenth-century products and techniques to Arthur's England at a "moderate" royalty for the Yankee of forty percent. The Yankee, in short, was to be an amoral opportunist. There is no hint of his having a conscience or being interested in political reform. To a worried query from Mrs. Fairbanks about what he was doing to her beloved Arthurian story, Twain replied he did not intend to besmirch Malory's beautiful characters but only to contrast the life of Arthur's time with that of his own time. Then he added rather curiously that the book was to be his holiday amusement for six days every summer for the rest of his life. "Of course," he said, "I do not expect to publish it."[4] What seems clear is that he really did not know what he was going to make of the narrative. So, as was his custom when puzzled in this way, he pigeonholed the manuscript and did not return to it until the summer of 1887 when he wrote chapters 4–20, excluding chapter 10.

These sixteen chapters carry the story through the eclipse the Yankee uses to terrify Arthur and his court, his rise to the exalted office of Boss, and the trip with Sandy that includes visits to the castle of Morgan le Fay and to what Sandy calls an Ogre's castle but what to Hank seems only a pigsty. Most importantly, before Mark Twain puts the manuscript aside for a second time, the Yankee's purpose has changed from making a fortune for himself to nothing short of ridding Arthur's kingdom of its political and social injustices. As a result, the narrative begins to alternate between buffoonery and serious satire, and the character of the narrator begins to disintegrate.

One can account for the change in large part by noting what was happening to Twain during the interval between early 1886 and mid-1887. For instance, he changed politically from a Republican to a Mugwump. He supported Grover Cleveland and began speaking out for civil rights and against political dictatorship of every stripe. He welcomed the rise of unions as an equalizing power between owners and workers. But maybe more to the point for *A Connecticut Yankee,* he began turning into an anglophobe. He was no end upset that in England the aristocracy and landed gentry were carrying the day against the Liberal party whose principles corresponded in large measure with his own. Furthermore, he was irritated by Matthew Arnold's review in early 1887 of the *Personal Memoirs* of Ulysses S. Grant. Despite a generally favorable appraisal Arnold got nit-picky in criticizing Grant's confusion of *shall* and *will.* This was more than Twain could stand, especially since Grant had been a close friend, and the *Memoirs* had been published by Twain's own firm. In April 1887, just weeks before he turned back to the *Yankee* manuscript, Twain blasted the English author in a speech before the Army and Navy Club, which took on an anti-English cast when Twain listed over twenty-five English authors who were guilty of faulty grammar—and added to the list Arnold himself. Howard Baetzhold, the major authority on Mark Twain's relations with the British, however, believes that George Standring's *The People's History of the English Aristocracy,* which Twain read for the first time in May 1887, was perhaps the primary cause for his turning against the English, especially their ruling classes.[5] Standring vividly attacked such political phenomena as the feudal laws of primogeniture and entail and the British adherence to what he considered to be the "fetish" of nobility. The only solution, he argued, was for England to become a republic. Soon Twain was linking Standring's book with Hippolyte Taine's *Ancient Regime,* Louis St. Simon's *Memoires,* and Carlyle's *French Revolution* as his favorite works. He even proposed publishing them.

The change is evident throughout the chapters he wrote in the summer of 1887. Alternating with continuing burlesque and buffoonery are passages satirizing the English and their laws and practices. The knights no longer have a noble mien. Instead, they are ignorant and superstitious and coarse. So are their ladies. When Hank is undressed before Queen Guinevere, he is the one who is embarrassed. The English, moreover, are so superstitious that the Yankee can easily convince them that he is responsible for the eclipse of the sun that fortuitously begins just as he is about to be burned at the stake. Still the entrepreneur, though, he demands—and gets—an office just below the king's and one percent of such revenue as he can succeed in making for the state. When Merlin, who is now the villain of the story instead of a bumbling fool, spreads rumors that the Yankee is a fake, Hank with the help of Clarence "invents" gunpowder and blows up Merlin's tower.

In chapter 8, however, the narrative takes a fundamental turn. Speaking directly for Twain, the Yankee begins to attack the laws and customs that protect English royalty, nobility, and the Established Church at the expense of the common people. Thus Hank Morgan the entrepreneur begins to give way to Hank Morgan the reformer. Quietly he establishes a patent office; opens up factories and schools; begins a "teacher factory," and military and naval academies; and "invents" the telephone and telegraph. He does this without fanfare because he is afraid to stir up the Church before he is ready for a confrontation with it. He realizes, however, that he is creating a "serene volcano" with a smokeless summit but "rising hell" in its bowels (chap. 10).

In his trip around the county with Sandy he encounters a group of ragged freemen, so-called, who must work from sunup to sundown for the pittance that is left after the king and the nobles and the church exact their taxes: "Why, it was like reading about France and the French, before the ever-memorable and blessed Revolution, which swept a thousand years of such villainy away in one swift tidal-wave of blood" (chap. 13). At the castle of Morgan le Fay he is further horrified by the callousness of the ruling class to human suffering. He sets free the forty-seven poor wretches in her dungeon, some of whom have been there so long no one can remember the charges against them. A young farmer is being stretched on the rack for killing a deer that had been ravaging his own property. In one of the more poignant passages the delightful Sandy flings herself on some muddy pigs, embraces them, and calls them by noble names. She is sure that they have been en-chanted. Borrowing words from Huck Finn, Hank Morgan says, "I was ashamed of her, ashamed of the human race" (chap. 20).

Near the beginning of chapter 21, Mark Twain ran out of steam and again put the manuscript aside. His book, despite its intermittent buf-foonery, had been permanently altered into an attack on the English and English history. "My kind of loyalty," says Hank/Mark Twain, "was loyalty to one's country, not to its institutions or its office-holders" (chap. 13). It was a comment that spoke to Twain's desertion of the Republican party as well as to sixth-century affairs.

Mark Twain wrote chapters 21–36 when the family was at Quarry Farm in the summer of 1888 and the remainder of the book in Hartford between that fall and the spring of 1889. Although he wanted to finish the book quickly—he needed the income—illness in the family and business problems posed major distractions. Most worrisome were his two major business ventures, the Charles L. Webster Publishing Company and the Paige typesetting machine. After two enormous successes—*Huckleberry Finn* and General Grant's *Personal Memoirs*—the Webster company began slipping, in part because Twain kept dipping into its capital for funds to pay the mechanics in Hartford who were constructing the typesetter under the eye of its quirky inventor, James W. Paige. Just about the time the machine seemed finally about ready to go into operation, Paige would think up some new frill and have it torn down again. It was costing Twain three thousand dollars a month, enough to upset a man far calmer than Twain. Yet, like his own Colonel Sellers, he was sure the typesetter would eventually make him millions. He saw an almost mystical relation between the book and the machine. Justin Kaplan puts the relationship this way: "The ambivalences, disillusions, destructive fury, and, finally, homicidal tantrums of the novel were fire drills in his imagination for the actual failure of the machine, machine values, and his dream of capitalist democracy in which he expected to be a tycoon among tycoons."[6] Fortunately, Twain did not wait for the success of the typesetter before completing his book, for the machine was ultimately a failure and a frightfully expensive one.

During the delays in composition Twain's reading continued to reinforce his contempt for the English upper classes. His notebooks show him reacting almost violently to Matthew Arnold's "Civilization in the United States," an article that appeared in the April issue of *Nineteenth Century.* He was especially irritated by Arnold's charge that a lack of reverence among Americans resulted from the American press and the American "addiction to the funny man." In a speech given at Yale where he received a Master of Arts degree, he retorted in what could have been a preface to *A Connecticut Yankee* that the humorist's real purpose is "the deriding of shams, the exposure of pretentious falsities, the laughing of stupid superstitions out of existence."[7] From the English newspapers of the time he got further information for attacking English laws, and from Mrs. Humphrey Ward's very popular *Robert Ellsmere* additional details for belittling snobbish English aristocrats. Details on outrageous treatment of the poor he found in W. E. H. Lecky's *The History of England in the Eighteenth Century* (1887–88), Charles Ball's *Slavery in the United States* (1836), and George Kennan's

accounts of slave labor under the czar (with graphic illustrations) in
Century magazine (1887–88). When he returned to his manuscript in
the summer of 1888 he was ready to mount an even more severe attack
on tyranny.

When Hank finally is able to pull Sandy away from her enchanted
porkers, the two join a group of pilgrims that are journeying (à la
Chaucer) to the Valley of Holiness. Sandy in all innocence describes
the great monastery at one end of the valley and the great nunnery at
the other, and "a fair great foundling asylum midway of the valley
between" (chap. 21). Then the effects of Twain's recent reading begin
to show. The pilgrims overtake a long line of slaves fettered together.
One young woman holding a baby stumbles from fatigue, and is immediately stripped and lashed by the slave master. The pilgrims comment only on the expert way in which the whip is handled. Restoring
the flow of water at the fountain in the Valley of Holiness turns into
another contest between Merlin and the Yankee, with the Yankee win-
ning with his greatest display yet of fireworks and blasting powder.
Back in Camelot the Yankee finds that the officer ranks in his new
army are being filled with nobles who, however stupid, could prove
that their titles go back at least four generations—no matter that the
titles were originally awarded to brewers or sons of royal mistresses. It
was a telling jab at contemporary as well as ancient England.

In chapters 27–38 the Yankee and the King travel across the countryside incognito, a device that gives the Yankee an opportunity to
associate with the poor and experience tyranny on the receiving end.
The episodes are wide-ranging. The King's eagerness to help a family
dying of smallpox convinces the Yankee that there is enough good
material in benighted people—even the Russians and Germans—to
build a republic. But the throne and the nobility have to be abolished,
and a long process of education must be started. The need for education
is especially evident to the Yankee when he finds it impossible to make
several craftsmen see the difference between wages and real income or
that protective tariffs, while they may raise wages, in the end lower
real income. (In such a passage Twain takes the narrative away from
the Yankee in order to school his own contemporaries.) He gives the
screw another turn when he has the King and the Yankee shackled as
slaves and thus in a position to report a young woman burned at the
stake to provide warmth for the other slaves, and another one hanged
for stealing a trifle in order to buy food for her starving baby. The

clergy approve of such hangings, and the nobility find them diverting. Soon, all of the slaves in the group to which the King and the Yankee are attached are to be hanged because the Yankee briefly manages to escape in order to call Clarence on a telephone. But, as we already know, Sir Lancelot and five hundred knights arrive in time to put a stop to the proceedings.

In chapters 39–44, the Yankee tries to destroy knight errantry, the bulwark of English aristocracy, in order to establish a republic with universal suffrage for both men and women. He starts out well enough when he lassos or shoots his opponents in a tournament, but then events go sour. He has married Sandy and she has given birth to a daughter they call Hello-Central, the Central after the original name for a telephone operator. When the child becomes ill, the parents take her to France for recuperation. While they are away Sir Lancelot corners the market on a railroad stock and forces many other knights to the wall. In retaliation, two of them tell King Arthur about the carryings-on between Lancelot and Queen Guinevere, and as in Malory a great civil war breaks out. To end it the church imposes the Interdict. Almost immediately, all of the Yankee's reforms come to a stop, and the kingdom slides back into the Dark Ages. When the Yankee returns to England he finds that only Clarence and fifty-two young knights are loyal to him. So that they will be of no use to anyone else (and will not remain an anomaly in English history) the Yankee blows up all of his factories and schools and mills (he had planted dynamite earlier for just such an exigency). Then with his loyal knights he retires to the cave in the Sand Belt, which he surrounds with a mine field and several strands of wire fencing which he electrifies. In addition, he diverts a mountain stream so that it will race through the ditch created when the land mines are detonated, and he places thirteen Gatling guns so that they can spew their bullets on any advancing army. Thus, when twenty-five thousand knights advance on the cave he slaughters them all in what he considers to be his grandest effect. Unfortunately for him, one dying knight stabs him, and Merlin, dressed as an old woman, manages to weave a spell that causes the Yankee to sleep for thirteen centuries. After this grisly holocaust, the narrative ends with a postscript by Clarence, who tells how Merlin backed into a charged wire and was electrocuted. In the closing part of the frame structure Mark Twain describes how the Yankee finally dies at Warwick Castle lamenting Sandy and his "lost land." Readers are left to decide for themselves whether the Yankee's destruction of the knights is the most damnable indication in the book of the immorality of the species, or whether it is the ultimate spectacular in a tall story that, as all tall stories, is essentially amoral.

Mark Twain completed the first draft of the book in the spring of 1889 and gave it to Fred Hall, the new head of the Webster Publishing Company. For an illustrator he chose Dan Beard, the well-known naturalist and later the head of the Boy Scouts of America. It was a happy arrangement, for Beard's drawings delighted Twain even though they overstressed the contemporaneity of the book. One illustration, for example, shows the king and a vassal becoming an American slave driver and slave, and they in turn becoming a bloated financier and a workman. In another illustration the slave driver of Arthur's time (actually there were no slaves in Arthur's time such as Twain describes) has the head of Jay Gould, the robber baron of the late nineteenth century. Beard usually shows Hank Morgan as an empty-headed Yankee Doodle with feathers sticking out of his top hat.

Although parts of *Life on the Mississippi* and *Huckleberry Finn* had been typed from the holograph manuscript, *A Connecticut Yankee* was the first of Twain's books to be entirely typed. Typed copy, Twain found, invites revision, and he made a number of changes in the *Yankee*, mostly for clarification. Especially he revised the portions of chapters 7 and 13 that were published in the November 1889 issue of the *Century* magazine. Twice he softened the preface to make it less offensive to the English, and even told Chatto, his English publisher, he could alter the final version if he wished.

Entitled *A Yankee in the Court of King Arthur*, the English edition appeared in December 1889 and the American edition four days later. American reviews were mixed; generally the more liberal the reviewer the more favorable the review. As might be expected, English reviewers castigated the work as a vulgar treatment of their beloved legend or, worse, ignored it. Pleading for a review that would take into account what he was trying to do, Twain wrote almost plaintively (and not very accurately) to Andrew Lang, a leading English critic: "Indeed I have been misjudged, from the very first. I have never tried in even one single instance, to help cultivate the cultivated classes. . . . but always hunted for bigger game--the masses."[8] In what served as a reply, Lang in the *Illustrated London News* for February 1891 praised *Huckleberry Finn* extravagantly but admitted that he had not read the *Yankee* because he believed Mark Twain did not have the knowledge to be a sound critic of the ideal of the Middle Ages. Later, Mark Twain's biography of Joan of Arc won back most of his English critics, but the *Yankee* has never been one of his most popular books in England. In America initial sales of the work were below those of *Huckleberry Finn* but over the years it has been steadily one of his five most popular works.

   Though an ingenious tale and a rich and varied satire, the novel is not an example of Mark Twain's highest literary art. At the center of its relative failure is the haphazard handling of the point of view. Initially Hank Morgan offers possibilities as a first-person narrator. Like Huckleberry Finn he is an outsider who is observant, commonsensical, humorless, and articulate. As a practical person who is supposedly barren of sentiment, he is an apt foil for the romantic Arthurian characters lifted from Malory, Tennyson, and Scott; and as an ardent democrat he is an equally apt foil for sixth-century (and nineteenth-century) autocrats. Moreover, as Henry Nash Smith has pointed out, with the Yankee as spokesman Twain has a chance to develop a new and exciting genre: a fable with a capitalistic hero of potentially epic dimensions.[9] Thus the possibilities in Hank Morgan as the narrator are not only promising but also daring and exciting. So what goes wrong?
   In the first place, Hank Morgan as a character is insufficiently realized. Many of the elements that gave Huck reality and individuality are missing here, especially his deep anxieties and psychological conflicts. Huck knows the jargon of the river and uses it; Hank Morgan, despite his long identification with the Colt arms factory, employs almost no shop talk. Twain seems able to perceive of the Yankee only as a stereotype, not as a flesh and blood Connecticut mechanic. What is more, it is a stereotype that he does not totally admire. Before the book is over, he attacks the excessively practical person, confiding to Dan Beard that his Yankee is "a perfect ignoramus."[10]
   Second, even if Twain had understood and respected his narrator, it is doubtful that he could have established a sharp identity for the character because his purposes in writing the book became too diverse and confused. No single narrator could do all that Mark Twain demands of Hank Morgan and remain believable. Among other things, as we now know, Twain requires Morgan to spin out an outlandish yarn, to get laughs out of the language, to perform trick effects, to play comic roles such as those of the tenderfoot and sufferer, to attempt to create a capitalistic utopia in medieval England, and to serve as a voice for

Mark Twain's satiric views of history, politics, economics, and religion. Inevitably the narrator becomes a bundle of contradictions. He is, for example, an intruder in a strange land and yet a know-it-all, an equalitarian and yet a boss, a person possessing great technical knowledge who uses it primarily for trivial effects, a humanitarian who frees the pathetic creatures in Morgan le Fay's dungeons, and yet an insensitive monster who massacres twenty-five thousand knights in the Battle of the Sand Belt.

The results of such contradictions and confusions in the point of view show up in the instability of the book's style. As in *Innocents Abroad,* such uniformity as the style of *A Connecticut Yankee* possesses it gains from its basic colloquialism, but it is a badly battered colloquialism before the book comes to an end. Because of the roles that Twain forces Hank to play, the narration displays the exaggerations, raciness, and wild climaxes of the Western raconteur; the overobvious contrivances of the burlesquer; the silly solemnities of the buffoon; the terse aphorisms of the crackerbarrel philosopher; the soggy emotions of the sentimentalist; and the sarcasms, broad irony, and vituperation of the satirist. Twain never allows the Yankee to serve as yarnspinner or burlesquer very long, for he is still observing the practice of alternating the comic and the serious. Invariably he turns him into the satirist with a serious purpose. Such satire takes many forms: aphorisms, incidents, essays, sermons, and bits and pieces of vituperation. Whatever the form, the style is almost always characterized by emotional excess. The character he dislikes especially he beats to a pulp. Morgan Le Fay, for example, becomes Satan, Vesuvius, and an ass; she is "loaded to the eye-lids with cold malice"; she is "tyrannical, murderous, rapacious, and morally rotten." On the other hand, the character for whom Twain feels sorry he grieves over unconscionably. One young woman unfairly condemned to be hanged is "friendless" and her case "piteous." As the noose is adjusted around her neck she "devours" the baby in her arms, "wildly kissing it, and snatching it to her face and her breast, and drenching it with her tears, and half moaning and half shrieking all the while."

Perhaps even more unsettling than such emotional excess is the tendency for such a passage without warning to dissolve into buffoonery. The attack on Morgan Le Fay, for example, for treating her slaves with unspeakable cruelty is completely blunted when Twain himself suggests that they put the musicians to death for playing "In the Sweet Bye and Bye," a tune he especially disliked. ("A little concession, now and then, where it can do no harm, is the wiser policy.") Similarly, he destroys the pathos of the situation when the toothless wretches are released from Morgan Le Fay's prison by having them followed by Sir Madox sellings Peterson's Prophylactic Toothbrushes. Sometimes several points of view coexist with astonishing results upon the style. In three consecutive paragraphs, for example, the Yankee narrator sounds like a Malory ("he lightly took his spear and gat him hence"), a sentimental novelist ("They could remember him as he was in the freshness and strength of his young manhood, when he kissed his child and delivered it to its mother's hands and went away into that long oblivion"), an American rustic ("when you can say that of a man, he has struck bottom, I reckon"), an essayist gifted with erratic literary elegance ("all gentle cant and philosophising to the contrary notwithstanding, no people in the world ever did achieve their freedom by goody-goody talk and moral suasion"). Despite its basic colloquialism the writing in *A Connecticut Yankee* is just about as patchwork a production as its unstable viewpoint would lead one to expect. Its appeal is in its profusion, in the variety and extremes of its effects. The style is almost never dull, but the excesses become tiring and lose their force.

Despite its buffoonery *A Connecticut Yankee* is a more bitter book than *Huckleberry Finn*. It is a book of the head and not the heart. There is no character in it capable of Huck's humanity or Jim's affection. The romance between Hank and Sandy at the end is simply a device to end the work. The *Yankee* is an antiutopian novel. Instead of picturing a harmonious society such as that in Edward Bellamy's *Looking Backward* (1887), it implies that sweeping reforms in human society are impossible. The Yankee is unable to establish a free-enterprise system that is just or a political democracy that safeguards human rights. Even technological wonders, he suggests, instead of hastening the millennium simply provide mankind with the power to self-destruct. What may be worse, they desensitize the individual to the suffering of others, as witness the kindly Yankee becoming so insensitive that he can view the slaughter of thousands as only a technological triumph. (What a foretelling of American insensitivity when the new atom bombs were dropped on Hiroshima and Nagasaki!)

For Mark Twain the sense of hopelessness can be traced to the theory that the universe operates on the principles of mechanical determinism. We do what we do because of the mindless activity of the atoms that determines our heredity and our training: "Training—training is everything; training is all there is *to* a person. We speak of nature; it is folly; there is no such thing as nature; what we call by that misleading name is merely heredity and training. . . . All that is original in us, and therefore fairly creditable or discreditable to us, can be covered up and hidden by the point of a cambric needle. . . ." (chap. 18). The sound heart so splendidly evident in *Huckleberry Finn* is now so negligible that it can be put under the point of the smallest needle. Such an unsettling thought burned deep in Mark Twain: if there is so little hope for human decency, why continue the charade? The only solution is that of the Sand Belt: kill off the race and be done with it. In a letter to Howells written just after finishing the *Yankee* Twain wrote: "Well, my book is written—let it go. But if it were only to write over again there wouldn't be so many things left out. They burn in me; & they keep multiplying & multiplying; but now they can't ever be said. And besides, they would require a library—& a pen warmed up in hell."[11]

Chapter Ten

The Tragedy of Pudd'nhead Wilson and *The Comedy of Those Extraordinary Twins*

In the issues it raises, *Pudd'nhead Wilson* is Mark Twain's most sophisticated book and yet one of his most carelessly contrived. A product of his blackest decade, the 1890s, it develops a surrealistic world in which there are few certainties and life is simply a tissue of ironies. Its underlying mood is one of despair. Yet it achieves this mood with a story that is melodramatic, often exuberantly comic, and sometimes downright silly. It is, as Malcolm Bradbury says in his introduction to the Penguin edition, "a bad book with a good book inside it struggling to get out, and in the end remarkable managing to do so."

In June 1891 the Clemenses moved to Europe in order to live more economically and to find relief for Twain's rheumatism and his periodic attacks of bronchitis. Also, he hoped to find more leisure for writing than Hartford allowed. After a winter in Berlin Twain settled them all in Bad Nauheim and then took off for New York on what was the first of a dozen trips across the Atlantic to see what could be done to salvage his investments in his publishing house and the Paige typesetting machine, both of which gave signs of failing. In the middle of July he returned, fairly confident that he could avert financial disaster. Encouraged, too, that the others in his family for once were all in good health, he plunged into writing, turning out *Tom Sawyer Abroad* and several short pieces, and beginning *Those Extraordinary Twins*, which was an outgrowth of a short farce he had written in 1869 about the original Siamese twins, Chang and Eng. He took the partly completed manuscript of the twins with him when the family moved in late September to Villa Viviana in Florence, and continued on it there. Soon, however, he realized that despite his intentions the story was changing. Without intending to, he was writing two books. He began the tale as a farce about the visit to Dawson's Landing in Missouri in the 1830s of a freak with two heads and four arms joined in a single body with a single pair of legs. Angelo, the blond twin is all good; Luigi, the dark one, is a scoundrel. Other characters included a silly miss named Rowena and two flighty middle-aged ladies named Aunt Patsy Cooper and Aunt Betsy Hale. But as the story spread, other characters entered and took over: a stranger named Pudd'nhead Wilson and a mulatto woman named Roxana, and these two pushed into prominence a young fellow named Tom Driscoll. By the time he finished the book, the original characters were all but forgotten. He had on his hands, he confessed, a farce and a tragedy. So he pulled out the farce and left the tragedy. In addition, he separated the Siamese twins and made two men of them. There was no reason, then, for their having foreign names, but "it was too much trouble to remove them all through, so I left them christened as they were and made no explanation." As a result of this "literary Caesarian operation," he created the comedy of *Those Extraordinary Twins* and the tragedy of *Pudd'nhead Wilson*.

There is little need to spend much time on the former, for it has no purpose but to "exhibit that monstrous 'freak' in all sorts of grotesque lights." It/they are exhibited, for example, as it/they dress, eat, and play the piano. During a duel for which Luigi is responsible, power over the legs transfers to Angelo (it transfers from one twin to the other once a week) and it/they run away. Angelo gets baptized, and Luigi catches cold from the immersion. Angelo campaigns for the Teetotalers' ticket, but just before the final parade Luigi takes a good snort of whiskey and thus Angelo is half seas over while leading the parade. Ultimately fed up with all the trouble Luigi is causing, the town hangs him. What happens to Angelo is unnecessary to record. Since many of the transitions in the story were ripped out during the Caesarian operation, Twain had to reinsert some in brackets, thus making the narrative even more artificial. Most publishers printed it in the same volume with *Pudd'nhead* because it cannot stand satisfactorily by itself. Parts of it, however, are first-rate farce, and in its crude way it suggests the interdependence of good and evil.

Pudd'nhead Wilson is something else. For the first time in his fiction Mark Twain confronts the slaveholding South head on. And given his fast-rising cynicism in the 1890s he sees such a culture, despite his nostalgic memories of it, as the ultimate absurdity of human existence. Anticipating such writers as Joseph Heller and Kurt Vonnegut, he creates a world in which irrationality is the norm, and humor the offspring of irony. On the surface there is a devil-may-care attitude about implausibilities, an unabashed use of stock characters and stock situations, and an undisguised manipulation of material for melodramatic tableaux at the ends of chapters. The characters seem to exist primarily to suggest the idiocy of human behavior. There is only one of them— Roxana—for whom the reader develops any sympathy, or even concern. Yet in its crazy way, the book becomes a sermon on the hopelessness of a society that accepts slavery. There is God's plenty to laugh at in *Pudd'nhead Wilson,* but it is not a book to laugh off.

Briefly, it is the story of the happenings that take place in the mid-1800s in Dawson's Landing, a Mississippi River town in Missouri. Roxana (or Roxy), an attractive slave who is fifteen-sixteenths white, exchanges her baby, fathered by a Virginia gentleman, with that of the well-to-do Percy Driscolls for whom she works. As a consequence the Driscoll child grows up as Chambers, a slave, and her own child grows up as Tom Driscoll. Since the false Tom is only one thirty-second black, no one detects the exchange, especially as his parents both die when he is quite young, and he is adopted by his uncle, Judge York Leicester Driscoll. David Wilson, however, a young lawyer from the state of New York, whom everybody calls "Pudd'nhead" because on his arrival he tells a story no one understands, lays the foundation for later disclosure by fingerprinting the babies. Thoroughly spoiled by Roxy, the false Tom grows up to be a reprobate who even sells his mother down river to obtain money to pay his gambling debts. When Roxy escapes from her master and returns to Dawson's, she reveals to Tom his real identity and blackmails him into finding enough money to buy her freedom. To do so he robs the Judge and kills him with a jewel-studded knife he has stolen from Luigi, an Italian twin whom the Judge has previously fought in a duel to protect the family honor. Although the evidence seems to point to Luigi as the killer, Wilson, having just discovered the exchange of the babies by means of his slides, is able to prove not only that the false Tom is in truth Roxy's son but also that he is the murderer. Thus the false Tom is convicted. He would be given life imprisonment except that his creditors successfully argue that by imprisoning him the court would be depriving them of valuable property; hence he is sold down the river and the creditors get the proceeds. The real Tom takes his rightful place as a Driscoll but cannot act the role because of his training as a slave. The Italian twins return to Europe, and Roxy, now bent and heartbroken, finds solace in church activities. Pudd'nhead is apparently delighted to be absorbed by the townspeople who have ridiculed him for twenty-three years, and the townspeople, we may assume, settle back to enjoy their rose-covered cottages and their slaves.

In the first sentence of the book Mark Twain calls the work a "chronicle." It is, therefore, a record of certain happenings in Dawson's Landing in the first half of the nineteenth century as told by the narrator in the third person. The point of view, however, is more complex than that of a typical chronicler. On the surface the style gives the impression of relatively objective reporting. The chronicler confines himself to the happenings, avoids irrelevancies, and even prides himself jokingly on eliminating references to the weather that might slow down his account. Although the author intrudes in the chronicle to provide. transitions between parts, he rarely intrudes, as he does in *A Connecticut Yankee,* to interpret or judge specific events. Some readers feel that he is so noncommital that by the end of the book they do not know whether he is for or against slavery or miscegenation. Such detachment might suggest that Twain was beginning to imitate the objectivity of Zola or Flaubert. But such is not the case. *Pudd'nhead Wilson* is a highly subjective book, for in it Twain is attempting not to judge particular individuals or institutions but the entire culture. In brief, he finds the entire life of Dawson's Landing absurd, not just special parts of it. To support this conclusion he attempts to show that it is a tissue of ironies, that in it one cannot be permanently certain of even one's own identity, that there is no such things as freedom, and that moral absolutes are nonexistent. The combination makes for a tragicomedy that has uncomfortable applications far beyond the life of Dawson's Landing. *Pudd'nhead Wilson* begins an assault that culminates with *The Mysterious Stranger.*

The ironies begin with the town. At first glance, Dawson's Landing is much like the St. Petersburg (Hannibal) of *Tom Sawyer,* for it is a small village on the west bank of the Mississippi River. Its name comes from Hannibal, for Dawson's was one of the schools the young Sam Clemens attended. But Mark Twain is not bringing back St. Petersburg *in toto* for this new chronicle. Dawson's Landing is a half day's journey by steamboat south of St. Louis, not north of it, and is therefore more of a Southern town than a Western one. Its flowers are more lush, its normal life more easygoing, and its slaves far more in evidence. Indeed, slaves are central to this story, they and their ambiguous relationships with the whites. On the surface, life in Dawson's is one of mindless contentment, symbolized by the cat in the first paragraph curled up on a sill beside boxes of moss-roses and geraniums. But slavery creates such a moral chaos underneath the surface that the contentment easily explodes into horror. Once the guilty parties are discovered, however, and in the opinion of the town properly dealt with, the town just as quickly settles back into its mindlessness. The social structure remains what it was. No one has learned anything except that fingerprints differ. No one can conceive of sweeping social reform because there are no moral certainties upon which to base it. The title, thus, might well be "The Tragedy of Dawson's Landing."

The leaders of the community, those who pride themselves on being descendants of the First Families of Virginia, are described by Twain as being stately, brave, and majestic. One of them—York Leicester Driscoll—is a county judge and a freethinker, attributes that suggest the model was Mark Twain's father. These are the men who bring civility and culture to Dawson's Landing. They are, on the whole, decent and honorable. In fact, committed to the chivalric code, they make a fetish of honor. But—and here the irony enters—these "good" people are the slave holders of the town. Their relation with their slaves rests on injustice and, at times, violence. Their code of honor, similarly, rests on violence, since it institutionalizes the duel. Because of the position of leadership they gain from owning slaves, the F.F.V.s, however fine their manners, are vain, pretentious, and hypocritical.

The whites of Dawson's Landing without F.F.V. credentials are fiercely democratic. They are a noisy crowd who love their town meetings and parades and elections, and preen themselves on being Sons of Liberty. But their democracy stops at the color line. A black among the Sons of Liberty would be unthinkable. So these lusty democrats are also hypocrites.

The major characters in the book live through the years covered by the chronicle ensnared in one irony after another. Brought up as a slave, for example, the true Tom Driscoll lives a pathetic existence through no fault of his own. The more helpful he tries to be to the false Tom, the harder he gets cuffed and kicked. When at the end of the story he suddenly finds himself free and rich, he is more miserable than ever. Because of his ignorance, his slave speech, and his uncouth manners, he cannot join the society of whites, and because he is white he can no longer share the society of blacks. He is the pathetic victim of an exchange prompted by mother love. So is Roxy's child, the false Tom. Denied nothing by his doting mother, he grows up to be worse than the stock scoundrels of river-boat melodramas. He lies, gambles, steals, sells his mother down river, and murders his foster father. As already indicated, he is finally convicted of murder but saved from imprisonment because as property he can be sold and his creditors repaid.

An irony of a different order is that the false Tom, scoundrel though he is, is the only character in the book who attempts to muse about the nature and effects of slavery. The day after Roxy tells him that he is her child, he asks himself, "Why were niggers *and* whites made? What crime did the uncreated first nigger commit that the curse of birth was decreed for him?" (chap. 10). For the first time he thinks of the true Tom as a "poor wretch" who has done him no harm. So it is the stock villain who senses the insanity of a society that tolerates slavery.

One would expect David Wilson, the educated outsider, to be the questioner, the interpreter, possibly even the reformer in the chronicle. In *Those Extraordinary Twins* he is something of a crackerbarrel philosopher from the East, and still serves that function in *Pudd'nhead Wilson* as the author of the epigraphs at the chapter beginnings. Otherwise he is little more than a functionary, or so Mark Twain believed. In 1894 he wrote to Livy that a lecturer had said that "Pudd'nhead was clearly & powerfully drawn & would live & take his place as one of the great creations of American fiction." Mark Twain was delighted. He continued, "Isn't that pleasant—& unexpected! For I have never thought of Pudd'nhead as a *character,* but only as a piece of machinery—a button or a crank or a lever, with a useful function to perform in a machine, but with no dignity above that."[1] With Wilson Twain tried to capitalize on the current rage for Sherlock Holmes and on the curiosity about fingerprinting that was developing after the publication of Francis Galton's *Finger Prints* (1892). Yet he stops short, as he suspected, of making Wilson much more than "a piece of machinery." Originally Wilson comes to Dawson's Landing, of all places, to make his fortune as a lawyer. And he stays for over twenty years performing only small jobs, reading palms, and taking fingerprints. His eventual fate after solving the murder of Judge Driscoll is not to become, at long last, a sage in the village, but simply another townsperson, presumably as mindless as his peers. He has often been described by critics as a grown-up Tom Sawyer. Although he does not have Tom's drive and flair for self-advertisement, he is admittedly like Tom in wanting to be accepted by the community and in being willing in the end to acquiesce to its values. He loses the nickname of "Pudd'nhead" but, ironically, assumes the reality. That is his tragedy.

Roxy, the most appealing character of all, is irony personified. She looks white but talks and acts black. She know she looks like a Southern belle, and is proud of it. She possesses a haughty grandeur, and she shares the white prejudices even about blacks. But she knows, too, that she must accept the role of a black slave. In Dawson's Landing, and elsewhere in the South, her one sixteenth of black blood outweighs the fifteen sixteenths of white blood. To confuse things still further, she plays at least four stereotypical roles for black women. At first she is the black wench, sassing Jasper, a coal-black young male. Shortly she turns into the black mammy, spoiling her boy rotten, until he turns against her and sells *her* down the river. When she returns to Dawson's she is the black bitch, drinking and blistering her son for what he has done to her, and in the heat of her anger even spitting on him. Finally, when her guilt is disclosed in the courtroom, she becomes the devout Negro churchwoman, asking God for forgiveness and finding solace in church affairs. Her troubles start because of the lust of a Virginia "gentleman" and they multiply because of her own mother love. From the time she exchanges the babies her story is like that of a Greek tragedy. Everything leads toward the very happening that she most wants to avoid.

Probably because he was so unsure of his own identity as a person or as a writer, Mark Twain kept coming back to the subject of identity in book after book. Characters are forever playing roles or altering identities by changing clothes. *Pudd'nhead Wilson* is the first work, however, in which Twain attacks identity as a universal, ongoing problem. There is no major character in *Pudd'nhead Wilson* without a problem of identity. David Wilson's concern is living down the reputation of being a numskull and becoming one of the townspeople. The F.F.V.s face the problem of maintaining their image as gentlemen of honor despite the fact that some of their practices are a good deal less than honorable. To enlarge the scope of the problem, Mark Twain for the first time introduces the subject of racial identity. Frequently he had dealt with blacks and whites before, but he had never raised the question of the blurring of the line between them because of miscegenation. In *Pudd'nhead Wilson* he does exactly that, showing how racial ambiguity can lead to confusion and misery, and how under the proper circumstances it can be manipulated by so simple a ruse as exchanging the clothes of two babies. Such confusions and miseries as Roxy's, Tom's, and Chambers's are bound to multiply, the narrative implies, because the guardians of the "purity" of the races, the male whites, are the very ones who create the problem by sleeping with black women. Any confusion of identity in *The Prince and the Pauper* or *Huckleberry Finn* seems like playacting compared with the real problems raised by *Pudd'nhead Wilson*. As whimsically constructed as it is, this book brings out firmly that identities are always in the process of change, that they are subject to manipulation, and that something so simple as the misfiring of a joke can alter one's identity for years. In short, except for their fingerprints, human beings can never be permanently sure of who or what they are.

A grimmer aspect of life in Dawson's is that no one, white or black, has any significant personal freedom. The blacks are simply chattel subject to their owners' whims. Although their work seems not too onerous, there is always the threat of being sold down the river to a big plantation that scares them witless and keeps them in line. Less obvious but just as exacting is the enslavement of the whites by their economic and social systems. *Pudd'nhead Wilson* stresses two of these systems, slavery and the chivalric code of the town's leaders. Both create mindsets that are monolithic. With respect to slavery the book offers no deviation from the opinion that blacks are an inferior race and must be treated like children; that if an individual has a black as a forebear, no matter how many generations back, he or she is a black; and that slaves are property. The F.F.V.s, in addition, are slaves to the chivalric code, which allows no deviation from such adamantine precepts as these: honor comes before all else, even Christian doctrine; honor is the prime characteristic of a gentleman, and must be preserved at all cost; if honor is besmirched by an insult, the insult must be avenged, either by a duel (when the besmircher is another gentleman), or by a flogging or similar humiliation (if the besmircher is not a gentleman).

Over and beyond the inescapable requirements of such man-made institutions, Mark Twain indicates that all of the characters, black and white, are inexorably trapped by their training. His belief in this doctrine of environmental determinism had been strengthening ever since the 1870s. Evidences of it appear in *Huckleberry Finn,* though under the influence of William Lecky they are countered by instincts that are innate. Thus Huck, it will be remembered, is torn between his conscience (values resulting from his training) and his heart (values with which he was born). Four years later, in *A Connecticut Yankee,* what is left of the heart can be put under the point of a cambric needle. In

Pudd'nhead Wilson the heart is not mentioned. Presumably the characters are totally the result of their training. Thus the townspeople, though often kindly, are all provincial, prejudiced, and relatively mindless. Among the individual characters, the real Tom Driscoll is undemanding because he has been brought up a slave. The false Tom is selfish and profligate because he has been brought up to believe he will get what he wants. After more than twenty years in Dawson's Landing David Wilson has come to accept its institutions and its values. And the whole community accepts the institution of slavery because they have been trained to do so. All life in Dawson's Landing, in short, is determined by what Dawson's is and has been.

Some readers see two exceptions to this seemingly irrevocable power of fate. One such exception occurs in chapter 14 where Roxy blames Chambers's cowardice on "de nigger" in him. If she is speaking for the author, a racist doctrine does indeed intrude on the deterministic one. On the other hand, if she is seen as simply parroting what her white masters would say in such a situation, she is giving evidence of her training and reinforcing the book's determinism. The other possible exception occurs in those places where the Italian twins display a Manichaean duality that could hardly be the result of the environment. The twins, however, are in the book because Twain was too lazy or careless to alter the Siamese monstrosity he created in *Those Extraordinary Twins,* other than to convert it into two separate human beings. In this volume the Italians are certainly not important enough to carry the weight of a philosophical position. Even if we give some credence to these alleged exceptions, the book shows the inhabitants of Dawson's Landing in one way or another sadly enslaved. As in the naturalistic novels of the time, the pathos of the situation is that the characters do not realize they are trapped.

What ultimately makes Dawson's a mad world is that the characters have no chance to reform, for there are no moral certainties upon which reform can be established. Furthermore, there is no source where moral certainties can be found. There are no "truth sayers" whose values transcend the self-serving ones imposed by the community's dominant class. There is no minister who at least enunciates the Golden Rule. There is no vernacular character, such as Huckleberry Finn, whose heart and common sense can provide folk truths. There is not even an outsider as knowledgeable as Hank Morgan who can correct the provincial prejudices of the locals. The Pudd'nhead Wilson who authors the aphorisms that head the chapters could be such a person, but, as we already know, the Wilson of the story has neither the wit nor the insight displayed in these aphorisms. In short, the people of Dawson's Landing have no place to turn for moral perceptions superior to their own. As a result, the place is doomed to moral chaos.

Probably the final irony is that the effect of *Pudd'nhead Wilson* on the reader is not nearly so depressing as the themes would lead one to believe. There are several reasons for this. One is that, with one exception, the characters are neither strong enough nor realistic enough to carry the weight of such concepts. For the most part they are stock characters from melodrama and tend to trivialize the ideas. The exception is, of course, Roxy. Made to play dissonant roles and to feature in one melodramatic situation after another, she nevertheless turns out to be a genuinely appealing character. Moreover, since she is nominally black, Twain is able to sidestep his usual psychological block in depicting female characters sufficiently to suggest that Roxy is sexually attractive. Not so believably and warmly drawn as Jim in *Huckleberry Finn,* Roxy is nevertheless one of Twain's most interesting black characters—and the most interesting female character in all of his fiction.

Finally, Twain in *Pudd'nhead Wilson* is still up to his old tricks in alternating the serious and the comic. By no means is all of the comic material of the black, surrealistic variety. There is light comedy as in chapter 2 where Roxy and Jasper sass each other; light satire where the Judge takes out the Italian noblemen to show off Dawson's Landing's graveyard and jail, and where judicious citizens insure themselves against the fire company rather than against fire; and out-and-out farce where at the meeting of the Sons of Liberty Luigi kicks the false Tom off the platform and on to the Sons sitting in the first row, and they in turn pass him back over their heads to those in the second row, and so on. One of Twain's funniest scenes shows these same Sons attempting to flood the building with water enough to annihilate forty times the fire that burns there. As late as chapter 21, Twain cannot resist turning the courtroom scene into a parody of such events. In short, while *Pudd'nhead Wilson* reveals Twain's growing cynicism, it shows also that it has not yet wholly squelched his urge to play the clown.

Chapter Eleven
Late Works, 1892–97

Pudd'nhead Wilson, though undoubtedly impaired by Mark Twain's anxiety over his financial affairs, was the only major work he published between 1892 and 1897 that was not a potboiler. Even *Joan of Arc,* though a labor of love, was intended as a profitable venture. To use the old cliché, Mark Twain's chickens had come home to roost. He was an impulsive investor and an untrained business man. He kept pouring money into the Paige typesetting machine long after it should have been clear to him that Paige was an eccentric and the machine too complicated to be dependable. Moreover, he insisted on making impractical demands on the Webster Publishing Company that slowed down production and resulted in the publication of books that did not sell. In even the best of times both of these ventures would probably have failed, but following the Panic of 1893 they certainly did. The publishing house went into bankruptcy in 1894, and a year later Twain had finally to admit that the typesetting machine was a lost cause. At the age of sixty, therefore, he found himself a bankrupt with a debt of well over a hundred thousand dollars. Almost desperately during the mid-1890s he turned to the only means of making money that he knew: writing and lecturing. Not counting *Pudd'nhead,* he wrote five books, and traveled around the world on a lecture tour. With the income from these ventures and with the valuable financial advice of Henry H. Rogers, a Standard Oil vice president, he eventually managed to pull himself out of his self-dug hole—but not until 1898. The first seven years of the decade were years of constant anxiety—and mediocre books.

The American Claimant

Of all of Mark Twain's potboilers written during this period, *The American Claimant* is the most clumsily contrived and the least interesting. Into it he jams an idealistic young English viscount who comes to America to support any rightful claimant to his father's earldom,

scenes from a play about Colonel Mulberry Sellers that he and Howells
had collaborated on in 1882–83, and parts of essays he had previously
pigeonholed. The young viscount, Lord Rothmere, disguises himself
as an American democrat and as such wins the hand of the excessively
romantic Sally, Colonel Sellers's daughter. When the old earl comes
over to Washington to stop the marriage, he and Sally get along so
well that he consents to the marriage. Then Sally temporarily balks
when she discovers that her fiancé is an aristocrat in disguise. But love
conquers all. They marry, and after the wedding they all, including
Colonel and Mrs. Sellers, are to board a train for New York and then
a ship for London. At the railroad station, however, the Colonel is
missing. He sends a note saying that he is working on a plan to control
sun spots. He promises that while the others are crossing the Atlantic,
he will parade a vast spot across the sun which will be his love sign
saying, "Mulberry Sellers throws us a kiss across the universe." Clearly,
Colonel Sellers, instead of being the impractical dreamer of the *The
Gilded Age,* is now a lunatic. It was a tribute to Mark Twain's reputation that McClure's Syndicate should pay $12,500 for the magazine
rights. In book form the work was brought out in 1892 in the United
States by the Webster Publishing Company, and in England by Chatto
and Windus. The return on both editions was small.

Tom Sawyer Abroad

When compared with the *Adventures of Tom Sawyer,* both *Tom Sawyer
Abroad* and *Tom Sawyer, Detective* come off rather badly. In the *Adventures* Mark Twain looks back upon his boyhood days with affection, and
his humor is warmhearted. In *Tom Sawyer Abroad* the relation between
the author and his characters is a slight one. The characters no longer
represent people out of his past but provincial states of mind. In *Tom
Sawyer, Detective* the tone is one of indifference. Tom and Huck have
simply been inserted in an old Danish murder mystery for whatever
profits their antics may bring.

However lacking in the qualities of high literary art, *Tom Sawyer
Abroad* is a witty attempt at science fiction, one of the first in the
United States. Narrated by Huck Finn but "edited" by Mark Twain,
it tells how Tom, Huck, and Jim happen to be aboard the gondola of
a power-driven balloon when it is launched. Once in the air, the inventor of the contraption, who is also aboard, begins to rail at those
who had made fun of his invention. To prove how ingenious he has

been, he teaches Tom how to manipulate the controls. In the middle of a storm at night when they are over the Atlantic ocean he attempts to throw Tom overboard, but Tom outmaneuvers him and pitches the inventor into the sea. Tom then sets their course due east with the result that the first land they strike is the Sahara Desert. There Huck is almost caught by a lion as he hangs from the rope ladder. They see a caravan attacked by robbers and rescue a baby for its mother. They come upon a second caravan, but all the people and animals have been killed in a sandstorm. At an oasis they drop down to drink and swim, Huck again being almost caught by a lion. They sight a third caravan and hover above it in friendly fashion until it too is overtaken and engulfed by a sandstorm. As a fog lifts, a man's face as big as a house looks over the gunnel, and they realize it is the Sphinx. Then they visit Cairo and Mount Sinai. When Tom's corncob pipe falls apart, he sends Jim back to St. Petersburg for another one, but Jim gets caught by Aunt Polly and returns to Mount Sinai with instructions for the boys to come home immediately. In such fashion the story collapses.

Twain wrote the book in Bad Nauheim during the period when he was working on *Those Extraordinary Twins.* His plan was to make it the first in a series of books about the travel of Tom and Huck and Jim to various parts of the world, but he never carried through on the idea. He hoped the tale would appeal to every boy and "any man who has ever been a boy." But after it appeared first in Mabel Mapes Dodge's *St. Nicholas Magazine* it became known almost exclusively as a story for young people. After being published as a six-part serial in *St. Nicholas* between November 1893 and April 1894, it was issued as a book by Twain's own publishing company in the United States and by Chatto and Windus in England. Ironically, a copy of the American edition was filed for copyright on the very day that Webster and Company went bankrupt. What Mrs. Dodge published, unfortunately, was not the book as Mark Twain wrote it. Conceiving of herself as the arbiter of taste for young readers in America, Mrs. Dodge bowdlerized the text scandalously. References to drunkenness were deleted, and the boys were not permitted to slobber or be sick. Jim became a "darky," slurs on religion were cut, and references to death reduced in number (a bird was not allowed to perch on a dead limb). Twain's state of mind, already shaken up by the *St. Nicholas* text, was hardly improved when he discovered that the first nine chapters of the American edition were set from the *St. Nicholas* printing that contained Mrs. Dodge's prissy alterations. Despite being reviewed unfavorably, when it was reviewed at all, the book sold rather well in England and America and was translated into almost twenty other languages.

There is little in *Tom Sawyer Abroad* that reflects its author's personal experience. Most of it comes from his reading, especially his reading of Jules Verne's *Five Weeks in a Balloon*. Although Verne's balloon is free-floating instead of power-driven and headed westward instead of eastward, there are so many parallels between the two works that Mark Twain might well be accused of plagiarism. Verne has three main characters: one (like Tom) who is knowledgeable and imaginative; a second (like Huck) who is practical-minded; and a third (like Jim) who is a faithful slave. Parallels in events are numerous: taking advantage of air currents, for example, and sighting caravans, falling from the gondola into the water of an oasis, observing a battle between native groups, seeing a mirage, encountering lions, hovering over a caravan while both people and animals are entombed by a sandstorm, and so on. Other happenings are mined from the Bible, the *Arabian Nights,* Scott's *The Talisman,* and Verne's *Dick Sands.* Mark Twain, moreover, is not reluctant to lift such items from his own works as Egyptian scenes from *Innocents Abroad,* the story of Horace Greeley and the cab driver from *Roughing It,* and from the travel books generally the combination of sentiment and satire in reporting foreign scenes. Finally, the nature and relationship of the three characters are similar to those in the frame portions of *Huckleberry Finn.*

Yet the book is not so drearily secondhand as these borrowings might suggest. Its best feature is the talk of Tom, Huck, and Jim. Indeed, some of the discussions of the "erronorts" on such diverse topics as maps and fleas and mirages are as comic as any such discussions in earlier works. Tom is invariably disgusted with what he thinks is the obtuseness of Huck and Jim, and they are irked by what they think is Tom's lack of common sense.

Tom Sawyer, Detective

In writing *Tom Sawyer, Detective* Mark Twain brought together what he believed would result in a book with surefire appeal: the popular detective-story genre, the point of view and language of Huck Finn, the setting of the Mississippi River region, and his famous characters Huck and Tom (the manuscript shows that he even dallied with the notion of including Jim). He says he heard the story told by the wife of an American diplomat at a social gathering in Paris, but it would be astonishing if he heard it only that once because it follows so closely the Danish novel, *The Minister of Veilby,* published in 1829 and written by Steen Steenson Blicher. Blicher's novel, in turn, was a fictionalized version of the tragic life of a seventeenth-century Danish Pastor, Sören Jensen Quist, who was executed for a crime he undoubtedly did not commit. What apparently caught Twain's fancy was that the Danish story would lend itself so nicely to being transferred to Arkansas with Tom Sawyer's Uncle Silas as the accused pastor—except that instead of being executed he would have him saved as the result of another of Tom's dramatic courtroom defenses. It would allow also many of Twain's favorite fictive devices, such as swindles, disguises, murder, reversals of fortune, and a dramatic trial. Tom and Huck, moreover, would make excellent stand-ins for Sherlock Holmes and Mr. Watson. Twain was so excited about the story's possibilities that he set to work immediately in January 1895 and finished the account in three weeks. He sold it to Harpers, who published it first in *Harper's New Monthly Magazine* in August and September 1896, and in book form in *Tom Sawyer Abroad, Tom Sawyer, Detective and Other Stories* in November of 1896. In England it was issued the same month by Chatto and Windus as *Tom Sawyer Detective as Told by Huck Finn and Other Stories.* It was not a commercial failure though it is impossible to measure the degree of its success since it has usually been published with one or more other works. Mark Twain's own estimate of its literary worth is thrown into question by a jotting he made in his notebook for 1 June 1896: "What a curious thing a detective story is. And was there ever one that the author needn't be ashamed of, except 'The Murders in the Rue Morgue'?"

Briefly summarized, the narrative tells how Tom Sawyer and Huck Finn at the request of Aunt Sally leave St. Petersburg for the Phelps's farm in Arkansas. On the trip down the Mississippi they encounter Jake Dunlap, a neighbor of Aunt Sally's, who has just stolen two diamonds from a pair of fellow thieves. When he discovers that the other thieves are also on board, Jake slips off the boat at night as it nears the Phelps's place. The other thieves follow, and in a sycamore grove on Uncle Silas's farm, they catch up with Jake and kill him. They do not find the diamonds, however, for the jewels are hidden in the heels of Jake's boots. Jake's brothers, Brace and Jubiter, come upon the body, but do not recognize Jake because the night is dark and Jake has been so mutilated. To pin the murder on Uncle Silas, Jubiter disguises himself in Jake's clothes, and they bury the body. (The reason for their

wanting to do in Uncle Silas is that he has been preventing Brace
Dunlap from marrying his daughter Benny. Moreover, they know that
Uncle Silas, who is not quite balanced, can be convinced that he killed
Jubiter, whom he does not like, while sleepwalking.) In a short time
Tom figures out all this, and in a dramatic courtroom scene exposes
the Dunlap brothers and clears Uncle Silas, who has indeed confessed
to the murder. As an added fillip, Tom produces the diamonds in the
heels of the boots that Jubiter is wearing. The judge praises Tom lav-
ishly, and Tom gets the two-thousand-dollar reward offered for the
diamonds. He gives half of the money to Huck, as Huck knew he
would.

The narrative leaves much to be desired. The plot is not especially
easy to follow, partly because Mark Twain throws in material from
another mystery he had been writing but did not publish. Tom and
Huck are interesting as takeoffs of Sherlock Holmes and Dr. Watson,
but show none of the authenticity or human complexity that formerly
established them as two of the most memorable characters in American
literature. Tom's extraordinary ratiocinative powers destroy the reader's
willingness to believe, and Huck's admiration for Tom makes a fool
out of the boy we had come to admire in *Huckleberry Finn.* The other
characters are cardboard. But Huck's dialect still appeals. And something of Twain's cynicism shows through when he makes another re-
production of the Quarles farm—the Eden of his youth—the center for
fear, near madness, and murder.

Personal Recollections of Joan of Arc

In one sense *Joan of Arc* was a potboiler because Mark Twain very
much wanted it to be successful in helping him retire his debts. In
another sense, however, it was a book he dearly wanted to write almost
regardless of its commercial prospects. He had been attracted to Joan
ever since the early 1850s when he found a leaf from a biography of
her on a Hannibal street and had to ask his brother Henry whether she
was real. He started his own biography of her at Étretat, Normandy,
in the summer of 1894, and finished it in Paris in April 1895. At
Twain's insistence, *Harper's Magazine* published it anonymously so that
readers would not expect a humorous account. But, of course, the author was immediately recognized. When Harpers brought out the story
as a book in May 1896, they ascribed it to Twain on the binding. As
late as 1908 Twain was still sentimentalizing about it: "I like the *Joan*

of Arc best of all my books; & it *is* the best; I know it perfectly well."[1]
Certainly he had had to work harder on it than on his other books
because it required considerable historical research. But his high estimate was more likely the result of his belief that Joan was the only
historical figure whose actions corresponded with her principles. And
whether he realized it or not, he was writing about Susy, his favorite
daughter.

The story follows the basic historical facts with reasonable accuracy.
Book 1 describes Joan's girlhood in Domremy, where she is partly the
pretty, laughing girl and partly the serious maiden whose voices are
already telling her she must be the savior of France. In book 2 she
struggles for military support from the Dauphin, and finally getting
it raises the siege of Orleans and follows that with victories at Jargeau
and Patay. Then, accompanied by the king, she marches on Rheims,
sweeping all remnants of English and Burgundian forces aside. At
Rheims the Dauphin is crowned Charles VII. When he offers to give
Joan anything that she wants, she asks only that Domremy no longer
be taxed. Over the protests of the Chancellor and other nobles Joan
starts to march toward Paris. But the king forbids an attack when she
is at the very gates of the capital. Oddly her Voices tell her to remain
at St. Denis. There follow eight months of drifting while the king
dances and frolics. Finally, with a group of cavalry she returns to fight,
but at Clairvoix her forces suddenly become disorganized and she is
captured. After two months as a captive of Burgundy, she is ransomed
by the English. Showing no gratitude for what she has done, the
French make no attempt to buy her freedom.

Joan is taken to Rouen near the end of 1430 to be tried for heresy.
The trial, which occupies the last third of the book, follows the records
of the historical trial, except when Twain adds many comments about
the perfidy of the clerical judges and the shrewdness and resoluteness
of Joan. The treacherous Archbishop Cauchon and the other priests lie
and trick and threaten and shout until Joan's strength is spent, and
with her mind wandering she signs a paper confessing she is a sorceress
and a blasphemer of God. Forty-two clerical judges pronounce her a
relapsed heretic, and condemn her to be delivered over to the English,
who constitute the secular force in Rouen. In the last chapter she is
burned at the stake.

Mark Twain had a hard time getting this book started. He says he
made six wrong starts, and each time when he offered his wife the
results she responded with the same deadly criticism—silence. But at

last when he got the right form, he knew what she would say, and she said it without doubt or hesitation.[2] The right form undoubtedly was to have the tale told by a narrator on the scene, hence the full title, *Personal Recollections of Joan of Arc.* For the narrator he selected Sieur Louis de Conte, Joan's page and secretary. He then has de Conte's fourteenth-century French translated by Jean François Alden. (It is incomprehensible that Twain could believe the readers would not see any humor in a book translated by a John Alden.)

Concerning the composition and sources of the book, Twain wrote to H. H. Rogers, "I have never done any work before that cost so much thinking and weighing and measuring and planning and cramming, or so much cautious and painstaking execution. . . . The first two-thirds of the book were easy; for I only needed to keep my historical road straight; therefore I used for reference only one French history and one English one—and shoveled in as much fancy-work and invention on both sides of the historical road as I pleased. But on this last third I have constantly used five French sources and five English ones, and I think no telling historical nugget in any of them has escaped me."[3] (In a note at the beginning of the book Twain lists eight French and three English "authorities examined in verification of the truthfulness of this narrative.")

As a narrator Sieur Louis de Conte is limited because he adores Joan. The view he offers, therefore, is grossly oversimplified. It never occurs to him that the opposition might occasionally have had a point. That the narrator has grown up with Joan gives Twain a chance to fictionalize about her home, the customs and folklore of the country, and something of Joan's inner conflicts because he is someone in whom Joan can plausibly confide. Joan, as he depicts her, is forever appealing in her femininity and admirable in her moral and spiritual strength; her antagonists are invariably flunkeys, insects, and the blackest of villains. Louis de Conte, therefore, is not a reliable witness. But being young, his ignorance of history, of medieval warfare, and the intricacies of the feud between church and state serve partly to obscure Mark Twain's own ignorance of these elements. Besides, his boyish enthusiasm or depression when events go well or badly provides an excuse for Twain's not maintaining a scholarly reserve.

The narrative comes alive only when Mark Twain inserts a Western character: the Paladin, whose bragging about his feats grows more incredible with every repetition; Noel Rainguesson, who expresses himself in overdrawn clichés; or the Dwarf, a huge fighter who lays about him with his ax so devastatingly that soon he is encircled by stacks of corpses. Twain, however, is not so adept as Scott or even James Fenimore Cooper in capturing the clash of great forces. To catch the high pitch of battle the narrator writes as though everyone in the opposing armies knows at the same instance how the fight progresses, and as one man roars in triumph or groans in despair. Moreover much of the suspense, for the reader, is dissipated because Joan's Voices too often inform us ahead of time whether she will prevail or fail.

Yet before we belabor *Joan of Arc* unduly, we must remember that the historical events themselves were preposterous. How can a writer picture a seventeen-year-old girl first as general of the French armies and then as victim of the Inquisition, and remain unmoved? Mawkish as it may be, *Joan,* especially in the trial scenes, reports the fundamental facts and can be read, therefore, as another of Twain's attacks on the Establishment. The English, especially, did not dismiss it as romantic sentimentalizing. The book won back for Twain many of those who had been turned off by his *A Connecticut Yankee,* for in his *Joan of Arc* he makes the French clerics the major villains, whereas most of the earlier biographers of the Maid of France had placed the onus on the English.

Following the Equator

Following the Equator is the last of Mark Twain's five travel books. In it he relates the events of the thirteen-month lecture tour he and Mrs. Clemens and Clara took in 1895 to help reduce the debt that he was determined to pay off fully. Financially it was a highly successful trip, though he probably would have made just as much or more by lecturing in the United States. But the trip was another of his grand effects. Unhappily it ended in tragedy. The Clemenses had returned as far as London when they received a letter from Hartford saying Susy was ill. By the time Livy and Clara got back, Susy had died of meningitis. Twain, who had to stay in London to meet his last lecture commitments there, was devastated. He had somehow managed to grapple with his other losses, but this one—the death of his favorite daughter—was almost more than he could bear. Yet he would not have brought her back to life had he been able. "She has found the richest gift that this world can offer; I would not rob her of it."[4] Nothing less than the universe, he felt, had attacked him. He turned to writing *Following the Equator* to make money—and to forget.

As in his earlier travel books Twain follows the actual journey but feels free to insert notes from his diary, memories from his boyhood, anecdotes, local legends, and tales told by people whom he meets. In addition, he pads the work generously with material from guidebooks and other works. Even Julia Moore, the Sweet Singer of Michigan, gets quoted again. He says little about his lectures, but does mention several breakdowns in his health. Something of the emphases in the book can be gained from a rough chapter count: eight about the three-week trip out, seventeen about Australia, eleven about New Zealand, one about Ceylon, twenty-four about India, three about Mauritius and the trip to Durban, and five about South Africa. He is especially fascinated by the hill country in Australia, the animals there, and the Melbourne Cup races. India, however, he finds even more fascinating, especially because of the scale of its mountains and plains, of the crowds, and the incredible human losses resulting from famines and plagues. The day of his trip down a mountain on a handcar he called "the most enjoyable day I have spent in the earth" (vol. 2, chap. 20). And he is entranced by at least the name of Sri Matparamahansaparivrajakacharyaswamibhaskaranandasaraswati. It must be admitted, however, that the writing, though agreeable and often amusing, is flatter than that in his earlier travel books. Exceptions are the passages in which he drops into Western exaggeration or vents his anger at the stupidity and cruelty he encounters. Particularly he becomes incensed with European colonial policies and with native fakirs, thugs, assassins—and the mass of people who drink and bathe in the foul gush of the Ganges thinking it will purify them. The attacks on European colonial policies anticipate the more biting attacks mounted in such shorter works as "To the Person Sitting in Darkness" (1901) and "King Leopold's Soliloquy" (1905). Howells praised *Following the Equator* for "noble seriousness" in places and for "justice and mercy" throughout.[5] Such praise is overgenerous, but given the bitterness of Twain's mood in the aftermath of Susy's death the book as a whole is surprisingly temperate and humane. Since Twain's trip around the world, and the reasons for it, were so widely publicized at the time, the work had for Twain a gratifying immediate sale. But in the long run it has not been one of his most popular works.

Chapter Twelve
Late Works, 1897–1910

Following the Equator was the last long book that Mark Twain attempted. From 1897 to 1910, the date of his death, his life was too crowded with triumphs and anxieties and tragedies to permit sustained literary effort. Besides, he continued to suffer from rheumatism and, in the last years, from angina pectoris. His public life during this period was a steady round of speeches, dinners, and honors, both in the United States and abroad. When he returned from England in 1900 he received what can only be called a national welcome. In the following years Yale, Missouri, and Oxford universities recognized his contributions to the world of letters with honorary degrees. Newspapers printed even his most casual remarks, and he became the country's commonsense philosopher, just as Will Rogers became in later years. After his seventieth birthday Twain made himself even better copy for photographers and journalists by adopting the trademark of white suits. (At Clara's wedding to Ossip Gabrilowitsch, the pianist and composer, he wore his orange-red Oxford gown.) His last big "effect" was to build Stormfield, an Italian villalike home designed by John Howells, the son of William Dean Howells, at Redding, Conn.

During these years of public adulation, however, the private man experienced days, and especially nights, of living hell. Tragedy followed tragedy in his life. Jean's epilepsy resulted in the loss of her happy personality, Livy died in Florence in 1904, both Clara and Jean had to spend periods in sanatoriums, and Jean died on 24 December 1909, the morning after helping her father trim the Christmas tree. Even though with the help of Henry H. Rogers he paid all of his debts by 1898 and was once more becoming a rich man, Twain remained guilt-ridden and bitter. He found his past too humiliating to contemplate, partly because he was sure that he was personally responsible for all the tragedies of the family. He blamed himself for the family's loss of fortune and the fact that they had to spend so much time in Europe to economize. He blamed himself for Susy's death. If he had not been so proud about paying off his creditors, Twain and Livy would not have taken the around-the-world lecture tour, and Susy would probably have not contracted meningitis. He blamed himself for Livy's invalidism and for the wandering of her Christian faith. He could not believe in God, and yet he felt he should. He did believe in the doctrine of mechanical determinism, and yet he believed he should not. He believed that an individual's actions should correspond to his or her principles, and realized that his did not. Twain began to have terrifying dreams in which, as in "The Great Dark," he and his family are lost in the dark on board a ship with no pilot and no rudder. He confessed that he "was never quite sane at night."

What saved him from possible insanity was not so much the public esteem as his writing. He wrote constantly, even though he did not finish much of it. The writing served as therapy, for it gave him a chance to distance himself from the subjects that plagued him. He wrote (or dictated) his autobiography in the form of disconnected sketches and essays; he tried to put his dream world down on paper; he finished "Extracts from Captain Stormfield's Visit to Heaven" begun some thirty years before. Chiefly, though, he wrote on affairs of the day or on philosophical ideas that fascinated him. Such works include essays on literary affairs such as "In Defense of Harriet Shelley" and "Fenimore Cooper's Literary Offenses"; satires on political and economic affairs such as "King Leopold's Soliloquy" or on social developments such as "The United States of Lyncherdom"; and diverse treatments of biblical and religious affairs such as "Eve's Diary," "God," and *Christian Science*. The wars of the time evoked his strongest diatribes: "To a Person Sitting in Darkness" on the rape of China by Western nations; and "The War Prayer," "Battle Hymn of the Republic (Brought Down to Date)," and "As Regards Patriotism" on aspects of the Spanish-American war. Perhaps the works of this period that are still most widely read are those on the nature of the human race and the universe and the Being responsible for both. These include "What Is Man?" "Letters from the Earth," "Report from Paradise," "The Damned Human Race," "The Man That Corrupted Hadleyburg," and *The Mysterious Stranger*. The last two deserve special treatment.

"The Man That Corrupted Hadleyburg"

"The Man That Corrupted Hadleyburg" is a story in which Mark Twain attempts to demonstrate that those who believe they can overcome what is basic in their nature are fools. This argument rests on the belief that life is determined by training and temperament, and that freedom of choice is a delusion because members of the human race always select what is to their personal advantage. The argument is weakened, however, because, though taking the position of a determinist, Twain cannot drop his lifelong role of moralist. As a moralist he assumed that men and women can make choices and are responsible for those choices. From an autobiographical point of view, therefore, the story is important for dramatizing a basic contradiction in Mark Twain's thought. The story tells of the undoing of Hadleyburg (Hannibal again), a town that prides itself on being honest and upright because it has eliminated temptation. A vengeful stranger, who once suffered an unspecified slight in Hadleyburg, leaves a sack he says contains gold coins with an elderly couple named Richards. He requests that it be given to a townsman who was kind to him. To claim the coins, however, this townsman must identify himself by repeating the remark he made to the stranger and which is now contained in a sealed envelope within the sack. Following instructions, the Richardses advertise the offer and ask everyone who thinks he made the remark to write it out and give it to Mr. Burgess, formerly the town minister. Although they believe that the remark was probably made by a Mr. Goodson, who has since died, nineteen of the leading citizens of the town, including the Richardses, determine to make a try for the gold by inventing a remark. Before they do, however, each gets a letter saying the remark was, "You are far from a bad man; go and reform."

At a packed meeting Mr. Burgess, to the immense delight of the crowd, reads what each of the leading citizens has written, and of course everyone has written the same thing. Because Richards had once done him a great favor, Burgess does not produce Richards's letter, and hence the crowd thinks there are only eighteen frauds. When the sack is opened, it is found to contain nothing but gilded lead slugs. A stranger in the crowd buys up the slugs and proposes to stamp on each the names of the eighteen frauds and to sell them as rarities. To save himself from being so defamed, one of the richest of the eighteen buys the discs from the stranger for $40,000. The next morning the stranger gives almost all of the money to the Richardses, who are hailed now as the only honest leading citizens in town. Troubled more by their fear of exposure than by their consciences, the Richardses begin reading things into what their neighbors say and do, and soon fall into a delirium in which they confess that they too had submitted a letter containing the fatal remark. After they die the city fathers delete the work "not" from the town motto, causing it to read, "Lead us into temptation."

"The Man That Corrupted Hadleyburg" is the only short fiction by Mark Twain that can properly be called a short story rather than a tale or sketch. It has the unity of action and mood, immediacy, coherence, acceleration, and culmination typical of the genre. It contains three clearly drawn groups of characters. First, there are the functional characters, the stranger and Mr. Halliday, the town clown. The stranger is the Outsider who knows that the leading citizens of Hadleyburg are basically greedy and sets up what amounts to a laboratory experiment to expose their weakness. Mr. Halliday conveys to the reader the reactions of the leading citizens after they are confronted with the temptation of a bag full of gold coins. The second group comprises the nineteen leading citizens whose reputations are ruined by the Outsider's experiment, eighteen by being publicly jeered and one, Richards (and his wife), by his fear of exposure. The third group consists of the rest of the townspeople, more specifically the crowd at the town meeting, who act as a kind of vulgar Greek chorus that scoffs at the "respectable" citizens for yielding to temptation. The narrator of the story, like the Outsider, knows that the nineteen are by nature greedy and thus anticipates how the experiment must inevitably turn out. Yet he seems to enjoy and approve of the scoffing they take from their neighbors. Since Mark Twain makes no attempt to disassociate himself from the narrator, we must assume that he too both recognizes the inevitability of what the leading characters do and blames them for doing it. In falling into this contradiction Twain joins such American literary naturalists as Frank Norris and Theodore Dreiser who picture their characters as victims of inexorable forces—their environment and their genes (as we would call them today)—but nevertheless often praise some and blame others instead of showing understanding and pity for them all. Despite its inherent contradiction, however, "The Man That Corrupted Hadleyburg" is a powerful study of humanity's common doom.

The Mysterious Stranger

In a letter to William Dean Howells, dated 13 May 1899, Mark Twain tells what he was trying to do in *The Mysterious Stranger*:

What I have been wanting was a chance to write a book without reserves—a book which should take account of no one's feelings, no one's prejudices, opinions, beliefs, hopes, illusions, delusions; a book which should say my say, right out of my heart, in the plainest language & without a limitation of any sort. I judged that that would be an unimaginable luxury, heaven on earth. . . . It is under way, now, & it *is* a luxury! an intellectual drunk. Twice I didn't start it right; & got pretty far in, both times, before I found it out. But I am sure it is started right this time. It is in (story) tale-form. I believe I can make it tell what I think of Man, & how he is constructed, & what a shabby poor ridiculous thing he is, & how mistaken he is in his estimate of his character & powers & qualities & his place among the animals.[1]

Intentionally or not, Twain did not publish any of the book before he died. It was first published posthumously in 1916 by Twain's official biographer and literary executor, Albert Bigelow Paine, and Frederick A. Duneka of the publishing firm of Harper and Brothers. Their version, which was an incredible hoax, remained the accepted text until John S. Tuckey in *Mark Twain and Little Satan* (1963) revealed that it was not as Twain wrote it, and William M. Gibson in *Mark Twain's Mysterious Stranger Manuscripts* (1969) revealed what he did write. Paine and Duneka added to one long fragment a separate chapter that they found elsewhere among Twain's papers, and turned an arrogant priest (Duneka was a pious Catholic) into an astrologer. Then they wrote all the transitions that such an alteration made necessary, and further cut and bowdlerized unconscionably. Finally, they foisted the results on a trusting public as a children's gift book!

Mark Twain's suggestion that he started *The Mysterious Stranger* three times is supported by the fact that three fragments exist. (Actually four if one counts a false start on the first fragment.) In addition, there is the separate chapter that Paine found. Twain's claim that the fragments are a dumping ground for his ordure, though overstated, should be taken seriously, for the fragments contain all of Twain's major animadversions of his late years. The result of his personal disasters, his reading in eighteenth-century philosophy and nineteenth-century biology and physics, and his reflections and notetaking, the fragments are the best possible introduction to Twain's last attitudes toward the human race and the universe itself. There is a humorous yet melancholy glitter to the writing that reveals the author as a humorist, moralist, cynic, romantic, determinist, and solipsist.

The first fragment, "The Chronicle of Young Satan," is a narrative of 55,000 words written in three periods from 1897 to 1900. The first part was written in Vienna; hence the Austrian setting. The action takes place in Eseldorf (Assville) and concerns three Austrian boys who are visited by an enchanting young man named Satan, the nephew of *the* Satan. The story gains suspense by being told by one of the boys, who is constantly being astounded by Satan's magical feats and horrified by his amorality. Possibly the most moving part of the action involves kindly Father Peter, who is so hounded by Father Adolf that he loses his mind, the happiest thing according to Satan that can happen to a man. During the course of the narrative Satan instructs the boys in the true nature of the human race. This instruction gives Twain an opportunity to parade his basic ideas without seeming to be over-didactic. Included among the points advanced by Satan are the evil of the moral sense (it is responsible for the race's cruelty and unhappiness), the triviality of human beings (they are to Satan as red spiders are to an elephant), and the inferiority of human beings to what they in their presumption call dumb brutes. He charges also that human beings live a life of self-deception, and that they are like sheep (thus recalling the speech of Colonel Sherburn in *Huckleberry Finn*). In two ways Satan tries to convince the boys that life is determined. He compares it with a row of upended bricks that inevitably fall one by one when the first is knocked over, and he demonstrates the point by changing a small detail in the lives of several characters and shows how by that one small change their entire destinies are altered. He ridicules papal infallibility, prophesies the continuation of wars (each started by "a loud little handful"), and blasts the Western powers for what they will do in China in the twentieth century. Additionally, he attacks those who will be responsible for the Boer War. The story, such as it is, peters out in India with Satan exposing a native magician.

The second fragment, "Schoolhouse Hill," consisting of 16,000 words, was written in the fall of 1898. Narrated in the third person, it tells of the arrival of young Satan, now called Forty-four,[2] at the school in Petersburg Village that Tom, Huck, and Sid Sawyer attend. Forty-four performs the amazing feat of learning everything in a book just by riffling through its pages, and of recalling everything that was done and said during a period in the school. He easily beats up the school bully and mashes the hands of the bully's father. He stays at the home of Mr. and Mrs. Hotchkiss (Hotchkiss is another reincarnation of Orion Clemens) where he produces historical characters, rescues townsmen buried in the snow, and leaves a beautiful suit filled with coins on his bed. He explains to Hotchkiss that he was born before Adam and Eve, and confesses his uncle's error in having them eat the apple because it conferred on them not only the knowledge of good and evil but also a passionate disposition to do evil. The fragment ends when he departs to go around the earth to study its people, and leaves behind a little devil to help the Hotchkisses and their two somewhat uneasy slaves. Apparently meant to be more humorous than the first fragment, the second is less packed with thematic material.

The third fragment, "No. 44, The Mysterious Stranger," is 65,000 words long and has been called the Print-Shop Version because it is laid in a print-shop in Austria in 1490. The fact that Twain wrote it during various periods between 1902 and 1905, and even a late chapter in 1908, may account for its diffuseness. He himself was so aware of this weakness that he burned 30,000 words. Once more the story is told by a young lad, August Feldner, an apprentice printer who, of course, becomes the special friend of No. 44 (whose full name is now Number 44, New Series 864,962). The kindly Father Peter and the dogmatic Father Adolf are brought over from the first fragment but do not feature so importantly in this one. Doangivadam is a character who wins respect because of his common sense and independence of spirit. No. 44 is roundly abused by the union printers, performs amazing tricks but in such a way that they are attributed to the neighborhood astrologer, and once more bests the local bully. The central story line, if it can be called that, involves a strike of the printers against their boss at a time when he needs to get out a large order quickly. No. 44 produces duplicates of the printers who see to it that the work is done speedily and exactly. The line between the real world and the dream-world begins to grow thin. It grows even thinner when Marget, August's secret love, ignores August's Waking Self but passionately loves his Dream Self. Soon August is passing through walls and closed doors. The fragment ends with a flight back in time to the Pharaohs. Most of the major themes are familiar ones: the triviality of man, the superstition and cruelty of the church, and the belief that everything is foreordained and that the human mind originates nothing, the last a central contention in "What Is Man?" What is newly stressed is that individuals have dream selves, waking selves, and souls. Actual life has become a dreamy affair.

The separate chapter that Paine found after Twain died and attached to the first fragment is more appropriately attached in the new edition by William M. Gibson to the third because it stresses the notion that life is a dream. In it Twain launches his most devastating attack on the universe and on God himself. No. 44 announces that he is going away, that all along he has been only a dream, that the narrator is only a thought, and that life itself is only a vision, a dream. The chapter ends with the conclusion that life as we know it is too insane to be anything other than a dream.

"It is true, that which I have revealed to you: there is no God, no universe, no human race, no earthly life, no heaven, no hell. It is all a Dream, a grotesque and foolish dream. Nothing exists but You. And You are but a *Thought*—a vagrant Thought, a useless Thought, a homeless Thought, wandering forlorn among the empty eternities!"
He vanished, and left me appalled; for I knew, and realized, that all he had said was true.

Mark Twain was happy with the "Mysterious Stranger" pieces. And well he might have been, for they offered him threefold protection against the guilt feelings that galled him daily. They attack the moral sense, or conscience (why pay any attention to it if it is evil?). They assert that everything is preordained (why feel guilty if the individual is not responsible for what he or she does?). And they assert the doctrine of solipsism (why worry if the self is the only reality and everything else is a dream?). There is much confusion and faulty argument in the "Mysterious Stranger"fragments, but there are also many examples of penetrating and honest insight. They are among the most poignant exhibits of a tortured spirit ever written. Incredibly, they are also among the most comic depictions of human and cosmic affairs. Life may be a bitter joke but it is still a joke. One cannot help admiring the tired and elderly author for his dogged determination to understand and explain the universe that he thought had laid him low.

Worn out in both body and spirit, Mark Twain died at Stormfield on 21 April 1910, the year of the return of Halley's comet. He had predicted the time of his death. "I came in with Halley's comet in 1835," he had told Paine the year before. "It is coming again next year, and I expect to go out with it. It will be the greatest disappointment of my life if I don't go out with Halley's comet. The Almighty has said, no doubt: 'Now here are these two unaccountable freaks; they came in together, they must go out together.'"[3] Apparently the Almighty agreed, for Mark Twain died within twenty-four hours of the comet's perihelion. The greatest tribute to him appeared in an essay by his old friend William Dean Howells: "Emerson, Longfellow, Lowell, Holmes—I knew them all and all the rest of our sages, poets, seers, critics, humorists; they were like one another and like other literary men; but Clemens was sole, incomparable, the Lincoln of our literature."[4]

Chapter Thirteen
Afterword

Since the year of his death Mark Twain has become an American legend. His pictures continue to appear in newspapers and magazines, and he continues to be quoted and alluded to in books and articles and on television and radio. His popularity is not limited to this country, for he is still one of the best-known and widely read American authors abroad. Possibly the surest proof of his persisting popularity is that he is still exploited commercially, a phenomenon that would not occur if he were not well known and widely respected. Advertisers have used his picture on spreads for such items as cigars, collars, sardines, flour, soup, and whiskey. The owners of the *Delta Queen* invariably include his picture in advertisements for their Mississippi River cruises. Approximately 70,000 persons annually visit his former home in Hartford, and 200,000 his boyhood home in Hannibal. First editions of his works are among the most highly sought after. His books, particularly *Tom Sawyer* and *Huckleberry Finn,* continue to be reprinted and sold by the hundreds of thousands. Nor has critical interest in him dwindled. Between 1868 and 1975 five thousand books and articles were written about him and his works, and this production has continued at the rate of over fifty works a year.

His writings remain a delight—and a reminder that in its vanity the human race has botched the job of living. C. H. Webb, the publisher of Mark Twain's first book, was so right: Mark Twain was both the Wild Humorist of the Pacific Slope and the Moralist of the Main. As he grew older, Twain's humor became blacker and his moralizing more pessimistic, but his twin roles never separated. In the first fragment of the *Mysterious Stranger* Satan tells the boys the human race in its intellectual and moral poverty has only one "really effective weapon—laughter. Power, Money, Persuasion, Supplication, Persecution—these can lift at a colossal humbug,—push it a little—crowd it a little—weaken it a little, century by century: but only Laughter can blow it to rags and atoms at a blast" (chap. 10). Mark Twain might falter in his literary achievement—he was quite capable of writing one of the nation's worst novels as well as one of its best—but he never faltered in using humor both to amuse and to serve the cause of human dignity.

Notes and References

Chapter One

1. *More Maxims of Mark* (N.p.: privately printed, November 1927), 14.
2. The house now is enclosed in the Mark Twain Shrine in Perry, Missouri. It is open to the public.
3. Quoted in Dixon Wecter, *Sam Clemens of Hannibal* (Boston, 1952), 84.
4. *The Autobiography of Mark Twain,* ed. Charles Neider (New York, 1959), 41.
5. Orion, Pamela, Sam, and Henry. Benjamin had died in 1842.
6. *Early Tales and Sketches,* ed. Edgar M. Branch and Robert H. Hirst, Iowa-California Edition, 2 vols. (Berkeley, 1979), 1:62. This is the same Jim Wolf who appears in the much more famous sketch entitled "Jim Wolf and the Tom-Cats."
7. Ibid., 1:92.
8. Walter Blair shrewdly views this letter as a rehearsal for the Sunday School scene in *Tom Sawyer; Mark Twain and Huck Finn* (Berkeley, 1960), 67–68.
9. Paul Baender, "Alias Macfarlane: A Revision of Mark Twain Biography," *American Literature* 38 (1966):187–97.
10. *Autobiography of Mark Twain,* 291.
11. Besides the two discussed here, there were a gothic tale laid in Germany and a ghost story that takes place on a Mississippi River steamboat. Neither of these was published until *Early Tales and Sketches,* 1:134–41, 146–51. The *Quintus Curtius Snodgrass Letters,* for many years attributed to Clemens, have been found to be the work of a writer on the *New Orleans Daily Crescent.*
12. *Early Tales and Sketches,* 1:144. The editors provide a useful set of explanatory notes for the burlesque on 449–52. The *Twilight* was a real steamboat, the other two were fictitious.
13. *Life on the Mississippi* (Boston, 1883), chap. 18.
14. Speech in Hartford to the Ancient and Honorable Artillery Company of Massachusetts in *Mark Twain Speaking,* ed. Paul Fatout (Iowa City, 1976), 108.
15. *Roughing It,* ed. Franklin R. Rogers, Iowa-California Edition (Berkeley, 1972), 154. The endpapers of this edition contain useful maps showing the stage route from St. Joseph to Carson City and the Washoe Silver mining region in 1862.

16. This treatment of Rice was a rehearsal for Mark Twain's later handling of Mr. Brown in travel letters from Hawaii and Europe.

17. *Early Tales and Sketches,* 1:195.

18. Since we are primarily concerned with the man as writer, from this point on we refer to him by his pen name, Mark Twain.

19. *Mark Twain's Letters* (New York, 1917), 1:182–83.

20. Franklin R. Rogers, *Mark Twain's Burlesque Patterns* (Dallas, 1960), 22–25.

21. *Early Tales and Sketches,* 2:91–93.

22. Mark Twain, for example, owed "Baker's Blue-jay Yarn" and "The Burning Shame" to Gillis.

23. In different versions the anecdote had been a favorite for years among yarnspinners, and had even appeared in print in *The Spirit of the Times* and at least two California newspapers. See Walter Blair, *Native American Humor* (New York, 1937), 156. There is no reason to suppose, however, that Mark Twain knew the story before hearing Ben Coon tell it.

24. Originally entitled "Jim Smiley and his Jumping Frog" (*Early Tales and Sketches,* 2:282–88), Mark Twain changed the title of the sketch to "The Celebrated Jumping Frog of Calaveras County" in the version included in his first book, *The Celebrated Jumping Frog of Calaveras County, and other Sketches* (New York, 1867). The title has also appeared as "The Notorious Jumping Frog of Calaveras County." After the initial publication Mark Twain dropped the salutation to Artemus Ward.

25. Quoted from the *Alta California* in *Early Tales and Sketches,* 2:271.

26. The statement occurs in "How to Tell a Story," first published in *Youth's Companion,* 3 October 1895. For a detailed explanation of how this story exemplifies Mark Twain's theory of humorous storytelling, see Paul Baender, "The 'Jumping Frog' as a Comedian's First Virtue." *Modern Philology* 60 (February 1963):192-200.

27. *Mark Twain's Letters,* 1:101.

28. Ibid., 1:103.

29. *Mark Twain, Business Man,* ed. Samuel C. Webster (Boston, 1946), 89.

Chapter Two

1. *Traveling with the Innocents Abroad,* ed. D. M. McKeithan (Norman, Okla., 1958), 315.

2. Dewey Ganzel offers interesting evidence, however, that she may have been on the *Quaker City* during its run from Bermuda to New York. See *Mark Twain Abroad: The Cruise of the "Quaker City"* (Chicago, 1968), 321–22.

3. *Mark Twain to Mrs. Fairbanks* (San Marino, California, 1949), 48.

4. Leon T. Dickinson, "Mark Twain's Revisions in Writing *The Innocents Abroad,*" *American Literature* 19 (May 1947):139–57.

5. *The Love Letters of Mark Twain,* ed. Dixon Wecter (New York, 1949), 165–66.
6. *Traveling with the Innocents Abroad,* 69.

Chapter Three

1. *Mark Twain's Letters,* 1:186. Some readers believe that Twain refers in this sentence to his brother. But since there are only two characters of importance and since the brother quickly loses significance in the narrative, Twain may have in mind the altering of the persona he has chosen for himself.
2. *Mark Twain's Letters to His Publishers, 1867–1894,* ed. Hamlin Hill (Berkeley, 1967), 68.
3. Henry Nash Smith, *Mark Twain, The Development of a Writer* (Cambridge, 1962), 52–54. All of chapter 3 in Smith's volume is a useful interpretation of *Roughing It.*
4. William Dean Howells, *My Mark Twain: Reminiscences and Criticisms* (New York, 1910), 113.

Chapter Four

1. *Mark Twain to Mrs. Fairbanks,* 184. Similar evidence appears in a letter to Dr. John Brown and in a marked copy prepared for William Seaver, a friend of Twain's.
2. A. B. Paine, *Mark Twain, A Biography* (New York, 1912), 1:477.
3. *Autobiography of Mark Twain,* 19.

Chapter Five

1. Justin Kaplan, *Mr. Clemens and Mark Twain: A Biography* (New York, 1966), 182.
2. *Mark Twain-Howells Letters,* ed. Henry Nash Smith and William M. Gibson (Cambridge, Mass., 1960), 1:22.
3. Ibid., 1:26.
4. Ibid., 1:34.
5. Ibid., 1:42–43.
6. Introduction to *Selected Shorter Writings of Mark Twain,* ed. Walter Blair (Boston, 1962), xx.

Chapter Six

1. *Mark Twain-Howells Letters,* 1:87–88.
2. Ibid., 1:91.
3. Ibid., 1:112.
4. These and other sources appear in Walter Blair, *Mark Twain and Huck Finn,* chap. 4.

5. Alan Gribben, "How Tom Sawyer Played Robin Hood 'By the Book,'" *English Language Notes* 13 (1976):201–4.

6. *Mark Twain's Autobiography,* ed. A. B. Paine (New York, 1925), 1:237.

7. *Mark Twain in Eruption,* ed. Bernard DeVoto (New York, 1940), 196.

8. A facsimile of the manuscript with a detailed introduction by Paul Baender is now available for those wishing to see how Mark Twain worked it over: *The Adventures of Tom Sawyer,* a facsimile of the author's holograph manuscript, 2 vols. (Frederick, Md., 1982).

9. *Mark Twain-Howells Letters,* 1:122–124.

10. The relation of Tom to the adults of St. Petersburg is well developed in Judy Fetterley's "The Sanctioned Rebel," *Studies in the Novel* 3 (1971):293–304.

11. *Mark Twain's Letters,* 2:477.

Chapter Seven

1. *Mark Twain-Howells Letters,* 1:290.

2. For detailed accounts of the book's sources see Leon T. Dickinson, "The Sources of *The Prince and the Pauper,*" *Modern Language Notes* 64 (February 1949):103–6, and the introduction to the Iowa-California Edition of the work by Victor Fischer and Lin Salamo (Berkeley, 1979), 19–25.

3. *Mark Twain in Eruption,* 206.

4. *The Love Letters of Mark Twain,* 166.

5. *Mark Twain-Howells Letters,* 1:34.

6. Horst H. Kruse, *Mark Twain and "Life on the Mississippi"* (Amherst, Mass., 1981), 165–66, 17, and *passim.*

7. *Life on the Mississippi,* Heritage Press Edition (New York, 1944), 411.

8. These passages appear with a note by Willis J. Wager in ibid., 383–418.

9. Guy A. Cardwell, "Retouching Mark Twain's Portrait," *Review* 6 (1984):106.

Chapter Eight

1. *Mark Twain International,* ed. Robert M. Rodney (Westport, Conn., 1982), 264.

2. *Mark Twain-Howells Letters,* 1:92.

3. Ibid., 1:144.

4. For a detailed treatment of the sources of *Huckleberry Finn,* see Blair, *Mark Twain and Huck Finn,* passim.

5. Ernest Hemingway, *The Green Hills of Africa* (New York: Scribners, 1935), 22.

6. These niceties of style were first commented upon by George Mayberry, "Reading and Writing," *New Republic* 110 (1 May 1944):608.

7. *Mark Twain in Eruption*, 202.

8. Albert E. Stone, Jr., *The Innocent Eye* (New Haven, 1961), 45.

9. Judith Fetterley, "Disenchantment: Tom Sawyer in *Huckleberry Finn*," *PMLA* 87 (1972): 69–74.

10. *The Autobiography of Mark Twain*, 68.

Chapter Nine

1. *Century Magazine* 31 (December 1885):193–204. On his visits to Missouri, first after his return from California in 1866, second with Osgood in 1882, and then with Cable on their speaking tour in early 1885, Mark Twain undoubtedly encountered criticism of his failure to fight for the Confederacy. "The Private History" can be read as a response to his critics. That he should encase it in a humorous sketch would seem to show considerable moral uncertainty.

2. See Howard Baetzhold, "The Course of Composition of *A Connecticut Yankee*: A Reinterpretation," *American Literature* 33 (May 1961):195–214.

3. *Mark Twain's Notebooks and Journals*, vol. 3, ed. Robert Pack Browning, Michael B. Frank, and Lin Salamo (Berkeley, 1979), 78.

4. *Mark Twain to Mrs. Fairbanks*, 258.

5. Howard Baetzhold, *Mark Twain and John Bull* (Bloomington, Ind., 1970), 111–13.

6. *Mr. Clemens and Mark Twain*, 281.

7. Quoted in Baetzhold, *Mark Twain and John Bull*, 120, from *Hartford Courant*, 22 July 1888, p. 5, col. 1.

8. *Mark Twain's Letters*, 2:527.

9. Henry Nash Smith, *Mark Twain's Fable of Progress* (New Brunswick, N. J., 1964), 39.

10. "Mark Twain, the Man, as Dan Beard Knew Him," *San Francisco Examiner*, 25 April 1910, 16; quoted in the Norton Critical Edition of *A Connecticut Yankee in King Arthur's Court* (New York, 1982), 309.

11. *Mark Twain-Howells Letters*, 2:613.

Chapter Ten

1. *Love Letters of Mark Twain*, 291.

Chapter Eleven

1. *Mark Twain, A Biography*, 2:1034.

2. *Mark Twain in Eruption*, 199.

3. *Mark Twain's Correspondence with Henry Huttleston Rogers 1893–1909*, ed. Lewis Leary (Berkeley, 1969), 124–25.

4. *Love Letters of Mark Twain*, 322.
5. *Mark Twain-Howells Letters*, 2:707.

Chapter Twelve

1. *Mark Twain-Howells Letters*, 2:698–99.
2. In his explanatory notes for "Schoolhouse Hill" William M. Gibson lists several possible explanations for the name "Forty-four," but he finds none of them wholly adequate. *Mark Twain's Mysterious Stranger Manuscripts* (Berkeley, 1969), 472–73.
3. *Mark Twain, A Biography*, 3:1511.
4. *My Mark Twain*, 101.

Selected Bibliography

This bibliography includes selected lists of Mark Twain's books, tales and sketches, and letters. Also included are titles of the present versions of his autobiography, collections of speeches, and bibliographical aids. Many of the most important secondary sources for information about Mark Twain appear in footnotes and are not repeated here. An exhaustive list of secondary sources can be found in Thomas A. Tenney, *Mark Twain: A Reference Guide* (Boston: G. K. Hall, 1977), and in supplements appearing annually in *American Realistic Literature*, usually in the August issue.

Section 2 lists the new authoritative editions of *The Works of Mark Twain* and the *Mark Twain Papers*. These editions have been carefully edited in order to bring each text into accord with what seems to be Mark Twain's last intent. Neither of these series is complete. All other sets of his work are out of print, including the "Definitive" edition, 37 vols. (New York: Gabriel Wells, 1923–25) and the "Stormfield" edition, 37 vols. (New York: Harper, 1929).

1. Books (in order of publication)

The Celebrated Jumping Frog of Calaveras County, and Other Sketches. New York: C. H. Webb, 1867.

The Innocents Abroad. Hartford: American Publishing Co., 1869.

Mark Twain's (Burlesque) Autobiography and First Romance. New York: Sheldon, 1871.

Roughing It. Hartford: American Publishing Co., 1872.

The Gilded Age. Hartford: American Publishing Co., 1873. In collaboration with Charles Dudley Warner.

Sketches, New and Old. Hartford: American Publishing Co., 1875.

The Adventures of Tom Sawyer. Hartford: American Publishing Co., 1876.

A True Story and the Recent Carnival of Crime. Boston: Osgood, 1877.

Punch, Brothers, Punch! and Other Sketches. New York: Slote, Woodman & Co., 1878.

A Tramp Abroad. Hartford: American Publishing Co., 1880.

Conversation, As It Was by the Social Fireside, in the Time of the Tudors. N.p., n.d. [possibly Cleveland: Alexander Gunn, 1880]. Also titled *1601*.

The Prince and the Pauper. Boston: Osgood, 1882.

The Stolen White Elephant. Boston: Osgood, 1882.

Life on the Mississippi. Boston: Osgood, 1883.

Adventures of Huckleberry Finn. New York: Webster, 1885.

A Connecticut Yankee in King Arthur's Court. New York: Webster, 1889.

The American Claimant. New York: Webster, 1892.

Merry Tales. New York: Webster, 1892.

The £1,000,000 Bank-Note and Other New Stories. New York: Webster, 1893.

Tom Sawyer Abroad. New York: Webster, 1894.

The Tragedy of Pudd'nhead Wilson and the Comedy of Those Extraordinary Twins. Hartford: American Publishing Co., 1894.

Personal Recollections of Joan of Arc. New York: Harper, 1896.

Tom Sawyer Abroad, Tom Sawyer, Detective, and Other Stories. New York: Harper, 1896.

How To Tell a Story and Other Essays. New York: Harper, 1897.

Following the Equator. Hartford: American Publishing Co. 1897.

The Man That Corrupted Hadleyburg and Other Stories and Essays. New York: Harper, 1900.

A Double Barrelled Detective Story. New York: Harper, 1902.

Extracts from Adam's Diary. New York: Harper, 1904.

King Leopold's Soliloquy. Boston: P. R. Warren, 1905.

Eve's Diary. New York: Harper, 1906.

What Is Man? New York: De Vinne, 1906.

The $30,000 Bequest and Other Stories. New York: Harper, 1906.

Christian Science. New York: Harper, 1907.

A Horse's Tale. New York: Harper, 1907.

Is Shakespeare Dead? New York: Harper, 1909.

Extract from Captain Stormfield's Visit to Heaven. New York: Harper, 1909.

The Mysterious Stranger. New York: Harper, 1916. A cobbled version that has no authority. For an authoritative version of the fragments as Mark Twain wrote them, see the Iowa-California Edition of the *Mysterious Stranger Manuscripts*, ed. William M. Gibson. Berkeley: University of California Press, 1969.

The Curious Republic of Gondour and Other Whimsical Sketches. New York: Boni and Liveright, 1919.

Sketches of the Sixties by Bret Harte and Mark Twain: Being Forgotten Material Now Collected for the First Time from the Californian 1864–67. San Francisco: John Howell, 1926, 1927.

The Adventures of Thomas Jefferson Snodgrass. Chicago: Pascal Covici, 1928.

The Washoe Giant in San Francisco: Being Heretofore Uncollected Sketches by Mark Twain Published in the Golden Era in the Sixties. Edited by Franklin Walker. San Francisco: George Fields, 1938.

Mark Twain's Travels with Mr. Brown: Being Heretofore Uncollected Sketches Written by Mark Twain for the San Francisco Alta California in 1866 & 1867. Edited by Franklin Walker and G. Ezra Dane. New York: Knopf, 1940.

Mark Twain in Eruption: Hitherto Unpublished Pages about Men and Events by Mark Twain. Edited by Bernard DeVoto. New York: Harper, 1940.

Letters from the Earth. Edited by Bernard DeVoto. New York: Harper & Row, 1942.
Mark Twain, Business Man. Edited by Samuel C. Webster. Boston: Little, Brown & Co., 1946.
Report from Paradise. New York: Harper, 1952.
Traveling with the Innocents Abroad: Mark Twain's Original Reports from Europe and the Holy Land. Edited by Daniel Morley McKeithan. Norman: University of Oklahoma Press, 1958.
Contributions to the Galaxy, 1868–71. Edited by Bruce R. McElderry, Jr. Gainesville, Fla.: Scholars Facsimiles & Reprints, 1961.
Forgotten Writings of Mark Twain. Edited by Henry Duskis. New York: Philosophical Library, 1963.
Simon Wheeler, Detective. Edited by Franklin R. Rogers. New York: New York Public Library, 1963.
Clemens of the Call: Mark Twain in San Francisco. Edited by Edgar M. Branch. Berkeley: University of California Press, 1969.
Tale of the Caliph Stork [by Wilhelm Hauff]. Translated by Mark Twain. Iowa City: Windhover Press, 1976.

2. Collected Editions (in order of publication)

a. Iowa-California Editions of *The Works of Mark Twain* (Berkeley: University of California Press)
Roughing It. Edited by Franklin R. Rogers and Paul Baender, 1972.
What Is Man? Edited by Paul Baender, 1973.
The Prince and the Pauper. Edited by Victor Fischer, Lin Salamo, and Mary Jane Jones, 1979.
A Connecticut Yankee in King Arthur's Court. Edited by Bernard L. Stein; introduction by Henry Nash Smith, 1979.
Early Tales & Sketches. Vol. 1, *(1851–1864)*. Edited by Edgar M. Branch, Robert H. Hirst, and Harriet E. Smith, 1979. Vol. 2, *(1864–1865)*. Edited by Edgar M. Branch, Robert H. Hirst, and Harriet E. Smith, 1981.
The Adventures of Tom Sawyer, Tom Sawyer Abroad, Tom Sawyer, Detective. Edited by John C. Gerber, Paul Baender, and Terry Firkins, 1980.
Adventures of Huckleberry Finn. Edited by Walter Blair and Victor Fischer, 1988.

b. *Mark Twain Papers* (Berkeley: University of California Press)
Mark Twain's Letters to His Publishers 1827–1894. Edited by Hamlin Hill, 1967.
Mark Twain's Satires and Burlesques. Edited by Franklin R. Rogers, 1967.
Mark Twain's Which Was the Dream? Edited by John S. Tuckey, 1967.

Mark Twain's Hannibal, Huck & Tom. Edited by Walter Blair, 1969.
Mark Twain's Mysterious Stranger Manuscripts. Edited by William M. Gibson, 1969.
Mark Twain's Correspondence with Henry Huttleston Rogers. Edited by Lewis Leary, 1969.
Mark Twain's Fables of Man. Edited by John S. Tuckey, 1972.
Mark Twain's Notebooks & Journals. Vol. 1, *(1855–1873).* Edited by Frederick Anderson, Michael B. Frank, and Kenneth M. Sanderson, 1975. Vol. 2, *(1877–1883).* Edited by Frederick Anderson, Lin Salamo, and Bernard L. Stein, 1975. Vol. 3, *(1883–1891).* Edited by Robert P. Browning, Michael B. Frank, and Lin Salamo, 1979.

3. Tales (in order of publication)
   These tales and others are included in *Mark Twain, Tales and Sketches,* ed. Louis J. Budd (New York: Library of America, 1987).

"The Dandy Frightening the Squatter." *Carpet Bag* (Boston), 1 May 1852.
"Petrified Man." *Territorial Enterprise* (Virginia City), 4 October 1862.
"How to Cure a Cold ('Curing a Cold')." *Golden Era,* (San Francisco), 20 September 1863.
"The Lick House Ball." *Golden Era* (San Francisco), 27 September 1863.
"A Bloody Massacre Near Carson." *Territorial Enterprise* (Virginia City), 28 October 1863.
"Whereas" ["Aurelia's Unfortunate Young Man"]. *Californian,* 22 October 1864.
"Lucretia Smith's Soldier." *Californian,* 3 December 1864.
"Advice for Good Little Boys." *Youth's Companion* (San Francisco), probably 1 July 1865.
"Jim Smiley and His Jumping Frog." *Saturday Press* (New York) 18 November 1865.
"The Pioneers' Ball" ["'After' Jenkins"]. *Territorial Enterprise* (Virginia City), 19 or 21 November 1865.
"My Late Senatorial Secretaryship." *Galaxy,* May 1868.
"Journalism in Tennessee." *Buffalo Express,* 4 September 1869.
"The Facts in the Great Landslide Case." *Buffalo Express,* 2 April 1870.
"The Facts in the Case of the Great Beef Contract." *Galaxy,* May 1870.
"How I Edited an Agricultural Paper Once." *Galaxy,* July 1870.
"John Chinaman in New York." *Galaxy,* September 1870.
"The Noble Red Man." *Galaxy,* September 1870.
The Indignity Put upon the Remains of George Holland by the Rev. Mr. Sabine." *Galaxy,* February 1871.
"A True Story, Repeated Word for Word as I Heard It." *Atlantic Monthly,* November 1874.

"The Curious Republic of Gondour." *Atlantic Monthly,* October 1875.
"A Literary Nightmare" ["Punch, Brothers, Punch"]. *Atlantic Monthly,* February 1876.
"The Canvasser's Tale." *Atlantic Monthly,* December 1876.
"The Great Revolution in Pitcairn." *Atlantic Monthly,* March 1879.
"Mrs. McWilliams and the Lightning." *Atlantic Monthly,* September 1880.
"The McWilliamses and the Burglar Alarm." *Harper's Christmas,* December 1882.
"The Private History of a Campaign that Failed." *Century Magazine,* December 1885.
"Letter from the Recording Angel." Unpublished; written before September 1887, probably January 1887. See Paul Baender, *What Is Man?* (Berkeley: University of California Press, 1973), 65–70.
"Is He Living or Is He Dead?" *Cosmopolitan,* September 1893.
"What Paul Bourget Thinks of Us." *North American Review,* January 1895.
"Fenimore Cooper's Literary Offences." *North American Review,* July 1895.
"The Great Dark." Unpublished; composed 1898. See John S. Tuckey, *Which Was the Dream?* (Berkeley: University of California Press, 1966), 102–50.
"Concerning the Jews." *Harper's Magazine,* September 1899.
"A Greeting from the Nineteenth to the Twentieth Century." *New York Herald,* 30 December 1900.
"To the Person Sitting in Darkness." *North American Review,* February 1901.
"The United States of Lyncherdom." Unpublished; written 1901. See *Europe and Elsewhere* (New York: Harper, 1923), 24–30.
"Does the Race of Man Love a Lord?" *North American Review,* April 1902.
"The Five Boons of Life." *Harper's Weekly,* 5 July 1902.
"Was It Heaven? Or Hell?" *Harpers Magazine,* December 1902.
"Saint Joan of Arc." *Harpers Magazine,* December 1904.
"Concerning Copyright." *North American Review,* January 1905.
"The Czar's Soliloquy." *North American Review,* March 1905.
"The War Prayer." Unpublished; dictated 1904–5. See *Europe and Elsewhere* (New York: Harper, 1923)
"The Turning Point of My Life." *Harper's Bazaar,* February 1910.

4. Letters (in order of publication)
Mark Twain Letters. Arranged with comment by Albert Bigelow Paine. 2 vols. New York: Harper, 1917.
Letters from the Sandwich Islands Written for the Sacramento Union. Introduction and conclusion by G. Ezra Dane. San Francisco: Grabhorn Press, 1937.
Letters from Honolulu Written for the Sacramento Union. Introduction by John W. Vandercook. Honolulu: Thos. Nickerson, 1939.
Mark Twain's Letters to Will Bowen. Austin: University of Texas, 1941.

Mark Twain's Letters in the Muscatine Journal. Edited by Edgar M. Branch. Chicago: Mark Twain Association of America, 1942.

The Love Letters of Mark Twain. Edited by Dixon Wecter. New York: Harper, 1949.

Mark Twain to Mrs. Fairbanks. Edited by Dixon Wecter. San Marino, Calif.: Huntington Library, 1949.

Mark Twain: San Francisco-Virginia City Territorial Enterprise Correspondent: Selections from Letters to the Territorial Enterprise, 1865–1866. Edited By Henry Nash Smith and Frederick Anderson. San Francisco: Book Club of California, 1953.

Twins of Genius. (Letters of Mark Twain and George W. Cable collected by Guy W. Cardwell.) Lansing: Michigan State College Press, 1953.

Mark Twain-Howells Letters. Edited by Henry Nash Smith and William M. Gibson. Cambridge, Mass.: Harvard University Press, 1960.

Mark Twain's Letters to Mary. Edited by Lewis Leary. New York: Columbia University Press, 1961.

Mark Twain's Letters from Hawaii. Introduction by A. Grove Day. New York: Appleton-Century, 1966.

5. Autobiographies
   Much of the biographical dictation is still in manuscript form at the Bancroft Library, University of California at Berkeley.

Mark Twain's Autobiography. Introduction by Albert Bigelow Paine. 2 vols. New York: Harper, 1924.

Mark Twain in Eruption. Edited and with an introduction by Bernard DeVoto. New York: Harper, 1940. (Contains material not in Paine volumes.)

The Autobiography of Mark Twain. Edited by Charles Neider. New York: Harper, 1959. (This work puts the contents in chronological order and contains material not in the the Paine and DeVoto volumes.)

6. Speeches (in order of publication)
Mark Twain's Speeches. Edited by A. B. Paine. New York: Harper, 1923.

Mark Twain Speaking. Edited by Paul Fatout. Iowa City: University of Iowa Press, 1976. This is the most complete collection.

Mark Twain Speaks for Himself. Edited by Paul Fatout. West Lafayette, Ind.: Purdue University Press, 1978.

7. Bibliographical Aids
Gale, Robert L. *Plots and Characters in the Works of Mark Twain.* Hamden, Conn.: Shoe String Press, 1973.

Johnson, Merle. *A Bibliography of the Works of Mark Twain*. New York: Harper, 1938.

Long, E. Hudson, and McMaster, J. R. *The New Mark Twain Handbook*. New York: Garland, 1985.

"Mark Twain." In *American Literary Scholarship,* published annually since 1962. Durham, N.C.: Duke University Press.

"Mark Twain." In *Bibliography of American Literature*. Vol. 2. Compiled by Jacob Blanck. New Haven: Yale University Press, 1957.

Mark Twain: A Reference Guide. Compiled by Thomas A. Tenney. Boston: G. K. Hall, 1977. Annual supplements in *American Realistic Literature*.

Mark Twain's Library: A Reconstruction. Compiled by Alan Gribben. 2 vols. Boston: G. K. Hall, 1980.

Union Catalogue of Clemens Letters. Edited by Paul Machlis. Berkeley: University of California Press, 1986.

Index

818.409
G 313

121050

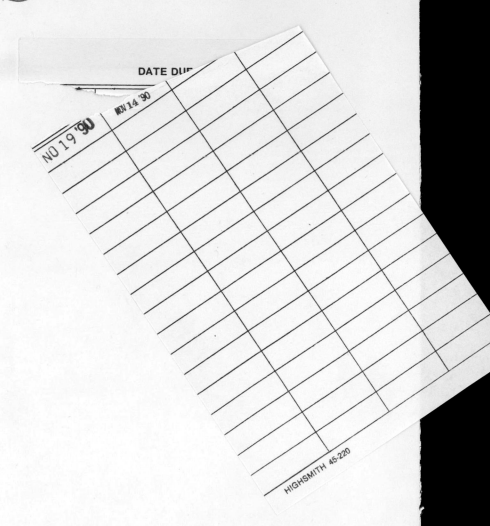

DATE DUE

NO 19 '90

NOV 14 '90

HIGHSMITH 45-220